Fanning the Flames

SUNY series in Japan in Transition
Jerry Eades and Takeo Funabiki, editors

Fanning the Flames

Fans and Consumer Culture in
Contemporary Japan

EDITED BY WILLIAM W. KELLY

STATE UNIVERSITY OF NEW YORK PRESS

Published by
State University of New York Press, Albany

For information, contact State University of New York Press, Albany, NY
www.sunypress.edu

Production by Kelli Williams
Marketing by Michael Campochiaro

Library of Congress Cataloging-in-Publication Data
Fanning the flames : fans and consumer culture in contemporary Japan / edited by
    William W. Kelly.
        p. cm. — (SUNY series in Japan in transition)
    Includes bibliographical references and index.
    ISBN 0-7914-6031-2 (alk. paper) — ISBN 0-7914-6032-0 (pbk. : alk.paper)
        1. Popular culture—Japan—History—20th century.   I. Kelly, William W.   II. Series.

    DS822.5b. F36 2004
    306'.0952'09049—dc22

                                                                    2004041740

10   9   8   7   6   5   4   3   2   1

Contents

Illustrations

Acknowledgments

The initial idea for this volume was hatched by Christine Yano and Carolyn Stevens, who organized a panel on "Intimacies, Identities: Fandom as Consumer Culture in Japan" at the annual meeting of the American Anthropological Association in Washington, D.C., on November 27, 1997. The coherence of the papers and the reactions of the audience then prompted me to organize a follow-up conference with several more contributors at Yale University on September 18–20, 1998. We are grateful to the Council on East Asian Studies at Yale for providing very generous funding from its Sumitomo Endowment to cover all expenses of the conference. All of the presenters at the conference are indebted to the thoughtful and supportive commentaries of Ted Bestor, Takie S. Lebra, Jennifer Robertson, and Merry White. At the Japan Anthropology Workshop meetings in Osaka in March 1999, several of us heard the presentation by Shuhei Hosokawa and Hideaki Matsuoka, which was so close in spirit to the other cases that we asked them to join us in this final volume. In preparing the final version of the manuscript, I benefited enormously from the assistance of Allison Alexy.

Finally, the authors and I appreciate the work of SUNY Press in producing this volume, especially Jerry Eades, series editor, Nancy Ellegate, senior editor, and Kelli Williams, production editor.

Introduction

Locating the Fans

WILLIAM W. KELLY

Who are the fans among the viewers, listeners, and readers of today's mass culture? To many nonfans, especially among the professional and upper middle classes, they are either the "obsessed individuals" or the "hysterical crowd" (Jensen 1992). They are condescendingly dismissed as incapable of discriminating admiration, prone instead to abject adulation. They are the "cultural dopes" of consumer capitalism (a phrase from Grossberg 1992), the most duped and ignorant of the already co-opted audiences of Culture Industry spectacles.

A deeper and more charitable appreciation of fandom has come only recently from some scholars within cultural studies. Fans, as Joli Jensen, Lawrence Grossberg, Henry Jenkins, and others have shown us, are those segments of mass culture audiences who most actively select from and engage with the performers, players, products, and productions of commodified culture. Their focused attentions are reworked into what John Fiske (1992) calls "an intensely pleasurable, intensely signifying" subculture that both shares with and is distinct from the experiences of more 'normal' audiences. Harlequin Romance reading circles, (Star) Trekkie conventions, Deadhead caravans, Madonna and Elvis fans, midnight audiences of The Rocky Horror Picture Show, Dallas viewers around the world, and diehard Chicago Cubs fans are all examples of the process, at once derivative and creative, of finding significance and taking pleasure from among the vast output of mass culture—in certain comic book heroes, film stars, B-grade movies, musicians, sports stars (or colorful failures), pulp fiction, and so forth.

Put simply, then, fans emerge out of mass culture audiences in search of intensified meanings and pleasures. They selectively appropriate from among this mass culture, and creatively rework their selections into a stylized matrix of practices and identities. They consume mass culture, but in their voracious and determined consumption, they produce both social communities and cultural artifacts. Fans' relations to the persons and products they "fan-tasize," to the Culture Industry itself and to the normal audience, are variously dependent and autonomous, even antagonistic. They, and the small worlds of "fandom" they create and inhabit in contemporary Japan, are the subjects of this collection.

Consumers and Fans in Contemporary Japan

The significance and the inherent fascination of the exuberant and commercialized popular culture of Japan need little justification. Since the 1980s, the mass cultural formations of media, leisure, and entertainment—and those who produce and consume their products—have been among the most vibrant areas of Japan studies, especially anthropology and literary studies. We now recognize that the forms and practices of music, sports, comics, film, fashion, and other areas of leisure and consumer culture are just as essential to fully understanding Japan as its factories, schools, and politics.

Thus, this volume does not allege to be a pioneer of dangerous and uncharted academic territory. To the contrary, we have drawn much inspiration from and we hope to make a distinctive contribution to a rich, emerging body of analysis. Within anthropology, Joseph Tobin's 1992 edited collection *Re-made in Japan: Everyday Life and Consumer Taste in a Changing Society* and Marilyn Ivy's 1993 essay "Formations of Mass Culture" were especially influential in spurring this past decade of research and publication. Jennifer Robertson's book on the Takarazuka Review (1998), Aviad Raz's book on Tokyo Disneyland (1999), Joy Hendry's study of Japanese theme parks (2000), works by Brian Moeran (1996, cf. 1989) and John McCreery (2000) on advertising agencies, John Clammer's book of essays on consumption patterns (1997), and the dissertations by Andrew Painter on daytime television production (1991, cf. 1996) and by Hiroshi Aoyagi on the production of "idols" (1999) are among a growing list of ethnographic monographs of Japanese mass culture sites (which also includes books new and forthcoming from this volume's authors).

Beyond anthropology, important publications abound. Richard Powers and Kato Hidetoshi's *Handbook of Japanese Popular Culture* (1989) has been a stimulating compendium. Frederick Schodt's entertaining and informative overviews of *manga* (comic art magazines and books) and *anime* (film, video, and digital animations) (1986, 1996), Sharon Kinsella's detailed study of the manga industry (2000), and Susan Napier's literary analysis of Japanese animation (2001) are book-length studies of that sector of Japanese popular culture that is the most commercially profitable, best known, and globally influential. Mark Schilling's *The Encyclopedia of Japanese Pop Culture* (1997) and Robert Whiting's books on

Japanese baseball (1977, 1989) are representative of many nonacademic works by commentators long involved with and deeply familiar with particular areas of Japanese entertainment and leisure.

Even broader arrays of perspectives, analysts, and topics have been introduced through a number of recent valuable scholarly collections, including those edited by Sepp Linhart and Sabine Frühstück (*The Culture of Japan as Seen Through Its Leisure*; 1998), by D. P. Martinez (*The Worlds of Japanese Popular Culture*; 1998), by John Whittier Treat (*Contemporary Japan and Popular Culture*; 1996), by Lise Skov and Brian Moeran (*Women, Media and Consumption in Japan*; 1995), by Tōro Mitsui and Shuhei Hosokawa (*Karaoke Around the World*; 1998), by Tim Craig (*Japan Pop!*; 2000), by James Lent (*Asian Popular Culture*; 1995), and by Joy Hendry and Massimo Raveri (*Japan at Play*; 2002). In short, even the titles alone catalogue the explosion of critical interest in the cultural politics and social patterns of producing and consuming leisure and entertainment in Japan.

Our own claim to a distinctive contribution to this new direction in Japan studies is our shared perspective and focus. We are all fieldworkers and ethnographers who have worked closely with the people and sites about which we write, and we aim to communicate with intensity and critical empathy the particularities (and often peculiarities) of those fan worlds. Ian Condry spent many long nights with the teenagers who frequent the small clubs and huge concerts of Japanese rap music groups and spent daytime hours in the recording studios and record shops. Christine Yano spent several years with the middle-aged women who compose fan clubs of Mori Shin'ichi, attending concerts together, sharing their lives both within and well beyond their club gatherings. Carolyn Stevens initially had a part-time job with The Alfee organization and through that came to know that subset of the band's audience who were tenacious loyalists and eager consumers of band products.

I myself spent parts of several baseball seasons in the right-field bleachers of Kōshien Stadium, amid the noisy, colorful, and irreverent fan clubs of the Hanshin Tigers. Lorie Brau accompanied *rakugo* (traditional comic storytelling) aficionados to countless performances and group meetings, discussing with fans and performers alike the nuances of rakugo performance. R. Kenji Tierney, whose dissertation fieldwork was based in one of the sumo world's wrestling stables, had sustained interactions with the patrons and supporter clubs of this and other stables. Matthew Thorn, himself both an academic and a professional translator of Japanese manga, joined the massive throngs at the Comic Market conventions that featured displays and sales of amateur manga artists and the "aisle theater" of costumed attendees acting out their favorite characters. And Shuhei Hosokawa and Hideaki Matsuoka, both with long-standing interest and knowledge of the jazz scene in Tokyo, pursued the aims and strategies of dedicated collectors of jazz records through long interviews and extended observations.

For us, however, ethnographic representation is not a matter of mere picaresque detail, but of deliberate and illuminating specificity. Within more literary cultural studies, for instance, there are many fine textual studies and many important analyses of broad sectors of popular culture. Neither is our objective here, which is rather a direct engagement with those people—the fans—who stand at the very heart of popular culture, between the performers and productions, on the one hand, and the more passive spectators and consumers, on the other hand. Theirs is an activity, a way of being-in-the-world, the fair representation of which requires close encounters of the extended kind. The volume's juxtaposition of different kinds of fans in music, sports, visual media, and theater is a strategy to tease out some of the commonalities and distinctions of these lifeways.

Culture, Consumption, and Cultural Studies

Our perspective on fans can be located not just within Japan studies but within a broader scholarly orientation toward modern consumption and mass culture that extends over many disciplines, from anthropology and sociology to history, literary studies, and communication and media studies. It is an orientation most frequently known as "cultural studies," a broad term that signifies to adherents capaciousness and eclecticism and, to detractors, flabbiness and pretentiousness. Perhaps most neutrally stated, the rubric has come to cover the critical analysis of the production, transmission, and consumption of mass culture in the modern era. Clearly, fans are to be found here, and their small lifeworlds are suspended within the lineaments of power and meaning of this mass culture.[1]

The present state of cultural studies seems to me to be an increasingly transnational hodgepodge of what were previously more distinct—and more distinctly national—fields of debate. Its German origins were in the Frankfurt School of Theodor Adorno, Max Horkheimer, Walter Benjamin, and others—and now Jürgen Habermas and his critics. French strains were theorists like Roland Barthes, Jean Baudrillard, Pierre Bourdieu, Michel de Certeau, and Michel Foucault. Its English roots were with Richard Hoggart, Raymond Williams, and the Birmingham Center for Contemporary Cultural Studies' crowd of Stuart Hall, Paul Willis, and a host of others. And in post–World War II America, it was anticipated by critics from Dwight Mcdonald, Paul Riesman, and Herbert Gans through to Michael Schudson, John Fiske, Janice Radway, and many more.

Name-dropping and intellectual lineages aside, the current thrust of much of this work fuses two rather different perspectives on the nature and status of popular and mass culture, themselves composite positions. The first perspective is shared by American and German theorists. Much early postwar American criticism conceived of cultural productions in highbrow, lowbrow, and later middlebrow forms. Cultural production to them reflected class-stratified tastes, and consumption was the passive expression of these tastes, which ranged from the critical, contemplative, and refined to the crude, the raucous, and the sensational.

Popular culture, by this interpretation, was the popularly cultured. Depending on the analyst, it was lamented or celebrated as mindless or spirited, vulgar or vivacious. By either view, however, it was irreverent but derivative and dependent on highbrow sources, and formulated and fed by highbrow interests.

This dependency of the popular on established interests and elite tastes was shared by German theorists of the Frankfurt School, who elaborated a critique of the central organs of culture production and transmission, the "culture industry," which manufactured diversions and entertainments for the masses as the bread and circuses of modern society. In Theodor Adorno and Max Horkheimer's famous phrase, "the might of industrial society is lodged in men's minds" (1972:127). Cultural production to them was deceptive and manipulative, and consumption was its passive and regressive reception by a disempowered and helpless population. Popular culture, in this scheme, was subsumed by hegemonic culture as the propaganda of the culture industry; no genuine popular culture could exist beyond the industry's pale.

A second perspective, rather different from American and German viewpoints, was shared by British and some French critics, despite their disagreements about much else. Stuart Hall, in part from his socialist political stance, rejected the Frankfurt School notion that a consumer public would necessarily be cowed into acquiescence; he explored instead the manifold popular responses by subordinate classes to the mass culture produced by dominant interests. Indeed, for Hall and for his colleagues at the Birmingham Center for Cultural Studies (from which the current rubric took its name), popular culture was to be distinguished from mass culture. The latter was formed of the products generated by the media and entertainment industries, while the former was the terrain of class struggles over meanings of that mass culture. Mass culture "encoded" establishment interests as implicit messages in books, magazines, music, sports, and so on, while popular culture "decoded" and "recoded" those messages. One of Hall's (1980) influential formulations was to identify three broad patterns of such decoding; "dominant" responses were those which accepted the intended messages of mass products and productions; "negotiated" responses, he proposed, were those that accepted the broad framework while rejecting certain parts of the message; and "oppositional" responses more radically reject the messages and that which produces them.

In France, Roland Barthes's significant contribution was the extension of semiotic analysis to the imagery and forms of popular culture (including photography, boxing, cycling, wrestling, and food). The structures that Barthes uncovered were not those of the political-economic forces of production but the linguistic systems of signification. The elements of a "fashion system" (1983) or a sporting event like a wrestling match (1972:15–25) are not objects produced, by forces whose interests determined its meanings, but signs to be understood, whose meanings were determined by their placement in converging semiotic grids (e.g., the cloth of fashion, the images of fashion, and the writing of fashion).

To the degree that there is any present consensus formulation of popular culture, it combines, in effect, the critiques of Culture Industry theorists and highbrow critics with the more populist celebrants of the lowbrow. It represents, one might argue, French and British operations upon the American and German debates. The production of mass cultural forms is judged to be intrusive and insistent in intent, but unpredictable and incomplete in its effects. Consumption is active, evasive, and resistant to complete co-optation. Popular responses to mass culture, therefore, cannot be collapsed into the interests of culture producers, but lie both beyond and within the reach of media and commodity capitalism, like a guerilla band operating furtively within a state. [For cultural studies in Japan, see Yoshimi 2001.]

Indeed, the guerilla is a favorite metaphor of popular culture theorists, no doubt because, as John Fiske notes, the essence of the guerilla is in not being defeatable (1989b:19). It has been used to particular effect by Michel de Certeau, for whom popular culture is "an art of being in between":

> Thus a North African living in Paris or Roubaix insinuates *into* the system imposed upon him by the construction of a low-income housing development or of the French language the ways of "dwelling" (in a house or language) peculiar to his native Kabylia. He super-imposes them and, by that combination, creates for himself a space in which he can find *ways of using* the constraining order of the place or the language. Without leaving the place where he has no choice but to live and which lays down its law for him, he establishes within it a degree of *plurality* and creativity. By an art of being in between, he draws unexpected results from his situation. [1984:30]

John Fiske has described, for instance, how Australian shopping malls are appropriated by joggers, poor and homeless, inveterate browsers, thrill-seeking shoplifters, and other mall rats who borrow and consume the space, heat, and goods of the malls while evading the hegemonic demand to consume through purchase (1989a:13–42). Janice Radway's group of women readers of Harlequin romances (1984) and Angela McRobbie's teenage girl dancers (1984) offer other examples of the creativity and liveliness of counterhegemonic readings of mass entertainment.

In short, cultural studies now give us a model of people seeking to make meanings out of the commodity system. Seldom are they merely duped or coerced into the meanings made for them. As Lawrence Grossberg puts it:

> For the most part, the relationship between the audience and popular texts is an active and productive one. . . . People are constantly struggling, not merely to figure out what a text means, but to make it mean something that connects to their own lives, experiences, needs, and desires. [1992:52]

Fans as Consummate Consumers

This new view of active reception and even agitated consumption that has come to define much of cultural studies both facilitates and complicates our challenge of locating fans. What is to specify fans amid the mass of consumers? Most simply and obviously, fans are excessive consumers. In disposition and behavior, they exceed the mass of ordinary spectators, viewers, and readers of mass culture in a number of ways: in focus, time, and energy and in the intensity of meaning they make and intimacy that they establish with their objects of attention. The television series, sports teams, celebrity singers, and vinyl recordings that are commodified forms of entertainment for most of us become vortexes of self-fashioning for fans. And of equal importance to their relation of excess to the object of consumption are the communities of mutual concern and shared commitment that fans form. Fans are inseparable from "fandoms," the small worlds of practice whose exchanges validate and intensify fan identity.

The chapters in this volume, individually and collectively, speak to these distinctive features of fans as identity and activity. By way of introduction, rather than summarize each contribution, I think it is more analytically useful to discuss how the studies variously support six propositions about fans that help us specify fans as social agents and fandoms as communities of meaning making.

1. *Fans are the most aggressive appropriators and the most brazen producers among consumers.* Certainly the kids who crowd into the small downtown hip-hop clubs that Ian Condry frequented quickly inhabit and animate them, creating a place of raucous vibrancy from a space of sparse dankness and pressing the barely definable stage with their pulsating bodies. Even more choreographed are the percussive routines of thousands of bleacher-seat fans at Kōshien, ignoring the "official" prompts of the stadium scoreboard and public address announcer for their own chanting rhythms throughout the game. The amateur manga artists who display their wares at the giant Comic Markets have gone even further in parodying the characters and story lines of their ostensible published sources, destabilizing the conventional norms of "straight" masculinity and standardized femininity. Like the "filking," or fan music making, and "slash" fan writings that Henry Jenkins (1992) and others have described for the United States, amateur manga art in Japan is an elaborate and ingenious response by inspired and enthused fans.

Viewing, hearing, reading, and buying may always require some degree of active "recoding." The cultural studies scholar Laura Mumford, for instance, proposed a continuum of soap opera viewers that ranged from the inexperienced (incompetent) viewer, the novice, the casual, the irregular, the competent, and the expert (1995:5). But fans, here and elsewhere, really are the guerilla vanguard of consumption, turning their "reception" of commercial entertainment into a resourceful, often irreverent, "production."

2. *Fans both know more and care more.* It is not just what they know but how they feel that sets fans apart from the rest of the audience. The Alfee fans rely on word-of-mouth, newsletters, and electronic communications to circulate fulsome reports of concerts, the smallest details of the band's routines, and tidbits of band members' private lives, but it is more the passion of commitment rather than depth of knowledge that identifies oneself or others as true Alfee fans. Rakugo aficionados can display tremendous erudition about the stories, allusions, and word play, but tend to measure their own sense of following by an ability to savor the rhythms of performance. The welling up of collective energy in the place and moment of performance (a concert, a game, an event like Comic Market) that is termed *moriagaru* (audience excitement) is often cited by fans as their ultimate satisfaction and standard.

Importantly, though, the intersection of knowledge and passion is unstable among fans; the proportions of objective detail and affective feeling vary widely. For example, I learned from the eighty or so games I have watched from the right-field bleachers of Kōshien that it is not easy to follow the details of the game from such a distance (300 feet) and in the midst of such frenetic activity. In fact it is quite impossible to attend closely to the game and to participate fully in the cheering at the same time. The chanting and clapping so necessary to sustaining the mood can be quite a distraction to the concentration required of appreciating the finer points of the action.

On the other hand, the pursuit and retention and display of ever more arcane knowledge can become a quite passionately *dis*passionate objective. Among those watching sumo, for instance, those who have the deepest appreciation for the strategic and technical dimensions of the sport are not the patrons but the reporters, some of whom have been studying sumo for decades, appreciating finesse and success but seldom exuding the partisan passions of the patrons and other fans. Thus, what and how much fans know and should know, and what and how much fans feel and should feel, are nervous issues even for the fans themselves.

3. *Fandom is serious play; it is about one's personal identity, not leisured entertainment.* Professional baseball plays to tens of millions of stadium spectators each year but very few of them come to an entire season of a team's 65 home games. The Alfee and Mori Shin'ichi have been selling out music halls for decades, but few in the audience follow their stars from concert to concert over the years. Jazz record sales have been substantial for three-quarters of a century, but those who "collect" records are but a fraction of those who "buy" records. Sports and music are consumed by a very large proportion of the national population—for entertainment. The fans among whom we have done our research seek much more than entertainment and they invest this "leisure" with much more drive and dedication.

Fans, we may say, are those who take leisure seriously. It becomes their arena for shaping meaning and organizing the routines of everyday life. The normal divide between work and play is abrogated. Indeed, the sharp division of work and play instigated by capitalist economic discipline has always been less compelling for children, students, housewives, and others outside the wage workforce, which may suggest that they are more likely than the office and factory workers to find identity in such pursuits.

Every chapter testifies to the centrality of identity construction. "Supporting Mori gives my life meaning," wrote one middle-aged woman, and Yano draws out the fans' self-fashioning as surrogate mothers to Mori. Tierney argues that the dense nexus of gifts that binds sumo patrons, stables, and wrestlers affirms the patrons' social presence and overcomes the impersonal transience of simple commodity exchanges like buying tickets and handing out calendars. Vinyl record collectors, Hosokawa and Matsuoka learned, spend years of their lives and considerable money to assemble complete sets of a particular artist or obscure label in part for the thrill of pursuit and a love of that particular sound but also to assert certain personal qualities of expertise, acumen, commitment, and taste. Takie Lebra suggested to us that the determination to fashion one's identity as fan could be a kind of social "time-out" for discovering and shaping an other in oneself; that is, for some, it is a way of taking a break from one's usual role-bound self, for a more self-indulgent, creative, playful identity.

4. *Fans seek intimacy with the object of their attention—a personality, a program, a genre, a team.* Christine Yano notes that fans of Mori Shin'ichi sometimes use the term *ittaikan* (feeling as if of the same body) to describe their sensation of physical–spiritual commingling with the star. This is an important opening into understanding just how fans' identities might be fashioned.

Fans are not satisfied with the formal performances, with the mediated and staged glimpses of stars. They seek to get behind the curtain, to know more about the performers, to "possess" them through tokens like autographs and handprints and bootleg tapes. Jazz record collectors do not just like listening to jazz; they want ownership, physical possession of the very material objects of jazz performance. They want the visual and tactile intimacies of ownership, beyond—and sometimes quite apart from—the pleasures of hearing the music. Thus, intimacy can inhere in the physicality of a momentary handshake and the materiality of vinyl and the unique tremolo of a voice but also in the more ephemeral and virtual. A Kōshien fan club that waves the banner of a certain Hanshin player when he is at bat feels a special intimacy and a distinctive identity by virtue of this role, but the felt connection is to a player, a persona, not a person.

Clearly, fans are set apart from others in seeking intimacy—and paradoxically, seeking intimacy in highly commodified settings. But how is intimacy possible with a baseball team, or a rock star, or a cult film? Or rather, what kind of intimacies can be fashioned out of such engagements? This is at the core of several of the chapters, especially those by Yano, Stevens, and Brau. Yano is most explicit in relating the feelings of intimacy to the charismatic powers of the star. The letters of her fan-informants communicated the intense feelings of pathos and sympathy they experienced toward Mori at his concerts.

Fandom, then, is a gesture of intimacy toward commodified culture, but our studies also show clearly that such intimacy is not to be confused with identity. For several reasons, fans are often involved in an intense play between identifying and distancing. For instance, keeping a certain social and physical distance is sometimes an acknowledgment of propriety. Stevens shows that The Alfee fans may well know the "rules of engagement" with stars even more than the casual audience—and may have even negotiated them through their previous behavior. Keeping one's distance may also be necessary for creative fantasy. As Merry White noted at our conference, intimacy may need proximity, but other fans—the manga costume players and amateur manga artists, for example—may be able to give play to their imagination only by maintaining a gap with the source of inspiration.

A third reason why intimacy does not collapse into identity is skepticism. By their very knowledge and passion, fans can be the most ardent of supporters but, equally, the most arch critics. Rakugo aficionados are not beyond criticizing performances that fall short of their expectations, and the fickleness of Tiger baseball fan clubs toward the team and its management is well-known (and feared by the team owners). Amateur manga artists adore the artists and characters they seek to imitate, but are unabashed in recoding the originals in quite unexpected and unconventional ways. We might say that fans emerge out of audiences by establishing their own—sometimes individual, sometimes collective—terms for what Albert Hirschman (1970) called, in a different context, "exit, voice, and loyalty."

5. *Being a fan can be a solitary, private pursuit—or a richly collective sociality.* Intimacy, then, may be sought and gained as a fan among fans as well as a fan toward the object of adulation. Producing meanings and pleasures through acts of both social and aesthetic discriminations, fans often create and sustain communities of shared practices.

The circles of Mori fans, the cheerleading clubs at Kōshien, the *ren* (networks of amateurs) rakugo fans, the patron associations of sumo stables, and the manga-writing groups are all manifestations of the social and intensely sociable nexus that forms around a shared passion. Fans are not class fractions or demographic niches or market segments; indeed, it is surprising just how diverse the composition of the fandoms is in most of these cases. It is only the hip-hop club goers and the sumo patrons who seem homogenous by gender or class or age.

Of course, we realize that to emphasize the group orientation of fans—the sociality of fandom—is to risk reinforcing some powerful popular imagery about Japan as a collectivist society, a population inclined to self-negation, seeking identity through empathetic and indulgent merging with others. Are not Japanese inclined to be fans by national character? If they are, then the obvious and striking parallels of Japanese fan group dynamics with those in Euro-American mass cultures would require similar inferences about those societies. Fans emerge out of commodified entertainment genres, not out of national gene pools.

To be sure, there may well be certain historical and contemporary features of social practices in Japan that give impetus and form to certain fan patterns. Ted Bestor reminded us at our conference of some of them: that consumption has produced elaborated aesthetics of fine discriminations and gradations of taste for a millennium from Heian to Harajuku; that modern Japan as a self-anointed "information society" has placed a premium on data gathering, processing, and examination that may well support the pursuit of the arcane and the data technologies of fandoms; that the long-standing centrality of *kata* (explicit forms) as learning-frame devices may promote the fixed routines of fan display; and that the importance accorded to uniforms and other role markers may predispose some styles of fan identification.

But those styles are not necessarily collective because at the other end of the spectrum, fans can also be among the most solitary, the most "self-consumed" of consumers. Hosokawa and Matsuoka note one obvious reason: a strong sense of competition. Fellow record collectors may be the only ones who can really appreciate and acknowledge one's collecting accomplishments, but they can also be one's most dangerous competitors for the same records. They are both one's essential reference group (and thus the more one shares with fellow collectors, the richer the mutual support) and one's bitterest rivals (thus the less information shared with them, the greater one's odds of success). In that sense, of course, solitary fans may not sustain a sociable community, but even they comprise a social network.

Thus, competition as well as the absorbing demands of knowing ever more and caring ever more lead some fans to an "externalizing" project of attaching themselves to a performer or a performance mood or a like-minded circle. The same motivations, though, draw others to internalize a persona or a genre into a sometimes quite claustrophobic world of one's own. This leads to my final proposition about the fan's condition.

6. *Fans test the limits of the excessive and the obsessive. They tread a fine line between the pleasures of fan-tasy and the pathology of fan-aticism.* One of the most noxious and notorious criminals of Japan's recent past was the serial child-killer Miyazaki Tsutomu. The 26-year-old worker was arrested in 1989 for the savage mutilations and murders of four girls. Police searching his house uncovered caches of girls' comics, pornographic movies, and animation video. Miyazaki was labeled an *otaku*, the term that had been adopted within manga fans and amateur artists to identify the weirdos among them but which had less dysfunctional and sometimes

even endearing connotations in other fandoms. As several chapters attest, otaku were and are nerds and geeks and loners, perhaps a bit more "into" something than other fans, but not necessarily psychologically unstable and criminally inclined.

The Miyazaki arrest changed public use of the term. Sharon Kinsella (1998) astutely analyzed the Miyazaki case in the broader contexts of establishment fears about youth and of the amateur manga movement of the1980s. She recognized the public uproar around the arrest and trial as a media-generated "moral panic," galvanizing public concerns about societal directions (e.g., family decline leading to directionless and isolated individuals) and public fears about an unlicensed and licentious mass culture. All the meanings of otaku were elided into a condemnation of the extremes by the nervous and outraged public: lonely individual meets lurid mass culture and civil order is under attack.

The criminal zealotry of Miyazaki thus created its own panic backlash, but his case and others of the recent past do raise a more general anxiety about fans: Just when and how does intimacy become idolatry? What is the line beyond which passion becomes pathological and participation becomes illegal? These are serious questions, but most difficult to resolve. It is easy to identify and condemn the criminal perversity of an obsessed individual like Miyazaki (one can easily cite fan crimes in the West, like the physical attacks on tennis star Steffi Graf and figure skater Nancy Kerrigan by self-declared "fans" of their rivals, or the collective violence of English soccer hooligans). But just where is the line to be drawn, beyond which the excessive becomes the obsessive? The issue is rendered even more complex because society's official agents, the mainstream population, and the fans themselves may have incommensurate standards of normalcy and morality.

It is, in any case, a question that we do not address here, in part because we seldom encountered those who seemed clearly obsessed beyond absorbed. Normalcy is certainly tested, often deliberately, by fan behavior and belief, but the fans, in these chapters at least, seldom exceed the unconscionable and the socially sanctioned. Their purposes may be narrowly conceived, their enthusiasms may be one-dimensional, and their investments of time, money, and energy may flaunt the conventionally rational. But it is not clear to me that their excesses are different in intensity or effect from the excesses of dedicated corporate workers or exam-driven students—except perhaps in their pleasures.

The powerful structures that produce the mass culture of our time, the multimedia of its transmission, its manifold content, and the consumption of that mass culture, both at the instant of reception and in its ensuing intrusions into daily life—these ramifying processes must be grasped as separately patterned and as mutually conditioning. It is no surprise that so many disciplines have brought their own methodologies to bear on this problem. Anthropology has no privileged insight over other disciplines, but we hope that the studies in this volume demonstrate that our sustained encounters of fieldwork and our attention to ethnographic representation create a distinctive and essential perspective from which to identify, engage, and interpret the fans and their fandoms within mass culture.

These chapters help to explicate why it is that fandom is the unstable core of commodified culture (and its cultural commodities): because fans are dangerously poised between the forces of production and the sites of reception, inclined both to disrupt with rude distortion and to comply with exemplary consumption. Fans represent the fondest hopes and worst fears of a culture capitalist. And what all of our studies show too is just how paradoxical is the life of the fan, who seeks both detailed knowledge and intense feeling about the object of his or her obsession. Within the larger population of spectators, fans are the most unreflectively passionate yet most analytically critical, both avid consumers and often irreverent producers of mass culture. Their excesses reveal to us the nature of the hold that mass culture has over the Japanese and ourselves. Let us now encounter some of them in the worlds they have fashioned.

References Cited

Adorno, Theodor W., and Max Horkheimer
    1972   The Culture Industry: Enlightenment as Mass Deception. In Dialectic of Enlightenment. John Cumming, trans. Pp. 120–167. New York: Herder and Herder.

Aoyagi, Hiroshi
    1999   Islands of Eight Million Smiles: Pop-Idol Performances and the Field of Symbolic Production. Ph.D. dissertation, Department of Anthropology, University of British Columbia.

Barthes, Roland
    1972   Mythologies. Annette Lavers, trans. New York: Farrar, Straus and Giroux.
    1983   The Fashion System. Richard Howard, trans. New York: Farrar, Straus, and Giroux.

Clammer, John
    1997   Contemporary Urban Japan: A Sociology of Consumption. Oxford: Blackwell.

Craig, Timothy J., ed.
    2000   Japanese Pop! Inside the World of Japanese Popular Culture. Armonk, NY: M. E. Sharpe.

de Certeau, Michel
    1984   The Practice of Everyday Life. Berkeley: University of California Press.

Fiske, John
    1989a   Reading the Popular. Boston: Unwin Hyman.
    1989b   Understanding Popular Culture. Boston: Unwin Hyman.
    1992   The Cultural Economy of Fandom. In The Adoring Audience: Fan Culture and Popular Media. Lisa A. Lewis, ed. Pp. 30–49. London: Routledge.

Grossberg, Lawrence
    1992   Is There a Fan in the House? The Affective Sensibility of Fandom. *In* The Ador-
            ing Audience: Fan Culture and Popular Media. Lisa A. Lewis, ed. Pp. 50–68.
            London: Routledge.

Hall, Stuart
    1980   Encoding/Decoding. *In* Culture Media, Language: Working Papers in Cultural
            Studies, 1972–1979. Stuart Hall, David Hobson, A. Lowe, and Paul E. Willis,
            eds. Pp. 128–139. London: Hutchinson.

Hendry, Joy
    2000   The Orient Strikes Back: A Global View of Cultural Display. Oxford: Berg.

Hendry, Joy, and Massimo Raveri, eds.
    2002   Japan at Play: The Ludic and the Logic of Power. London: Routledge.

Hirschman, Albert O.
    1970   Exit, Voice, and Loyalty: Responses to Decline in Firms, Organizations, and
            States. Cambridge: Harvard University Press.

Ivy, Marilyn
    1993   Formations of Mass Culture. *In* Postwar Japan as History. Andrew Gordon,
            ed. Pp. 239–258. Berkeley: University of California Press.

Jenkins, Henry
    1992   Textual Poachers: Television Fans and Participatory Culture. London: Routledge.

Jensen, Joli
    1992   Fandom as Pathology: The Consequences of Characterization. *In* The Adoring
            Audience: Fan Culture and Popular Media. Lisa A. Lewis, ed. Pp. 9–29. Lon-
            don: Routledge.

Kinsella, Sharon
    1998   Japanese Subculture in the 1990s: Otaku and the Amateur Manga Movement.
            Journal of Japanese Studies 24(2):289–316.
    2000   Adult Manga: Culture and Power in Contemporary Japanese Society. Richmond,
            Surrey: Curzon Press.

Lent, James A., ed.
    1995   Asian Popular Culture. Boulder, CO: Westview Press.

Linhart, Sepp, and Sabine Frühstück, eds.
    1998   The Culture of Japan as Seen through Its Leisure. Albany: State University of
            New York Press.

Martinez, D. P., ed.
    1998   The Worlds of Japanese Popular Culture: Gender, Shifting Boundaries and
            Global Cultures. Cambridge: Cambridge University Press.

McCreery, John
    2000   Japanese Consumer Behavior: From Worker Bees to Wary Shoppers. Hon-
            olulu: University of Hawai'i Press.

McRobbie, Angela
    1984   Dances and Social Fantasy. *In* Gender and Generation. Angela McRobbie and
            Mica Nava, eds. Pp. 130–161. London: Macmillan.

Mitsui Tōro, and Hosokawa Shuhei, eds.
  1998   Karaoke Around the World: Global Technology, Local Singing. London: Routledge.

Moeran, Brian
  1989   Language and Popular Culture in Japan. Manchester: Manchester University Press.
  1996   A Japanese Advertising Agency: An Anthropology of Media and Markets. Richmond, Surrey: Curzon Press.

Mumford, Laura Stempel
  1995   Love and Ideology in the Afternoon: Soap Opera, Women, and Television Genre. Bloomington: Indiana University Press.

Napier, Susan J.
  2001   Anime from Akira to Princess Mononoke: Experiencing Contemporary Japanese Animation. New York: Palgrave Press.

Painter, Andrew A.
  1991   The Creation of Japanese Television and Culture. Ph.D. dissertation, Department of Anthropology, University of Michigan.
  1996   Japanese Daytime Television, Popular Culture, and Ideology. In Contemporary Japan and Popular Culture. John Whittier Treat, ed. Pp. 197–234. Honolulu: University of Hawai'i Press.

Powers, Richard Gid, and Kato Hidetoshi, eds.
  1989   Handbook of Japanese Popular Culture. Bruce Stronach, associate ed. New York: Greenwood Press.

Radway, Janice
  1984   Reading the Romance: Women, Patriarchy, and Popular Literature. Chapel Hill: University of North Carolina Press.

Raz, Aviad E.
  1999   Riding the Black Ship: Japan and Tokyo Disneyland. Cambridge: Harvard University Press.

Robertson, Jennifer E.
  1998   Takarazuka: Sexual Politics and Popular Culture in Modern Japan. Berkeley: University of California Press.

Schilling, Mark
  1997   The Encyclopedia of Japanese Pop Culture. New York: Weatherhill.

Schodt, Frederik L.
  1986   Manga! Manga! The World of Japanese Comics. Tokyo: Kodansha International.
  1996   Dreamland Japan: Writings on Modern Manga. Berkeley: Stone Bridge Press.

Skov, Lise, and Brian Moeran, eds.
  1995   Women, Media and Consumption in Japan. Honolulu: University of Hawai'i Press.

Tobin, Joseph J., ed.
  1992   Re-made in Japan: Everyday Life and Consumer Taste in a Changing Society. New Haven: Yale University Press.

Treat, John Whittier, ed.
   1996   Contemporary Japan and Popular Culture. Honolulu: University of Hawai'i
            Press.

Whiting, Robert
   1977   The Chrysanthemum and the Bat: Baseball Samurai Style. New York: Dodd
            Mead and Company.
   1989   You've Gotta Have Wa: When Two Cultures Collide on the Baseball Diamond.
            New York: Macmillan.

Yoshimi Shun'ya
   2001   The Condition of Cultural Studies in Japan. *In* Cultural Studies and Japan.
            Steffi Richter and Annette Schad-Seifert, eds. Pp. 41–49. Leipzig: Leipziger
            Universitätsverlag.

Note

1. *Fan* may be derived from *fanatic* but fanaticism is hardly limited to fans. Fans share an intensity of commitment and taste with fanciers and the faithful, with connoisseurs and true believers. Indeed, can we say that one is a fan of Shakespeare? Is it useful to talk of fans of the Bible? A fan of Thanksgiving? A fan of one's Uncle Charlie? A fan of roast beef and Yorkshire pudding? Probably not, unless we are Lewis Carroll's White Queen. Fans, to us and to most analysts, are to be related to those leisure and entertainment pursuits that are mass in scale and commercialized in form. In short, fans are to be found among modern consumption practices.

1

B-Boys and B-Girls

Rap Fandom and Consumer Culture in Japan

IAN CONDRY

On July 7, 1996, about four thousand rap fans gathered at an outdoor amphitheater in downtown Tokyo to attend the largest Japanese hip-hop event to date. The showcase, called "Thumpin' Camp," featured over thirty rappers, DJs, and break-dancers from Japan's underground scene. Although the rain came down in buckets, it failed to dampen the spirits of the audience, who cheered and bounced and waved their arms throughout the three-hour show. The energy of the crowd was not lost on the performers. At one point, Mummy-D, a rapper with the group Rhymester, paused between songs to acknowledge the fans:

> I've got something to say today, so listen up. This hip-hop scene was not made only by us. It was not made only by the people on stage here today. I want you to give it up *(sasage yo)* for all the rappers, DJs, graffiti writers, and dancers in Tokyo! [cheers from the audience; the DJ starts the music for the next song, but the rapper yells] Wait, wait. Not yet, there's more. For all the B-Boys who came from outside Tokyo and who are planting the roots of hip-hop in other areas, give it up! [cheers] And last, the people who have come here, you who understand Japanese hip-hop, for all our supporters *(sapōtaa)*, give it up! [cheers]

With that, the DJ started the backing record. A plaintive bass line droned out a groove that was gradually met by a pounding back beat. The rappers started yelling the title line of their song "Mimi o kasu beki" (You better listen up!), and the audience yelled it back again in response. As the song continued, the rappers encouraged their youthful listeners to "follow the path to their dreams" and to "find the energy to leave something for the next century." It was an anthem to youthful vigor and commitment, and it was emblematic of these hip-hoppers' stance toward their fans.

This back-and-forth shouting between performer and fan is an apt place to begin a discussion of rap fandom, because it highlights that both performers and fans must listen, and that both must perform. The circuits of mass culture are given their vitality and meaning at least in part from the style of that communication. Fans and performers together create a feeling of community—in Japanese hip-hop terms, *shiin* (a scene)—but one wonders, in what sense can it be called a "community"?

For Rhymester, the scene emerges by planting throughout Japan the roots of hip-hop, a style of expression that includes rap, DJ, break-dance, and graffiti. Being in the scene means not only listening to the music but more actively taking part in performances and events. Mummy-D calls the fans *rikaisha-tachi* (those who understand) not only because they understand in an intellectual way what hip-hop is all about—from its origins in Bronx block parties in the late 1970s to its rise as global pop 20 years later—but also because they understand how to feel rap. Rap fans sense the building tension of a song or freestyle session. They anticipate the moments when a rapper will hold out the microphone for the crowd to fill in lyrics. They know when to wave their arms and cheer, and when to be quiet. The combination of understanding and action is the essence of being a B-Boy or a B-Girl, that is, a rap fan.

But between these moments of expectant silence and explosive release falls a shadow of doubt about the appropriateness of fans' attachments. The music industry blurs the line between culture and commerce, and draws into question the commitments of fans and the claims of performers. We recognize, for example, that communication between fans and performers is largely one-way, mediated by marketing teams bent on utilizing communicative technologies for profit. Fans generally have access only to the persona of the musicians, not the person. Musicians might flicker briefly on a distant stage or on a cathode-ray tube, or be immortalized as digital data on a CD, or offer their insights in music magazines, but they never drop by for a heart-to-heart chat. The relationship between fan and performer is a social one but it is a sociality limited by the form of the media and tinged with a profit-making aspect. In Japanese hip-hop, the media are primarily live shows at late-night clubs and record albums (vinyl or CDs). In more commercially successful forms of Japanese pop music, the main media are television and the karaoke box, and the relationship between artist and fan is somewhat different.

The mediated sociality of popular music evokes many of the anxieties of the modern world, and fits into expanding efforts to study consumption (Clammer 1997; Miller 1995a). Daniel Miller observes that consumers embody a state of rupture characteristic of modernity in that "to be a consumer is to possess consciousness that one is living through objects and images not of one's own creation" (1995b:1). This takes on particular significance, he argues, within an ideology that espouses authenticity through creation, and that includes the more mundane notion of natural ownership through labor:

> Within such a dominant ideology the condition of consumption is always a potential state of rupture. Consumption then may not be about choice, but rather the sense that we have no choice but to attempt to overcome the experience of rupture using those very same goods and images which create for many the sense of modernity as rupture. [1995b:2]

Fans offer a telling example of people "overcoming this sense of rupture." In many ways, fans epitomize both the rewards and the distortions of consumer culture. For fans, consumption is an end in itself. For a magazine writer or a sports gambler, an event is but a means to some other end—an assigned story or a winning wager. For the fan, the experience of an event is the primary objective. Such an experience will likely become productive in some sense, perhaps circulated as talk with friends, or as fan letters or even as a fanzine (Fiske 1992), but being a fan means, in part, to content oneself with the act of consumption. Fans can be viewed as ideal consumers, and thus provide a means of critically examining consumption in everyday life.

Being a consumer of cultural products is an active process of identity formation, as many have shown (e.g., McRobbie 1993; Radway 1991), but the tensions inherent in this process are not resolved simply through the assertion of identity. Part of being a fan is preserving some distance between oneself and the artist such that one can discriminate between excellent and lackluster performances. In this volume's introduction, Kelly notes that fandom entails instabilities on at least two axes: First, fans care more and know more, but this intersection of knowledge and passion is always shifting. The second axis, that of instability, is their involvement in the intense play between identification and skeptical distancing in enacting fandom. Fandom is a gesture of intimacy toward commodified culture, but intimacy is not identity. What lies within these notions of "rupture" and "instability" are the contradictions inherent in being a consumer and a fan. An additional source of instability that needs to be considered is the vague but ubiquitous condition of "information overload." One feature of media-saturated, late capitalist societies is the constant overflow of available information, which is part commodity, part resource and yet which always exceeds the consumer's grasp.[1]

One way we can observe how fandom relates to these modern consumer tensions is in the variety of Japanese words used to describe fans. At nightclubs, fans are most often called *okyakusan* (customer or guest), which strongly connotes someone being served and who is paying for the service. People more committed to a specific group or genre are called *fuan* (fans). Someone obsessed with collecting objects (e.g., records) would likely be termed *maniakku* (maniac). One of the most intriguing designations is *otaku*, which refers to a reclusive consumer of media-generated objects (e.g., video games, comic books, music, and animation). Otaku are regarded as obsessive fans who substitute the "real world" with closed-off, media-generated worlds, of which *anime* (Japanese animated movies) are the most representative case. I would suggest that these media "geeks" are more than the Other within mainstream society. There is reason to believe we are all becoming otaku.

In this chapter, I argue that 1990s Japan witnessed a transformation in the place of popular culture in society, and that this transformation can be observed in the self-organization of hip-hop fans. Put simply, there are two broad trends: one, an increasing massification of popular culture, and the other, an increasing diversification of niche markets with intensely specialized fans. With respect to music, for example, there has been a dramatic increase in the number of million-selling hit singles in the 1990s; as of 1996, there were eight, compared with none in the 1980s, two in the 1970s, and only one in the 1960s (Asō 1997:12–13). At the same time, specialized scenes in Japanese hip-hop, reggae, and techno, for example, are becoming more established as Japanese artists release more albums and even travel overseas to export their styles.[2] Some sociologists in Japan argue that cultural consumption no longer acts as a broad structuring process in and of society because a growing number of fans come to inhabit relatively autonomous "islands in space" (Miyadai 1994:231–274). If this is true (and I will try to show how this phenomenon appears in Japan's pop music world), then we need to reconsider whether cultural consumption retains the structuring power that Bourdieu finds in 1960s France. I believe the growing massification and increasing diversification of Japanese popular culture is leading to a broad restructuring in the meaning of consumption, and this has effects on social organization as well. I will show one way of understanding this transformation through the otaku characterization of fans.

To explore these issues, I begin with an ethnographic sketch of two concerts, each representative of divergent audiences for Japanese rap. Next, a brief history of postwar Japanese pop music allows us to observe some continuities and breaks between genres as reflected in contrasting attachments of music fans. Then I turn to two trends in consumer culture of the 1980s, namely, the contrast between *shinjinrui*, a "new breed" of conspicuous consumers, and otaku, the reclusive fans. These two ideal types embody different approaches to media, fandom, and social relations. Finally, I return to hip-hop fans to consider their process of self-definition in relation to more widely popular forms of mass culture. I conclude with a discussion of what these music fans tell us about the intersection of music, media, and fandom in late modern Japan.

Two Worlds of Japanese Rap and Their Fans

Rap fans in Japan are known as *B-Boys* (or *B-Girls*), a term that originally referred to break-dancers ("break-boys"), but now indicates anyone in hip-hop regalia: baggy pants, baseball caps, and expensive sneakers. They tend to be teenagers or in their early twenties, which is the age range for peak involvement with music consumption in Japan (Hayashi et al. 1984:152). Rap fans are concentrated in Tokyo, in part because there is little national coverage of the local rap scene, and because much of the information on shows and club events is found in flyers and free papers distributed in Tokyo record stores and nightclubs. Shibuya, a teen shopping district in downtown Tokyo, is where most of the major rap venues are located. The *kurabu* (nightclubs) are usually cramped and somewhat seedy underground bars with a DJ booth and a small stage, holding between 100 and 500 people. Clubs are regarded by artists, fans, and commentators alike as the actual site (*genba*) of the Japanese scene, where one must go to experience with one's body (*taiken*) the bone-rattling bass lines, and the charismatic delivery of the rappers.

Beyond these generalizations, however, the scene quickly diversifies, and it is the way the boundaries are drawn that offers the most insight into the nature of rap fandom. Two shows I attended during the summer of 1996 illustrate key contrasts between two main trends in the rap scene, namely, underground hip-hop and party rap. The Thumpin' Camp show provided a defining moment for the underground hip-hop scene, with its sold-out crowd and broad ranging participants. A week later, in the same outdoor amphitheater in Hibiya Park, the party rappers convened for their own sold-out showcase.

A caveat is important here. Most rappers object to the simplistic dichotomy between "underground" and "party" styles for a couple of reasons. Rap groups tend to be organized in loose networks, often called *famirii* (families), which perform together and collaborate on each other's albums.[3] These collectives are the most appropriate rubrics for understanding style affinities and differences, because they share the most in their approaches to music, performance, and their audiences. One criticism is that party/underground dichotomy overstates the commonalties among the families.

Another objection to the party/underground split is that all the artists tend to listen to the same music. Although they are likely to identify different "favorites," they all share a similar appreciation for American hip-hop as a whole. To divide J-Rap into two armies is analytically convenient, but according to rappers, it both overstates the similarities within the two camps, and obscures their shared musical foundation in American hip-hop.

With regard to fans who attend the shows, however, the differences between underground and party rap are undeniable. Most striking is gender. The audience for Thumpin' Camp was roughly 80 percent male, and this ratio was reversed for the Dai LB Matsuri (Big LB Festival). In both cases, teenagers were the bulk of the audiences, ranging from junior high school to college age, with a slightly higher average age apparent for the underground show. The baggy B-Boy clothing style was more prevalent at Thumpin' Camp, and almost everyone was wearing a hat (e.g. floppy Kangol or baseball caps or short brim golf hats). At moments of excitement, the Thumpin' Camp audience would nod their heads to the beat and wave their hands in a fawning motion toward the stage. At the Big LB Festival, hands were waved side to side (as I have seen at other pop-oriented shows) and a kind of full-body bob by bending at the knees accompanied the catchier tunes.

It was also striking to see the different approaches to performance, and the different ideas about what the audience should see and do. At Thumpin' Camp, the kind of propaganda that Mummy-D shouted—"We are all working at making hip-hop in Japan"—was echoed by other artists as well: "So many people are here, clearly a true scene has arrived" and "This is real hip-hop." Fans were encouraged to "spread the word and live hip-hop culture." Almost every group led the audience in a call-and-response ritual of "Say Ho!" The tone was macho, and slightly reckless, as when You the Rock announced, "The show is not over until I stage-dive into the audience." The standard greeting of the Kaminari outfit seemed to capture the sought-after emotional response: "Chōshi wa dō dai" (How are you?) and "Ikareta kyōdai" (My angry brothers). The performers presented an irate, confrontational stance aimed at unspecified others who threaten the individuality of the rappers and audience (and who threaten their shared commitment to hip-hop culture). The only overt political message came from K Dub Shine, a rapper with King Giddra, who called on the audience to shout at the Ministry of Health and Welfare building visible from the concert area in protest against the HIV-tainted-blood scandal that had dominated headlines in the previous weeks.[4]

At the Big LB Festival, the atmosphere was as different as the weather. A warm, sunny day made the free visors advertising the "LB Nation" a welcome present. The stage had two DJ platforms at the back and an enormous banner that read "Little Bird Nation." On the left part of the stage sat a large birdhouse. The tone was playful and upbeat. Although there were also several sessions of "Say Ho!," many of the activities between songs were aimed at getting the audience to laugh. For example, a couple of times a cannon blast went off, clearly startling whoever was on stage, and then a rapper from one of the other groups would come running out of the birdhouse with a sign reading "B-Boy *dokkuri*" (B-Boy surprise!), which elicited much giggling. Most performances had an element of self-ridicule. When Dassen Trio came on stage (a group of Osaka rappers who started out as comedians), two members were wearing white Elvis outfits with wigs and long, long tassels, and the third member, the self-proclaimed *debu* (fatso) MC Boo, was wearing a skin-tight Superman outfit. There were other nods to mainstream pop culture, such as a 15-minute skit that parodied a popular music information television show called *Waratte ii to mo* (It's good to laugh).

In sum, the two shows illustrate that style differences are reflected not only in the sound of music, but in the mode of communication between performers and fans. The self-important authenticity of the underground scene contrasts with the self-deprecating parody of the party scene. Before analyzing in greater detail the meaning of these style differences, however, we need to understand a little of the broader context of the popular music world. How do such fan–performer orientations relate to cases in the past?

Postwar Music and Fans

Throughout the postwar period, there has been a dynamic relationship between Western musical imports and Japanese-style appropriations. When such appropriations veer toward the commercial end of the spectrum, they tend to be defined as *kayōkyoku* (Japanese pop music). In other cases, such as early Japanese versions of folk, rock, and rap, musicians emphasize their *angura* (underground) status, namely, an oppositional stress on authenticity over commercialism. New genres tend to be defined in contrast to what is popular (commercially successful) at any given time, and rap is no exception. To understand rap fans, we need to get some sense of how they differ from more mainstream pop music consumers. Several studies of postwar pop music give us a look at these developments over time (Asō 1997; Hosokawa, Matsumura, and Shiba 1991; Miyadai, Ishihara, and Otsuka 1993).

In early years after World War II, jazz rose to prominence as the most popular genre, experiencing its first boom in the early 1950s (Hosokawa et al. 1991:13). A counterpoint to this "drunken-craze with American boogie woogie," however, was offered by then child-singer Misora Hibari, who restored a "melancholy voice to Japan, at a time of rapid economic growth and generally conservative cultural renaissance" (Tansman 1996:115). In 1952, at the age of 15, Hibari sang *Ringo no uta* (Apple Melody), a sad story of a young girl's longing for her country home, and sold a postwar record of 70,000 albums (Tansman 1996:122).

To a large extent, changes in Japanese popular music have followed on the heels of American and British imports. Three sociologists of youth culture trace the ways the evolution of Japanese popular music set in motion specific types of communication between musician and fan (Miyadai et al. 1993). In 1965, there was an "electric guitar boom," started in part by the Japan tour of the Ventures, an American surf music act that maintains a strong following even today. This music was "so strange, it was if the musicians had stepped off a flying saucer," and the music generated for its youthful fans a specific meaning of "us": We youth understand electric guitar music, while they (adults) do not (Miyadai et al. 1993:61). In 1966, The Beatles toured Japan and sparked a "group sounds" boom, prompting many bands styled after the Fab Four and ushering in a new kind of communication between musicians and fans. The *sōgo shintō* (mutual interpenetration) of *kanjōsei* (emotion) and *taiken* (experience) became an issue: "The only people who understand this music is us" (Miyadai et al. 1993:61). It was no longer simply the newness of the sound that made it cool to youth and opaque to adults, it was the specific emotional stake that a music style offered to its fans that became paramount.

The question of emotional stake also relates to the media by which musicians were experienced. In the early 1960s, singers like Misora Hibari were mostly seen on stage at large concerts or were heard on the radio. Through such media, it seems likely that although looks were not irrelevant, they were less valued than a powerful singing voice (Asō 1997:18–19). As the 1960s progressed, however, a new brand of teenage singers using youth slang and singing about high school life began to appear on television.[5]

In the late 1960s, folk music became popular among college students. The appeal of "college folk" was its connotation of being *tokai-teki* (metropolitan) as opposed to *inaka-teki* (rural), such that mouthing English lyrics and the harmonies of Peter, Paul, and Mary became the "urban" ideal. A hit song by the Folk Crusaders, a group assembled from a magazine talent search, sparked many folk-sounding versions of pop songs. This so changed the dynamic that afterward real folk represented anticommercialism, while kayōkyoku (including its folklike manifestations) was associated with commercialism (Miyadai et al. 1993:64). Hence, the new appellation *angura fōku* (underground folk) emerged, and the fan base of folk music widened to include working students and young working women. It is striking how the distinction between authentic and commercial appears time and again, often spurred by a noteworthy hit song, which is then decried as "inauthentic." This could be called the "paradox of pop," because the fruits of a group's success (popularity) also plant the seeds for a group's demise ("too commercial").

Television has played a large role in the development of Japanese pop music. In the 1970s, *aidoru* (idol) singers were largely supported by various "best ten" programs. In this world looks were paramount, and the quality of the singing became less important than the image conveyed. In the 1990s, there are also numerous "best ten" music programs, but the social context for viewing them has changed. Before, there was only one television in the house, and the head of the household controlled the channels:

> So when people watched a music program, it was the whole family together. It was an opportunity for the family to become closer through watching as a household. Nowhere in Japan could you find today's situation of a kid in his own room, talking on the phone with a friend, while watching "Hey! Hey! Hey!" on his own TV. [Asō 1997:24]

As a result, the big hits of the 1970s came mostly from music programs aimed at the whole family. In fact, a children's television show song from 1975 called "Oyoge! Taiyakikun" (Swim! Little Fish Cookie) held the record as the biggest hit single in Japanese pop music history (4.5 million sold), until 1999 when Utada Hikaru's "Automatic" sold eight million copies (Asō 1997:24). This kind of prime-time, mass appeal can be contrasted with late-night television associated with underground folk, which played folk music, and presented discussions of problems in love and school aimed solely at youthful viewers. Miyadai et al. argue that this solidified a new type of communication between fan and performer such that "only that person understands us [the fans]" (1993:64).

Television can be a unifying force, but depending on the content, it can air images that fracture society as well. In the winter of 1972, the nation sat transfixed, watching a live broadcast of the storming of a Red Army mountain retreat (Mizuki 1994:22–26). When the revolutionaries were finally apprehended, it came to light that the group had killed 12 of its own in a political purge. The repercussions were broad ranging: "The propriety of imagining an enemy as a means of generating individual enthusiasm and bringing together 'us' *(wareware)* as a group began to be seen as embarrassing, and the so-called 'reactionless era' *(shirake no jidai)* started" (Miyadai et al. 1993:66). According to Steinhoff (1992), this extraordinary event is even more shocking in light of an analysis that shows the purge was the result of ordinary social processes and normal individuals.

With regard to musical communication, one result was a declining sense of "we" and a more alienated sense of "I," which can be seen in the rise of the singer-songwriter. Thus in the 1970s, an aesthetic of *tezukuri* (handmade) folk emerged, along the lines of James Taylor and Carol King. Music that was made and performed by the same person was contrasted with nonhandmade, other-produced kayōkyoku. *Nyū myūjikku* (new music) grew out of this folk song tradition during the second half of the 1970s, and continues to the present. During the 1970s, professional songwriters and composers would hand over the songs for singers to perform. But the 1980s were an era of the artist who writes his or her own lyrics and plays his or her own music. They poured their energy into making albums rather than hit singles. They did not appear on television, and showed no interest in music-ranking programs, which gradually disappeared. As Miyadai et al. (1993) put it, the key distinction became "only this person understands me" (i.e., no longer "they understanding us"). At the same time, the aesthetic of *jisaku jien* (self-made, self-performed) took on ethical significance, a sensibility echoed by today's underground rappers. Yūmin is a representative "new music" star.

By the mid-1970s, however, a counterpoint to this stress on creating *orijinaru* (original) songs was the expanding use of *kaigyaku* (parody), such as the Crazy Cats who made a name with their gag songs, and Otaki Ei'ichi, a former rocker who turned to parodies of rumba and merengue. At the height of the new music era, this use of parody presented a reversal of values in musical enjoyment. Of particular interest is the way entertainment arises not from hearing something new and unique, but rather from recognizing the *in'yō* (musical references) to older work. In the current hip-hop scene, this latter kind of enjoyment is a central one, particularly for DJs, for whom identifying the *neta* (samples) that make up a given song is a popular pastime and the subject of articles and even a book (Murata 1997).[6]

According to a 1990 survey of urban college students, new music is the most popular genre (see Table 1.1). Rock music is popular as well, and parallels new music in the sense that Japanese rockers hold to the same ethic of "self-produced, self-performed." Rockers differ, however, in their rejection of melding of emotions

Table 1.1
"Music I Like" (Urban College Students), 1990

New music	31.2%
Rock	21.8%
Pops[7]	15.4%
Kayōkyoku	7.5%
Classical	5.2%
Black contemporary/soul	4.5%
House/Eurobeat	3.3%
Jazz	2.6%
Fusion	2.3%
Heavy metal	1.7%
Folk	1.7%

Source: Miyadai et al. 1993:59.

with their fans (c.f., new music: "only she understands me") and also rejected parody apparent in pops (Miyadai et al. 1993:76). Instead, they tend to emphasize their angura status as a means of asserting their authenticity. Whether it is the hard edge of X-Japan or the more mellow sound of the Southern All-Stars and The Alfee (see Stevens, chapter 3, this volume), a few Japanese rock bands have achieved large and devoted followings.

One of the contentions of this chapter is that popular music is moving toward both greater mass markets and more elaborately discriminated niche markets. We see evidence of greater massification in the emergence of global pop stars, like Michael Jackson and later Celene Dion, in the movement of Japanese popular culture overseas to Asia, especially the teen idols and singers modeled on them (Aoyagi 2000; Ching 1996), and in the rapid increase of million-selling hit singles in Japan in the 1990s. Asō argues that the rise in the number of these platinum hits is closely related to the appearance of the "karaoke box," that is, a room rented to a small group of friends for singing along to favorite pop songs. The boxes first appeared in 1986, and by 1988 over 10,000 rooms were in use during the day (Asō 1997:29). It was women 20–25 years old who became the main users of CD-singles (a most user-friendly format), and the songs primarily chosen were those associated with prime-time television "trendy dramas." For the purposes of understanding fans, we should note that for these kinds of hits, communication between artist and listener is less important than the other associations of the song.

Here, we don't see the stance of consumers who say, "It's because I like this artist." They like the sound, the way a song matches the taste of a drama, and that it is easy to sing as karaoke. It may not even matter who sings it. . . . We are in an era of "song hegemony," when hits are born with no relation to the artist. [Asō 1997:39]

It is interesting that these listeners take a very active role as consumers of music—they learn melodies, familiarize themselves with the lyrics, and even perform the songs—and yet they probably should not be considered fans. Absent any gesture of intimacy toward the artists, we are left with a kind of consumption that is, above all, concerned with riding the wave of what is popular and communicating with one's friends via these items.

The Little Bird Festival, with its references to mainstream pop culture (e.g., the television show) and the absence of assertions of promoting a separate hip-hop culture, fits more comfortably in this style of consumption. Party rap is best considered a subset of popular music, aiming for, if not yet achieving, a kind of karaoke-box-appropriate kayōkyoku. In contrast, the Thumpin' Camp audience is the group better identified as Japanese hip-hop fans. They are the protectors of a niche scene premised on the authenticity of the artists, and they define themselves against the hegemonic model of pop music consumption. This dichotomy can be observed in a broader transformation of Japan's consumer culture.

Consumer Culture Trends of the 1980s and 1990s: From Shinjinrui to Otaku

Japanese social scientists as well as workers in the culture industries identify a broad shift in consumer culture that has occurred between the 1980s and 1990s. The 1980s constituted the height of the "bubble economy," a time of rapid economic growth financed on the shaky ground of skyrocketing real estate prices in Tokyo. The dominant youth culture trend was that of the so-called shinjinrui. The word was coined in 1984 as a pun that could be read as shinjin-rui, connoting the type of "new faces," or shin-jinrui, connoting "new human race" (Chikushi 1986). They are the conspicuous consumers of the mid-1980s, symbolic of the wealth of bubble economy as well as a vivid display of its ills.

> They are people who link their "classy" code-like (oshare na kigō-teki) consumer practices with their interpersonal relations. By choosing the right car, the right fashion, the right places to eat, and the right spots to play, they choose their companions (aite o erabi) and automatically keep away the kinds of people they'd rather not see. They are also the type who hold a "brand manual" in both hands and communicate via merchandise language (shōhin gengo). [Miyadai 1994:153]

The emphasis is on a group of youth who unite through their sensitivity to what is trendy and fashionable. The notion of *oshare* (classy) speaks to a kind of elegance that signifies not class in Bourdieu's sense, but rather being "in the know." The novel *Nan to naku, Kurisutaru* (Somehow, Crystal) is emblematic of the era; it not only uses consumer items as a vehicle for the story, but also indicates in the endnotes where the items can be bought. The plot and characters are less central to the novel than the atmosphere created by brand-name items, a feature that both delighted readers and incensed critics (Field 1989).

A countervailing cultural trend was the emergence of the so-called otaku, who are also defined by their relationship with media and consumption, but who can be viewed as opposites of the shinjinrui: "Otaku. Youth who retreat from the shinjinrui-style of code-like interpersonal relationships. Instead, they inhabit distinctive 'worlds' *(sekai)* conveyed by media (anime, science fiction, amateur radio, dial-up message boards, . . .)" (Miyadai 1990:187). The definition is of fanatics who are extremely conversant within their own field of interest, but who tend to be asocial loners, "unbalanced specialists" with extreme manias (Miyadai 1990:187). The word *otaku* is essentially an honorific for "home" and hence means "your home" (because one never uses honorifics in reference to oneself or one's own group) and, by extension, "you." The politeness level conveys respect, but also makes clear a lack of intimacy between "me" and "you." It may also carry the connotation of someone's closed-up room filled with evidence of mania. The term can be used jokingly, or casually as an adjective *(otakii)*, but most often the term is a sign of repulsion and scorn.

Otaku became a particularly bad appellation after 1989 when a man named Miyazaki Tsutomi was arrested for murdering four elementary school girls. His room was found to be filled with thousands of slasher and child-pornography videos. When people began to question the accused's *seitai* (ecology), a public debate was initiated about dangers of youth who live in worlds conveyed by media as a substitute for reality (Miyadai 1994:153–154). Over time the idea of otaku as a type of person began to give way to a notion of otaku as a kind of cultural orientation.[8]

Miyadai argues that in the 1980s there was still a broadly shared sense of hierarchy in consumer culture, such that shinjinrui consumption was highly valued, at least among their 20-something cohort, and otaku-type specialists felt a kind of *kakko warusa* (uncoolness). He notes, for example, that the first disco boom of 1978 emerged from the popularity of *Saturday Night Fever*, while the second disco boom of the mid-1980s related to shinjinrui snobbishness: Those who hadn't gone to a disco were *inakamono* (country bumpkins) (Miyadai 1994:244). But, he adds, by 1989, things had changed. "Does one go out to a Eurobeat spot, or House, or maybe not go to disco at all? A new problem was that the groove might not be personally appropriate *(nori no chigai no mondai)*."

It became an era where one didn't feel an inferiority complex [for not going out] nor feel superior [for going out]. In the 1990s, this kind of tendency has become even more extreme in the club boom: hip-hop, reggae, new wave, hard core, jazz; or if it's a disco, "flashy" *(parapara)* style or rave style? Everything is lined up side-by-side, like dispersed "islands in space" *(shima uchū)*. Between these separate islands in space there is no sense of hierarchy among them, and moreover, they are mutually opaque [to outsiders]. [Miyadai 1994:244–245]

This idea of mutually exclusive "islands in space" is one way of understanding how consumer culture has changed in Japan. Japanese hip-hop is characteristic of today's splintering of youth movements into such islands. Within hip-hop, there are clear hierarchies and specific meanings, but it is striking how little these understandings are related to fans of other genres. The debate about authenticity— "real" hip-hop, from the street, underground, hard core—may carry deep meaning for Tokyo B-Boys, but it is a debate that garners no sympathy and little understanding from those outside the circle.

Miyadai argues that what makes Japan a "high level information society" is precisely the diversification of consumer culture. It is not that people are consuming more, but that more people are consuming differently (1994:142–143). In the late 1950s, everyone wanted the three S's (washing machine, electric rice cooker, vacuum).[9] In the late 1960s, it was the three K's (air conditioner, car, color television). But now the commonplace attitude is to wonder why in the world would anyone want that? Youth of all stripes are becoming otaku (extreme specialists within a media world), and moreover, this otaku-ization, if you will, of Japanese youth culture is altering the social meaning of consumption. The sense of superiority of the 1980s that shinjinrui felt over those who lacked the consumer skills they had is gradually disappearing in the 1990s as it becomes impossible to compare between closed off media worlds.

What does an otaku-like world look like? Miyadai offers the following generalizations.

(1) otaku within their own tribe are marked by the same jargon (meaningful words among their friends), the same active space, the same knowledge, and same media; but

(2) they are not warm to each other beyond acknowledging the others as "otaku" (whether they actually call each other otaku is not an issue);

(3) as seen from one otaku tribe's perspective, otaku from other tribes make no impression or are considered to be "weirdoes" or "another race"; and

(4) the various "islands in space" of different otaku groups are not hierarchically organized and have no feelings of superiority; rather, they are viewed as equivalent. [1994:245]

These features point to a way of understanding fan attachments within over-arching changes in the cosmology of consumer culture. With expanding media networks, it is becoming increasingly difficult to keep track of the wide-ranging possibilities for consumption, and hence more difficult to assess the social significance of different practices.

In Bourdieu's ethnography of 1960s France, upper-class consumers of culture reproduced their status through highbrow cultural practices. But in 1990s Japan, the compartmentalization of music genres is but one example of a larger trend in which cultural practices are opaque to outsiders, and are observed without any sense of superiority or inferiority. People are left *mukanshin* (unmoved) by the at-tachments of others, at least as long as those others remain confined in their is-lands in space. This forces a reconsideration of Bourdieu's characterization of cultural consumption and its role in structuring society.

> In cultural consumption, the main opposition, by overall capital value, is between the practices designated by their rarity as distinguished, those of the fractions richest in both economic and cultural capital, and the prac-tices socially identified as vulgar because they are both easy and common, those of the fractions poorest in both these respects. In the intermediate position are the practices which are perceived as pretentious, because of the manifest discrepancy between ambition and possibility. [1984:176]

This opposition assumes a widely shared understanding of cultural capital that may well be disappearing.

We can see evidence of a similar trend in the United States. Two examples are college degrees and luxury goods, classic examples of cultural capital. During the recent dot.com boom and the publicity given to 20-something Internet million-aires, the significance of a college degree was widely questioned: Why waste one's most precious years as a programmer on college? The luxury goods business pro-vides another example of the weakening power of cultural consumption to orga-nize society. Bernard Arnault, the businessman whose empire includes Christian Dior, Givenchy, and Louis Vuitton, has made luxury available to the masses, or at least to anyone with the money to buy it.

> In the luxury-goods business, the Era of Wealth has given way to the Age of Connoisseurship. The new elitism is predicated on taste, and it holds out an essentially middle-class notion: the promise of a meritocracy in which the hereditary ruling class is supplanted by an aristocracy of style. [Brubach 1998:26]

The notion of otaku-like islands in space is useful here. At one time, carrying a Louis Vuitton bag signaled an association with the elite, but now it can be seen merely as a matter of taste. This aristocracy of style has no power to inspire emulation. Brand-name fanatics are more likely to be ridiculed as just one island among many, as is the Japanese hip-hop comic (Chusonji 1996).

This subversion of the elite's power to set trends also diminishes the subversive potential of so-called subcultural forms. Hebdige writes of punk's revolutionary appropriation of everyday objects (e.g., the safety pin through the ear) that it is "through style, that the subculture at once reveals its 'secret' identity and communicates its forbidden meanings" (1979:103). In the islands-in-space scenario, however, these forbidden meanings became opaque; they are no longer a source of shock, but merely cause detached bemusement. As a result, the islands turn inward to build a realm of value predicated on the ideologies consonant with their interests. In the case of Japanese B-Boys, this means recognizing public performance, especially in clubs, as the ultimate enactment of fandom.

Hip-Hop Fans: "He's Just an Otaku" and Other Pleasurable Put-Downs

There is evidence that the kind of shift from 1980s-style to 1990s-style consumerism has occurred in the Japanese appropriation of hip-hop. In a February 1996 interview at his office, surrounded by pop idol posters and stacks of CDs, a Sony Records representative in his thirties described some differences between hip-hop in Japan in the mid-1980s compared with a decade later. He noted that when Run-DMC came out in 1986, the Adidas sneakers and trainers associated with rap music first appeared in the punk and new wave scenes: "In our era, there was everything within the subculture." But in the 1990s, things had changed:

> As more and more things came out, it became impossible to say "hip-hop" and stop with Run-DMC. Along with the changing era, each scene *(bun'ya)* became deeper. You had to say, "Run-DMC is not all there is to hip-hop. There are various styles, various artists." But there were too many things to keep track of. So what happened? This was the beginning of otaku. . . . In other words, now one chooses one genre—reggae, hip-hop, computers, animation—and goes deeply into that.

Two points are worth highlighting. One of the driving forces of this beginning of otaku is that "more and more things came out." The increasing diversity of niche cultures and an erosion of their hierarchical ordering is partly related to the expansion of consumer options. This expansion is itself an outgrowth of corporate, national, and global economic policies often predicated on an ideal of "consumer-led growth," as well as of broad-based shifts from Fordist methods of production to flexible accumulation. A second noteworthy point is that "it became impossible to talk" about hip-hop if you only knew Run-DMC. This reminds us that consumption is not only about securing a personal identity, but, perhaps more important, about having things to talk about with one's friends.

The hardening of the hip-hop niche in Japan appears in several ways. Rappers I interviewed remarked that what is different about the current generation of up-and-coming rappers is that they are into "hip-hop only," whereas the currently more established rappers grew up on a wide variety of musical styles, and the first generation of Japanese rappers all came from other genres of music, especially rock and punk.[10] In 1996, the magazine *Front*, which identifies itself "for hip-hop and R&B freaks," transformed from a once-in-a-while supplement to a monthly, and further closed the circle of Japanese B-Boys. The bulk of the magazine is interviews with American and Japanese rap artists, but it includes a section of columns aimed at discussing the current scene. The rapper MC Shiro with Rhymester writes a section called "B-Boyism" that discusses various aspects of Japanese pop culture (especially manga, movies, and action-figure toys) that converge with his notion of hip-hop culture. There are extended discussions of how hip-hop can best be put into practice in Japan.

Miyadai's (1994) characterization of islands in space notes that otaku use the same jargon, same active space, same knowledge, and same media. For hip-hop fans, we can see this in the use of American hip-hop slang, such as describing one's personal ability as "ill skill" (i.e., able lyricism and delivery), and new albums as *geki yaba shitto* (literally, "extremely bad shit," meaning "good songs"). The media ranges from the magazine *Front*, to flyers and free papers, as well as wider circulation fashion magazines focusing on "street style." Perhaps most important to understanding where these islands in space exist is the nightclubs. The clubs are the proving ground for rappers and their lyrical salvos, as well as the places where the knowledge and the jargon are most valued. It is no surprise that these are the places that everyone in the scene—rappers, DJs, magazine writers, and record company people—identifies as the genba of Japanese rap.

It is in the clubs that one can observe the type of community of fans that hip-hop as a genre provides. In attending monthly events sponsored by the various "families" of rap groups, one has a chance to meet (and have one's picture taken with) the artists, as well as meeting many of the other regular club goers. One revision needed in Miyadai's (1984) concept of islands in space is in his assertion that "otaku within the same tribe are not warm to each other, beyond acknowledging that they are mutually otaku." Having spent considerable time in clubs with what could be called "hip-hop otaku," I have found quite a lot of warmth, openness, and camaraderie among clubbers. Clubs specializing in one genre of music such as hip-hop are primarily urban phenomena. The people who attend these events from around midnight until the trains start running again at 5 a.m., are perhaps best thought of as "the Mobility" (to borrow a Thomas Pynchon phrase), often linked primarily by their attachment to a kind of music, rather than ties to a common place. Yet as fans, especially of the groups that regularly attend certain events, they can come to see each other regularly and form lasting friendships.

Rap music clubs, as islands in space, are also sites of contestation about what it means to be a fan. There is a spectrum of behavior that runs from casual consumer to active producer, and each step along the way involves an increasing engagement as a Japanese hip-hop fan. These decisions can be read as responses to the sense of rupture Miller (1995a, 1995b) identifies in peoples' projects of living through objects produced by others. They are also responses to the problem of how to choose among the plethora of consumer items out there, a rupture that seems to me more daunting to today's Japanese youth. The tensions inherent in being a fan appear most clearly in criticisms of fellow fans.[11]

The most common criticism of hip-hop fans is that "they only care about fashion." Although hip-hop-inspired clothing is a leading style for teenage boys, only a fraction of all the people sporting the baggy pants are actually consumers of the music, at least judging from the sales of Japanese rap. Fashion magazines like *Fine* have been active promoters of hip hop, but the emphasis is on *kakko ii* (cool style) rather than, as many rappers would prefer, a focus on music. On the other hand, buying music alone is often dismissed as a weak gesture of fandom, depending on the goal of buying. Itagaki Toshiya, the manager of Manhattan Records (a central hip-hop record store in Shibuya), is skeptical of his customers' intentions. "Only about 20 percent of them care about the music," he says. "Many of them just buy records to fill up their room." It seems, he explained, that having a lot of records impresses potential girlfriends. Even for those who bought records and went home and played them, Itagaki questions their commitment to hip-hop:

When I was in high school, it was electric guitar. Now it is a couple of turntables and a mixer that all the guys have. In college, they get a sampler and try making a few songs. But once they get a job, they'll turn to snowboarding. It's just about riding the wave of whatever is popular.

Some kids even come to the store and ask for the distinctive white-and-blue shopping bags to carry around, even though they don't buy anything. "I don't mind," he laughed, "After all, it's advertising for me, but it shows how unimportant the music is to them."

The discourse surrounding fans is in many ways a criticism of the vagaries of consumer culture. To buy is not enough to be a fan, one must actively engage with hip-hop culture, and this means finding one's own expressive style. Itagaki, and many DJs on the club circuit as well, note that lots of boys call themselves DJs, but when asked where they play, it turns out they only play in their rooms. "They're just otaku" is the common refrain. To prove one's commitment to hip-hop, one must perform in a club, the scene's genba.[12]

This belief that the true fan is also a producer highlights the performative aspects of fandom, and the range of possible performances. From simply buying
clothes to carrying around an empty record bag to buying records to listening to
and studying the music and artists, there is an increasing engagement as a "hip-
hop fan." Going to a club, becoming a regular at events, trying out one's own
hand at DJ-ing or writing rhymes or practicing break dancing in the park with
friends—these represent a deepening involvement. They also encourage some
"skeptical distancing," in that decisions about how and where to move deeper into
the hip-hop scene become unavoidable. Later, one can perform at a club during
freestyle sessions, DJ contests, or impromptu dance battles. At each step deeper
into the performative aspects of the genre's fandom, one confronts a tension between embarrassment (the risk of any performance) and seduction (the chance to
be noticed and appreciated), which heightens the emotional intensity (Frith
1996:214–215). It is small wonder, then, that there is criticism of those who fail
to take the plunge, or who go too far and give the genre a bad name. This is one
reason it is useful to see how the transgressions of fandom, such as the claim
"He's just an otaku," give us a deeper view of the complex identity issues involved.

Returning to the two concerts described at the beginning of this chapter, we can
see that "Japanese rap fans" are best thought of as those at the Thumpin' Camp
show. The performances of the rappers on stage emphasized a deliberately closed
space ("real Japanese hip-hop") that generates its own cosmology of value, meaningful to fellow B-Boys and B-Girls, but opaque and unimpressive to those outside
the circle of commitment. It is their voiced attachment to hip-hop that identifies the
showgoers as fans. In contrast, the show by the Little Bird Nation often veered far
from the realm of rap music, including a barbershop quartet, an unusual group
composed of a singer, guitarist, and DJ (Tokyo #1 Soul Set), as well as a variety of
rap groups aiming for a more pop-oriented sound. There, the audience was not expected to go out and "spread the word of hip-hop," since such ideologies of "authenticity" and "real" were far removed from the playful associations that reigned
at the Big LB Festival. As a member of Dassen Trio (the Elvis duo with Superman)
said, "It's OK to be 'real' if you've got anything to be real about. We just don't see
it." They would undoubtedly regard the rantings of self-important Thumpin' Camp
MC's as a sign that they were all merely otaku. In both cases, however, we can see
that fans are examples of contemporary struggles to find meaning in a media-saturated, consumer society, where the mainstream forms of cultural capital (a good
education leading to a good job leading to a good marriage) are losing their luster.

Conclusion: Consumption, Fandom, and Modernity

This chapter began with the proposition that fans epitomize the ideal consumer because for them consumption is its own reward. Although Miller (1995a, 1995b)

identifies an unease associated with consumption, it is worthwhile considering how widespread is this discomfort. In some cases, the ability to consume intelligently, finding the right clothes for a good price, for example, can be an empowering feeling. When Yuka, a dancer with the group Now, discovered that the clothing combination she was wearing was featured in a popular fashion magazine, she showed her friends the photo. "I felt like, 'I did it!'" *(yatta tte kanji)*, and, she added, "Each piece I bought only cost 1,000 yen [$10]." The job of searching through stores, comparing prices, and perusing magazines for the latest trends to gauge the ins and outs of fashion can be viewed as a kind of productive work in its own right.

This is particularly true in the case of DJs, where the boundary between consumption and production is difficult to demarcate. Their extensive record collections are the raw material of their late-night performances, which to a large extent involve strategies to get the audience excited (*moriagaru*), for example, by choosing a well-liked track. If, however, a song is *dasai* (overplayed), the effect is dulling. An unknown song can spark interest and even draw a few listeners up to the DJ booth to try to read the artist and title off the spinning disk. But too many unknown songs can alienate listeners as well. As an example of the kind of calculations required, DJ Etsu, a member of the group EDU, took great pride in an album he found at an outdoor record sale in the fall of 1996. It had the original version of a song recently remade by the global rap stars, the Fugees. Etsu paid a bargain price ($8) for the record, then scoured thousands of more titles filling the cardboard boxes for another three hours, finding nothing. Yuka and Etsu are two examples of the way that consuming something that someone else has produced is less a cause of "a sense of rupture" than the despair of there being too much to choose from, and too much uncertainty about what best to choose. Their moments of triumph are the exceptions that prove the rule. It is important to recognize, however, that their *kachi* (triumphs) would only seem so among friends within their own island in space.

The significance of the otaku in Japan, both as media geeks and as a description of the compartmentalization of today's popular culture, is that it points to a new understanding of the ways consumer culture relates to society in general. On one hand, concern over otaku as unbalanced specialists reveals the enduring anxiety about social relationships based on media-generated objects. Returning to Kelly's (see introduction, this volume) notion of fandom's axes of instability, we see that otaku exhibit a perversity of both knowledge and passion; they know too much and their feelings verge on the dangerous, occasionally spilling over into grotesque crimes. As one commentator puts it, "What makes a person an *otaku* is that no matter what genre they pursue, s/he never grows tired of it" (Asō 1997:55). This unending commitment represents the dangers of a social life built on consumer items that can become all-consuming.

On the other hand, otaku as a general description of the way consumer culture is becoming more compartmentalized contains an important insight. As worldwide media networks extend their reach, there is every reason to believe that two trends in mass culture will only intensify. In one direction are the increasing opportunities for huge global pop phenomena. A recent example is the movie *Titanic*, which grossed over $1.5 billion, the largest amount ever; two-thirds of these receipts came from overseas box offices (Riding 1998), and Celene Dion, who sings the *Titanic* theme song, has herself become a global music star. But any pronouncements that such examples augur an age of homogenizing global mass culture are decidedly premature because at the same time there is a quieter but equally deep-seated transformation underway. The growing ease of electronic communication and small-scale production (in music, magazines, and websites, for example) is spawning an increasing diversity of otaku communities. As Internet sites, cable and satellite television channels, magazines, and so on become increasingly specialized, the assessment of the worker at Sony will likely hold true for more people. You cannot say "rap music" and stop with Run-DMC; rather you need to choose one thing and go deeply into that.

The islands in space where hard-core fans can be themselves and enjoy a group of fellow travelers with similar interests deserve closer examination, not only in terms of their internal logic, but in comparison to the uses of more massified mass culture. *Community* may be too expansive a word for what fans create, but even in the case of hip-hop we can see how fellow fans and performers attempt to define and enforce norms of behavior within the group. We need more research to analyze how such media-based communities differ from locale-based ones, but it is critical that we move beyond the common attitude that they are all merely empty or alternatively fully dangerous. If we are all becoming otaku, this is all the more reason to be leery of discriminatory attitudes toward fan behavior, despite the anxieties that consumer society evokes.

References Cited

Aoyagi, Hiroshi
    2000   Pop Idols and the Asian Identity. *In* Japanese Pop! Inside the World of Japanese Popular Culture. Timothy J. Craig, ed. Pp. 309–326. Armonk, NY: M. E. Sharpe.

Asō Kōtarō
    1997   Breeku shinkaron (A theory of increasing music hits). Tokyo: Jōhō Sentaa shuppan-kyoku.

Bourdieu, Pierre
    1984   Distinction: A Social Critique of the Judgment of Taste. Richard Nice, trans. Cambridge: Harvard University Press.

Brubach, Holly
    1998   And Luxury for All. New York Times Magazine, July 12: 24ff.

Chikada Haruo
1998   Kangaeru hitto (Thinking about hits). Tokyo: Bungei shunjū.

Chikushi Tetsuya
1986   Young People as a New Human Race. Japan Quarterly 33(3):291-294.

Ching, Leo
1996   Imaginings in the Empires of the Sun: Japanese Mass Culture in Asia. In Contemporary Japan and Popular Culture. John Whittier Treat, ed. Pp. 169-194. Honolulu: University of Hawai'i Press.

Chusonji Yutsuko
1996   Wild Q. Tokyo: Magazine House.

Clammer, John
1997   Contemporary Urban Japan. Oxford: Blackwell.

Field, Norma
1989   Somehow: The Postmodern as Atmosphere. In Postmodernism and Japan. M. Miyoshi and H. D. Harootuian, eds. Pp. 169-188. Durham: Duke University Press.

Fiske, John
1996   The Cultural Economy of Fandom. In The Adoring Audience: Fan Culture and Popular Media. Linda Lewis, ed. Pp. 30-49. London: Routledge.

Frith, Simon
1996   Performing Rites. Oxford: Oxford University Press.

Hayashi Susumu, Hiroshi Ogawa, and Atsuko Yoshii
1984   Shōhi shakai no kōkoku to ongaku (Advertising and music in consumer society). Tokyo: Yūhikaku.

Hebdige, Dick
1979   Subculture: The Meaning of Style. London: Methuen.

Hosokawa Shuhei, Matsumura Hiroshi, and Shiba Shun'ichi
1991   A Guide to Popular Music in Japan. Kanazawa: IASPM-Japan.

McRobbie, Angela
1993   Shut Up and Dance: Youth Culture and Changing Modes of Femininity. Cultural Studies 7(3):406-426.

Miller, Daniel
1995a   Consumption and Commodities. Annual Review of Anthropology 24:141-161.
1995b   Introduction: Anthropology Modernity and Consumption. In World's Apart: Modernity through the Prism of the Local. Daniel Miller, ed. Pp. 1-22. London: Routledge.

Miyadai Shinji
1990   Shinjinrui to otaku no seikimatsu o toku (Analyzing the end of the century for Shinjinrui and Otaku). Chūō kōron 105:182-202.
1994   Seifuku shōjo tachi no sentaku (The choice of the school uniform girls). Tokyo: Kōdansha.

Miyadai Shinji, Ishihara Hideki, and Otsuka Meiko
1993   Sabukarucha shinwa kaitai (Dismantling the myths of subculture). Tokyo: Parco.

Mizuki Shigeru
    1994   Showa shi (8): Kōdo seichō ikō (History of Showa era, vol. 8: From the high-growth period on). Tokyo: Kōdansha.

Murata Tomoki
    1997   Shibuya-kei moto neta disc guide (A record guide to the original samples of Shibuya-Kei music]. Tokyo: Ohta shuppan.

Radway, Janice A.
    1991   Reading the Romance: Women, Patriarchy , and Popular Literature. Chapel Hill: University of North Carolina Press.

Riding, Alan
    1998   Why 'Titanic' Conquered the World. New York Times, April 26: sec. 2, pp. 1, 29.

Steinhoff, Patricia J.
    1992   Death by Defeatism and Other Fables: The Social Dynamics of the Rengo Purge. *In* Japanese Social Organization. Takie S. Lebra, ed. Pp. 195–224. Honolulu: University of Hawai'i Press.

Tansman, Alan M.
    1996   Mournful Tears and *Sake*: The Postwar Myth of Misora Hibari. *In* Contemporary Japan and Popular Culture. John Whittier Treat, ed. Pp.103–133. Honolulu: University of Hawai'i Press.

Notes

1. "Information" is in many ways a problematic category. We should be suspicious when information is discussed as if it has meaning outside of the social (or technological) context in which it is useful.

2. Evidence for the deepening of the niche scenes appears in an increasing number of record releases as well as overseas tours by representative acts: DJ Krush and Urbarian Gym's T.O.P. Rankaz appeared in New York (hip-hop); Chelsea tours in Jamaica (reggae); Ken Ishii is gaining increasing international fame (techno).

3. Examples of families circa 1996 include the Funky Grammar Unit (Rhymester, East End, Mellow Yellow), Kaminari (e.g., Rino, Twigy, You the Rock, DJ Yas), the Little Bird Nation, which is the "LB" of the party rap festival (e.g., Scha Dara Parr, Tokyo #1 Soul Set, Dassen Trio), and a less central (but more familiar to me) collection called Kitchens (e.g., EDU, Now, Cake-K).

4. In the early 1980s, the Ministry of Health and Welfare approved the use of unheated blood products for Japanese patients, despite warnings of the danger of contamination by the virus later identified as HIV. Over four hundred people, mostly hemophiliac children, were infected with HIV as a result. Collusion between the pharmaceutical company Green Cross and the ministry that squashed a report of the dangers came to light during the spring of 1996.

5. For example, Asō (1997:19) reports that up till the late 1960s appearance of these pre-idols, the informal forms for *boku* (me) and *kimi* (you) were never used in lyrics.

6. At club events, too, DJs spinning from the after-3-a.m. portion of the night will often play rare or relatively unknown old soul, jazz, and funk albums as *neta taimu* (sample time).

7. "Pops" is a rendering of the category *poppusu* in Japanese. Each of the four main genres—new music, rock, pops, and kayōkyoku can be viewed as "pop music" (as opposed to underground, alternative, indies, and so on) and so I have retained the strange English of "pops" to distinguish it from the larger category of "pop." It is not unusual to combine the categories "pops" and kayōkyoku, as is done in publications from the Recording Industry Association of Japan, and in the influential monthly *Music Magazine*.

8. Miyadai points out that initially the idea of otaku was as a kind of person without good interpersonal skills, but as groups of people began to consider themselves otaku who faced unfair discrimination, the term took on the connotation of a kind of culture (from *jinkaku ruikei* to *bunka ruikei*) (1994:162–166).

9. Three S's because of the Japanese words for these items: *sentakuki, suihanki, sōjiki*. The three K's were *kūrā, kā*, and *karā terebi*.

10. For example, Takagi Kan was a punk rocker. Chikada Haruo, who later took the moniker President BPM, had several rock albums to his name before starting a rap group called Vibrastone. He has since turned to ambient music, and is currently receiving acclaim as a J Pop music critic (Chikada 1998).

11. In considering criticisms of fans, it would be important to include outsiders' criticisms, but interestingly, there are few such critics. Except for the dismissive attitude, "they're just imitation New Yorkers," there are few outside critics of Japanese hip-hop fans. This seems to support Miyadai's (1994) claim that outsiders have no feeling one way or the other about other islands in space.

12. Unlike American rap, which has many references to residential neighborhoods as the source of a rapper's authenticity, in Japan the club is the primary locale referred to to contrast the true hip-hop culture from the crass commercialism of the market. Such assertions, however, cannot be taken at face value.

2

Letters from the Heart

Negotiating Fan–Star Relationships in
Japanese Popular Music

CHRISTINE R. YANO

It is an early Sunday evening in October, with sunlight beginning to wane and winds picking up in the gray skies above NHK Hall in the fashionable Shibuya district of Tokyo in 1992. I have wound my way out of the train station, past the statue of faithful dog Hachiko, whose loyal patience has been immortalized in bronze and whose surroundings have become a waiting zone for people meeting friends. Everywhere, it seems, I am surrounded by evidence of youth culture in the department stores, boutiques, sidewalk vendors, McDonald's, and coffee shops. Those around me stroll in pairs, threes, and fours, tea-hair-dyed browsers, dodging cars, buses, and taxis as they meander from store to store. I walk singly, hurriedly, and in the distance I see two older women in dark dresses, nylons, and low-heeled black shoes, whose steps match my own. We are headed for the same place, just beyond this maze of commerce, to the spot where the jumble of stores suddenly ends and vistas broaden to encompass trees, broad sidewalks, and the quiet, glass-enclosed pillars of NHK Hall.

By the time I enter the building, I am surrounded by other women, most of them the age of my mother but not quite looking like her. They murmur their greetings, they gaze over posters and recordings, they glance through souvenirs for sale— handkerchiefs, telephone cards, folding fans, T-shirts. For the most part, they linger only briefly before taking their seats in the darkened concert hall. They have come but incidentally to buy. They have come primarily to see before them live on stage the man whose voice fills their living rooms at home, whose songs, they say, sustain them, invoking notions of *ikigai* (give their lives meaning), *yasuragi* (soothe them), and *kokoro no sasae* (support their hearts and souls). In their words, they have come here to *au* (meet) him, even if that meeting takes place between one singer and thousands of fans. For many, this is not the first time.

The curtain parts, and suddenly there he is, Mori Shin'ichi, a lone 45-year-old tuxedoed figure on a big stage. "Mori-san!" enthusiastic fans call out to him. He launches into song. Some songs follow one another without a break; other songs are interspersed with light stage patter. He is not an expansive figure, but contained—striking a pose that is serious, shy, and slightly awkward. His songs speak of broken hearts and aching memories. His body moves very little throughout the performance, an arm raising the microphone to sing, a leg shifting his weight, his head lowered between numbers. After an hour and a half, near the concert's end, the lights dim and he launches into what has become his signature piece, "Ofukurosan" (Mother Dear). Suddenly his knees buckle slightly, his face contorts, and it seems that he may begin to cry. His fans rush to him.

Swept by the morbid curiosity that drives most anthropologists, I rush, too. I stand 20-women deep from the stage, reaching my hand out to touch his in mimicry of those around me. There is Mori, elevated but a stone's throw away. Here are fans, in the aisles, out of their orderly seats, crowding the stage, pushing slightly. In yearning toward him, they press against one another, arm to arm, leg to leg, abdomen to back. This chapter addresses both the yearning toward and the pressing against as forms of intimacy that give meaning to Mori Shin'ichi's fandom in contemporary Japan.

Thomas Kasulis points out that intimacy—that is, "an inseparability, a belonging together, a sharing"—may be considered a trope for religious, moral, and aesthetic values in Japan (1990:436). Intimacy animates the sociality of selves enmeshed within everyday lives. In this chapter I examine intimacy as an ideal form embedded in the commercialized relationships of fans to star in popular culture. It is the very appetite for intimacy—here, many to one, as well as to each other—that drives flocks of fans to the concert hall, to the music stores to buy Mori's latest CD, to the karaoke booths where they sing Mori's songs.

Enka and Its Reputation as the Heart–Soul of Japanese

The fan world I analyze here surrounds *enka*, an old-fashioned, sentimental genre of syncretic Japanese popular music originating in the early 20th century, stereotypically dubbed expressive of *Nihonjin no kokoro* (the heart–soul of Japanese). That heart–soul is said to rest not only in the chords, rhythms, and melodies that sound instantly old, but in the words that paint a picture of unremitting longing for lovers long gone and mothers in rural hometowns, and the images of scenes and singers that invoke the past and distant (Yano 2002).

Enka has the look and sound of a previous era, even as it is newly created. In fact, it is this very referentiality that lends its appeal so that each new song sounds strikingly familiar. Singers such as Mori embody old-fashioned values of *gaman* (endurance), *gambaru* (perserverance), and *giri-ninjō* (the internal struggle between duty and desire). The stereotype guarantees enka a place within the national imaginary, recuperated from the margins to claim center stage as indigenous popular song (cf. Ivy 1995).

Of course, the heart–soul abides as a marketing ploy as well [tugging at national heartstrings with carefully crafted tears for sale.] The marketing ploy has become increasingly desperate in recent years as the industry has watched sales shrink steadily from its heyday in the 1970s, dwindling from four percent in 1990 to less than one-tenth percent by 2000. And yet enka survives, primarily through karaoke, AM radio, and state-supported institutions such as Nihon hōsō kyōkai (NHK; Japan's public broadcasting corporation). NHK, in particular, provides critical airplay, both on radio and television. Enka still occupies the main stage at the annual New Year's Eve popular music bash, the NHK Kōhaku Uta Gassen (Red and White Song Contest), viewing of which has long been a national family ritual.

Enka's stereotype persists amid constant challenges from youth, intellectuals, and many others who disparage this "crying song" as awash in feudalistic values, outdated, out of step with the times. For these critics, enka is not merely out of step with the times, but dangerously so, pulling Japan back to a past that has never changed. The stereotype also persists despite several ironies: non–Japanese Asian singers from Korea and Taiwan singing this "heart–soul of Japan"; the continuing popularity of enka in other Asian countries in part as a legacy of Japan's colonial past; and suspicions that enka's origins were not in Japan, but in colonial Korea in the 1930s, where similar sentimental ballads are still popular (Yano 2001).

These challenges and multiple ironies go unheeded by enka's fans, primarily middle-aged and older adults. Many of these fans are indeed working class and from the country, but white-collar urban dwellers also listen to and sing these tearjerkers. Gender separates their fandom in time and space. Typically, women constitute the majority of fan club members; as such, they attend concerts, and occasionally parties; write song requests to radio and television stations; buy the singer's latest cassette or CD; and sometimes sing his songs, either privately or in the company of friends. Much of a woman's day can be spent on fan club activities, if she chooses. Men, meanwhile, participate in fandom in their own kinds of way, often after-work hours, such as singing at karaoke and listening at bars. For female fans (many of them housewives), [developing a relationship with an enka star, particularly a male one such as Mori Shin'ichi, becomes a means toward creating a sexualized, economic, affective identity built on the consumption of intimacy and celebrity.] The fan–star relationship frames these women's lives with a sense of purpose and focus.

Intimacy as a Model of Knowledge and Experience

Although Mori's fans share much in common with fans of other media stars and fantasy worlds globally, such as Elvis and *Star Trek*, I argue that the tie between fan practices and particular cultural values in Japan gives these fans a kind of legitimacy and authority that elsewhere might be far more subject to critique. One of these cultural values is the concept of intimacy that Kasulis describes as "a general orientation of Japanese religious values" (1990:433). Here, I deliberately extend intimacy to the realm of fandom in Japan, as one of many links that might be made between the fervor of religious and cult followers to the passion of fans of media stars. In both religion and fandom, a drive to intimacy impels individuals to act in ways that go beyond the bounds of self to seek greater communion with the object of their adoration. This drive forges the yearning and pressing of the concert hall.

Kasulis delineates five overlapping aspects of Japanese intimacy that revolve around types of knowledge, experience, and relationships: (1) intimacy as objective, nonpublic knowledge; (2) intimacy conceptualized as an internal relationship between overlapping parts, not as an external bond; (3) intimacy as affective knowledge; (4) intimacy as somatic knowledge and experience; and (5) intimacy as non-rational, intuitive knowledge (1990:436–439). All five aspects model fan–star interactions in Japan such as that of Mori and his fans.

First, fans enter a particular kind of fan–star relationship by joining a fan club, creating a sense of *uchi* (insider identification) with other club members. Within this context, intimacy may be marked by the degree to which members share and sometimes compete for objective, nonpublic (that is, not known to outsiders) knowledge. This knowledge ranges from the mundane (e.g., time and place of concerts, media appearances, fan club gatherings) to the esoteric (e.g., Mori's favorite animal, food, preference for mountains over oceans). Mori trivia, in fact, becomes the basis for competition at fan club gatherings in which members participate in a quiz game with prizes awarded to those who know the most about Mori. Intimacy requires the acquisition of this "objective, nonpublic knowledge"; thus being a fan means engaging in *Mori-benkyō* (study) and displaying the fruits of that study to other fans. Even if fans themselves take some of this in jest, the process includes the culturally lauded practice of *benkyō*, leading to mastery, expertise, and display of knowledge. This kind of parallel alternate universe of cultural values and practices shared with the larger society lends legitimacy to Japanese fandom. A Mori fan, then, may be distinguished as a Mori expert.

Second, through *omoiyaru* (empathy), fan members make the star's needs their own, in effect embracing the star within their own uchi. Fans talk of *ittaikan* (feeling as if of the same body) in describing the intimacy of their connectedness with the star. A relationship with the star, then, becomes internal—one part to another within a somatic unit. Intimacy in this way becomes an assertion of that uchi as an organic and thus naturalized bond. Self and star commingle as overlapping parts, not as self and other. This is not unlike the relationship of mother to child in a Japanese context, whose postuterine interactions assume the continuing tie of the womb. Here, fans become mother to son Mori. They have thus incorporated Mori within themselves, grandfathered in as an assertion of a retroactive womb, even as they dream of the fiction that he has somehow incorporated them within him.

Third, fans' actions find their basis in affect. Above all, emotion fuels their behavior, compelling them to listen, buy, cheer, clap, yearn, and press. Among the range of behaviors that distinguishes fans from mere listeners is establishing an affective bond with each other by joining a fan club. Within the club, a fan may take comfort as a member of a community built on emotion. The community in fact spawns even greater emotion fueled by the giddiness of shared passion. This bond of passion sometimes emboldens members to act in ways they might not otherwise individually—for example, rushing the stage—in a bout of emotional contagion (Hatfield et al. 1994).

Fourth, the fans' relationship to the star is often expressed in bodily terms— whether as pounding heart, loss of consciousness, or tears. Fans engage viscerally with the star's persona, even when that persona exists not in the flesh but in electronically mediated form. At concerts they cry with Mori; at home they cheer as they watch him on television. This bodily engagement authenticates the fan–star relationship as real by virtue of those tears and cheers. The tie of fans to star, as well as to each other, becomes that much more compelling because it is experienced sensually firsthand as the yearning and pressing of bodies.

Stars enable and encourage this bodily engagement by regularly, if formulaically, reaching out to fans. These activities include leaving the stage while singing and mingling with the audience, not as a spontaneous gesture, but one preplanned and orchestrated to systematically cover first one side of the auditorium, then the other, aisle by aisle, back to front. In this audience mingling, Mori does not move alone, but maneuvers surrounded by crouching assistants who pave his way and lead him through the territory of pressing middle-aged female fans, their arms outstretched, their hands waving. Body-grazing activities include these brief Mori encounters—a glancing touch of fingertips, a hasty locking of hands. They also include more formal handshaking sessions, sometimes held immediately after concerts, sometimes held at promotional events where fans purchase the latest CD and receive the opportunity to shake Mori's hand. They include photo sessions at annual fan club dinner parties where fans line up for the opportunity to stand one by one with Mori, and have that moment forever commemorated with a Polaroid shot. Photos such as these become particularly important treasures, capturing one moment as a visual mnemonic of not only the event, but an entire relationship. One fan excitedly showed me her collection of such photos, chronicling her relationship with Mori over the years. The photo of two people (and two people alone) standing side by side—shoulder to shoulder, and for the more daring, even cheek to cheek—in their party best, smiling before the camera could be that of any couple. In fact it is the very coupling, the fiction of the two-ness, that beautifully masks the lopsidedness of the relationship. Intimacy inheres within a dream of exclusivity performed by the photo.

Finally, the fan-star relationship gains cultural validity in its very nonrationality, as if its authenticity lies in not being subject to rational processes or pragmatic concerns. Fans' relationships with Mori rest in the extraordinary, and thus are above reason. So, too, is fans' knowledge of Mori; [they know him in ways that are embedded internally, prerationally if one is to follow the mother-child analogy, even preternaturally.]Explaining the relationship would rob the coupling of its status. Instead, it is a relationship built on the inexplicable, and its inexplicability gives profundity to the relationship. [These various aspects of knowing and being become the model of intimacy upon which the fan-star relationship is built.]

A further aspect of intimacy not covered by Kasulis's (1990) features is also important for the fan-star relationship in Japan—that of *migawari*, which means, literally, "body exchange" and refers to person, act, or state of substitution—in short, surrogacy. In Japanese society, self-other exchange—the *dainin* (surrogate) for the *honnin* (real person)—is a common trope of public life. As Takie Lebra explains, a designated dainin appears as a legitimate surrogate for the honnin in the following ways: (1) as a form of protection when the honnin is unable to perform a function; (2) as authentication that amplifies the actions and sincerity of the honnin; and (3) as implementation to rectify a status-role gap (1994:112–118). Through bodily practices such as karaoke, fans become surrogates for the star in public settings. Surrogacy, in fact, may be considered an extension of omoiyari in its empathic identification of dainin for honnin. Fan club members are thus encouraged by the record company that organizes and controls the club to sing Mori's latest song at karaoke as part of a promotional strategy, spreading its sound to *mimi ni hairu* (enter the ears) of the public and make it a hit. Ideally, one might hear Mori's songs sung by his fans or surrogates in karaoke bars and booths from Hokkaido to Kyushu. Of course this does not imply that any of these middle-aged and older female fans can remotely approximate Mori's husky voice—or perhaps some can—and idiomatic style. But though they may not provide true surrogate for Mori's sound, the indexicality of their effort pays tribute to Mori as a star. As one industry publication states, "An enka song must not only be sung by the original person [to be considered truly popular], but also by other singers and in karaoke" (*Konfidensu* 1992:24). A song thus needs migawari, its "shadow performance," to prove its status and validate itself. Likewise, Mori (honnin) needs his fan-surrogates (dainin) to establish and legitimate his worthiness. Through fans' surrogacy, a song and singer live not singly, but multiply, appearing and reappearing in ubiquitous form. This kind of surrogacy suggests that[fans and singer form a bubble of engagement, endlessly locked in small and large performances of intimacy on a public stage.]

Charisma and Fandom

Intimacy in its various complicated and overlapping dimensions is centered in and by the charisma of the star. According to Weber (Lindholm 1990), charismatic figures "are marked by a unique and innate capacity to display highly colored emotions, of whatever kind. [They] are imagined . . . to be more vivid than ordinary mortals; they appear to exist in an altered and intensified state of consciousness that is outside of mundane patterning and that is more potent than ordinary emotional life" (p. 26). Clearly, emotion rests at the heart of charisma, culminating in the "charismatic moment," defined by Weber as "a psychological state in the here and now" (Lindholm 1990:26). However, rather than take charisma to inhere within an individual or moment, I wish to embed charisma within a particularized relationship that is asymmetric, hierarchical, unstable, and interdependent. As Lindholm points out, "charisma is, above all, a *relationship,* a mutual mingling of inner selves of leader and follower" (1990:7). It is the social nature of charisma that is of interest: the phenomenon of one leader with numerous followers, one star with thousands of fans, each fan and follower personalizing that relationship for her or his own purposes. Whether in religion, politics, or entertainment, a charismatic relationship develops between a human figure and an image in human form that becomes mediated into a larger-than-life figure.

The asymmetry of the relationship rests on various aspects. For one, because it is a relationship between one and many, the depth, investment, commitment, and intensity can hardly be equal on both sides. The two meet in an imagined arena of intimacy, and one side of the equation must do far more of the imagining than the other. Practices of intimacy on the part of fans may be individual, spontaneous, and contextual, as well as ritualized and predetermined. Star practices of intimacy, typically one generated to provide for the needs of many, by contrast are formulaic and generalized—one size fits all.

Second, the statuses of the two parties in the relationship are, for the most part, unequal. In the case of religion, the statuses may be so uneven as to be between human and deity or quasi deity. In entertainment, status differences are marked by prestige, privilege, wealth, and celebrity create a chasm of inaccessibility. Both star and fan work to overcome this chasm, but to different effect. The star in the Japanese entertainment world must constantly bridge the distance with fans, or at least give the impression that he is doing so. As Hiroshi Aoyagi (1999) has pointed out, the Japanese public prefers their stars as *toshindai* (life sized); therefore stars should be human, rather than godlike. The work of the star, then, consists of a tightrope balance between the magnitude of the stage and tōshindai imaging, between performing larger-than-life feats of emotional expression and down-to-earth "aw-shucks" handshaking. Fans, too, work constantly to overcome the chasm, but their work is emotionally driven in a bid to establish and assert intimacy. This is the work of yearning and pressing.

Third, if the majority of Kasulis's aspects of intimacy revolve around knowledge, then the degree of knowledge of one party concerning the other is vastly different. The star's dearth of knowledge about individual fans contrasts greatly with the depth and breadth of knowledge of fans concerning the star. In fact, a fan's relationship with the star hangs by the very thread of her knowledge; therefore acquiring and displaying this knowledge is of vital concern to her. She must be the Mori expert, because only then can she establish herself as a fan rather than a mere listener.

Fourth, stars and fans differ in how each expresses her or his involvement in the relationship. A star sings songs on stage or in recordings, and that undifferentiated communication reaches out to fans. Fans, on the other hand, give individualized gifts of devotion to the star. They write personal letters to him. They sing his songs at karaoke as acts of both surrogacy and loyalty. By forming their lips around his words, they perform themselves as part of him. The asymmetry of their relationship does not deter fans. What matters more is that there is a relationship at all, in whatever form, surviving the most tenuous conditions.

Stars in Japan such as Mori constantly work against the asymmetry of the relationship. Instead of portraying themselves as superstars, they position themselves as servants to fans, thanking them for their support. Their biographies paint a picture of early hardship, whether derived from poverty or the uphill battle of making it as a star. Enka stars in particular must be carefully imaged to fit the genre; therefore their images emphasize humble beginnings in rural villages or, if from urban centers such as Tokyo, their ties to the most traditional parts of the city, dubbed *shitamachi* (downtown). In these ways, stars are not stars so much as everyday folk—toshindai—serving those who support them.

The degree of investment differentiates fans as a subset of general consumers. Fans are those consumers who have identified with and committed to a particular product through practices of intimacy. That investment then informs future decisions of consumption so that each decision is made within the framework of fandom. Fans do not consume uncritically. Rather, as various authors in this volume point out, fans consume and critique, perhaps with a greater sense of authority based on knowledge and even ownership. Moreover, fans consume on the basis of a preestablished relationship with a product (here, a singer). Fans consume as fans, highlighting their consumption with etched meaning as not only a symbolic act, but also a social act. Intimacy gives license to consume as an expression of their continuing relationship to the product, and their ongoing identity as a fan.

Fans produce as they consume, "poaching" texts, as Michel de Certeau (1984) puts it, to suit their needs and circumstances; here the text that fans poach is not limited to the words of songs, but extends to Mori himself as a symbol, to performance at concerts such as these, and to enka as a genre. The texts are multiple and moving, and its readers thus "nomadic," moving to new texts, producing new meanings (de Certeau 1992). Henry Jenkins delineates five different ways by which fans read texts: (1) intragenerically, in relation to others within a series of related texts; (2) transgenerically, across generic expectations; (3) extratextually; (4) subculturally; and (5) within the author's oeuvre (1992:37–38). I argue that the mode of reading with greatest impact on these fans' lives is extratextual, constantly linking up Mori's songs, performances, and Mori himself to their lives. At the same time, they link their lives to these texts. They do this by the very relationship that they assert, embedding Mori within the everyday.

The Practices of Intimacy

One of the primary ways fans have of asserting and subsequently negotiating that relationship is through fan letters, a select few of which are published in monthly newsletters. Fan letters are part of what Lawrence Grossberg calls "the mobilization and organization of affective investments" (1992:59). These "practices and texts" provide fans with "strategies that enable them to gain a certain amount of control over their affective life" (Ibid.: 65). Fan letters stake a claim to an active role in a fan–star relationship, as well as to the existence of the relationship itself.

In this section I analyze fan–star relationships negotiated in part through letters published by Mori Shin'ichi's *kōenkai* (support organization or fan club) over a two-year time span (1992–94). I consider these letters to document a shared, intimate relationship between one star and many fans. What makes this shared intimacy particularly noteworthy is the fact that most pop music fan clubs in Japan are organized and run not by fans themselves, but by production and record company promotion division. [Shared intimacy becomes a marketing tool, willingly engaged by fans, craftily conceived by promotional strategists, heartily welcomed by record company executives.] Fans find their own sources of pleasure and satisfaction in club activities that give them greater proximity to the star. Asserting their powers of consumption, housewives buy membership in a club, which purchases them intimacy through newsletters, parties, tours, and "infomercial" meetings. They write letters to the star, and these letters become testament not only to participation in a charismatic relationship, but also to the empowering effects of consumer desire.

True to Weber's (Lindholm 1990) characterization of charismatic figures, [Mori is known for his emotions and his sincerity and skill in displaying and conveying them.] Most importantly, Mori is said to be particularly adept at expressing (even sometimes embodying) *onna no kimochi* (the feelings of women) in songs that are either sympathetic to a woman's point of view or, more directly, to that most important woman in many Japanese men's lives, his mother.

Mori's signature song, "Ofukurosan" (Mother Dear), highlights some of the ways in which his music constructs and reaffirms motherhood. Here, an indebted son sings to an audience of wise, caring mothers who flock to concerts and buy recordings to hear these words—words their own sons might feel but seldom, if ever, express directly to them.

OFUKUROSAN [Mother Dear]
Lyrics: KAWAUCHI Yasunori
Music: INOMATA Kōshō
Sung by MORI Shin'ichi, 1971 (Victor)
(Translation C. Yano)

> Mother dear, mother dear,
> I look up to the sky and find memories of you.
> On rainy days, you are my umbrella;
> You taught me to become an umbrella
> For others in this world.
> I will never forget
> The truth of your words.

Huge numbers of women have joined Mori's fan club, and as club members, they write him letters that illuminate various aspects of fan–star interactions. On the one hand, the letters may be taken as private expressions of fans, as conduits of communication by which a relationship is established and shaped. Here is personal narrative by which a fan constitutes an event and makes sense of it. However, this is not a diary, but a letter; therefore the telling of the story is meant to communicate with another person. Moreover, the person to whom the letter addresses is a celebrity, and the purpose of the letter is to bridge the chasm between the ordinary world and the star. On another level, the letters as published in the monthly newsletter may be taken as documents of the fan club–publicity office whose goal is to spur fans to loyalty, make them believe in the power of their star, and establish a community of fandom with one another. These letters are selected (and some cynics may say even written) by employees who keep the goals of the organization in mind when doing their selecting. Upon publication, these letters become not private expressions, but carefully filtered public documents of a profit-seeking culture industry.

Mori's fan club is operated by his production company, in conjunction with Victor Records, to which he is contracted. Staff members of the fan club are not fans, as some have been quick to point out; however, the woman in charge of overseeing club activities is, in fact, a relative of Mori's. In 1992, there were approximately 10 thousand members, the majority of whom were middle-aged and older women in Japan.

Each month, the kōenkai sends out a *kaihō* (newsletter) to all members, which contains color glossy photos; information of upcoming concerts, television appearances, and record releases; a philosophical "talk essay" in which Mori ruminates on life in general, and a *fuan no hiroba* (fan section of letters and Mori's replies). The identities of letter writers are only partly revealed by their initials and place of residence, but even in this degree of individuation [each letter becomes authenticated as the voice of a particular fan whose experience may signify the experiences of many.] In these letters we selectively overhear individual fans establishing their own sense of intimacy with Mori and, in effect, with other club members.

Many of the letters evoke intimacy through their bodily knowledge (or at least contact) with Mori, reconstructed as "charismatic moments."

6/92, Y.E. from Kanagawa: To my surprise, at the end of your recent concert, I got to hold your hand when you came down to the audience section. Your hand was unexpectedly soft. It was a hand warm from moving people's hearts. I would like to make the memory of that day live in my daily life as nourishment for my soul.

9/92, K.O. from Osaka: I will never forget the warmth of Mori's hand at the handshaking gathering.

11/92, H.F. from Hyōgo Prefecture: In the second half of your concert, I was able to shake hands with Mori. I grasped your soft hand with both of mine. I was greatly moved. It was a night that transported me out of the fatigue of the day.

Mori: Thank you. The concert was a moving experience for me, too, and I felt the warmth of everyone's hearts.

12/92, M.K. from Osaka: I am thrilled to have a commemorative photo with Mori from the annual fan get-together. Afterward on the train home from the party, I would look at my photo and remember the warmth of Mori's cheek on mine. I felt so happy. I hold the warmth of Mori in my heart and promise to support you all the more from now on.

Mori: I, too, hold my fans' warmth in my heart.

In these letters, as well as in Mori's replies, one finds the rhetoric of intimacy—softness, warmth, heart. Yet, note the economy with which Mori (or the creators of the newsletter) writes. The fan's individuated expression is answered by generalized response, applicable equally to the letter writer herself, as to those other fans reading over her shoulder. "She" becomes "everyone," the warmth of one cheek becomes diffuse warmth held in one's heart.

Furthermore, the words used to describe Mori's physical presence are not those one typically associates with male sexuality, or at least the stereotypical *kōha* (tough guy) image. Instead of a hard body, Mori's hand is "unexpectedly soft"—a quality commented on by more than one letter writer. Fan letters describe Mori in feminized ways through comments about softness and warmth. The source of his warmth is the work of Mori—actively "moving people's hearts." Mori, in fact, fulfills the other Japanese male stereotype of *nanpa* (a romantic, "soft" guy), typified historically as feminized men, known for their great appeal to women through an almost simpering emotionality (Buruma 1984:143; Gilmore 1990:187–188; Yano 2003). The attractions of Mori, as well as other nanpa, lie not in sexual dimorphism, but on the contrary in their very proximity to women. Their bodies are slight, their faces pale, their touch soft. More important, they call out for care, begging the *amayakasu* (willingness to be depended on) and nurturance of women. In Mori's case, his virtues, described bodily as softness and warmth, echo those of women themselves. He nourishes his fans spiritually, even as they, at times, nourish him physically with gifts of food and general solicitations of care. Mori and his fans thus become mutual, alternating, though asymmetric, mothers.

Fans' letters of intimacy also describe being transported out of their everyday lives by Mori and his singing. In a sweep of passivity, fans portray themselves as victims to Mori's charms, listening captivated, mouthing his words enraptured.

> 2/92, H.T. from Kanagawa Prefecture: At Mori's Tokyo concert, without thinking of what I was doing, I found myself singing along with Mori softly to myself. Hearing Mori's heartful singing of "Usagi" brought tears to my eyes and I was enraptured.

Fandom becomes here a rape or rapturing of consciousness, fans submitting to something or someone more powerful than themselves. Of course there is no physical, or even emotional or spiritual, attack to this rape; rather, the rape occurs benignly and diffusely. Mori takes the stage and sings; his fans listen and are led to actions "without thinking of what I was doing." Mori's seductions take over fans' consciousness, leading their bodies to acts beyond rationality, whether singing along or crying with him.

The question arises, How exactly does Mori seduce? Fan letters describe Mori's seductions as founded in emotions—in other words, exactly in the charismatic capacity in which Weber writes (Lindholm 1990). He seduces by his vulnerability, singing of the lover he lost, or even more potently, of the mother he cherishes. His singing and sometimes his (near-)crying become both source and stimulus of tears.

1/92, T.H. from Tokyo: I was moved to tears . . . by Mori's songs. But if they are tears with such fine aftertaste, then it would be fine for them to flow however many times.

These tears embody a kind of affective utopia, "direct and vivid, not 'qualified' or 'ambiguous' as day-to-day life makes them," which Dyer analyzes as the basis of entertainment (1993:273, 276). Locked in mutual engagement, fans cry with, for, and through Mori.

7/93, Y.F. from Ehime Prefecture: [In concert] Mori sang with tears in his eyes, and his fans listened with tears in theirs.

7/93 K.K from Tokyo: We cried together with Mori.

[The mingling of tears becomes testament to common emotional ground, of the very intimacy upon which this fan–star relationship may be based.]
Fans' letters indicate that that intimacy may be conjured not only in person, but in electronically mediated presentations. Television and radio's very transcendence of spatial distance produces what Painter calls a "quasi-intimacy" that is both public and private, circulated widely and consumed in the home (1996:227). Fans bridge the gap between the mediated and unmediated by involving themselves bodily with Mori even when he is not there.

1/93, S.U. from Osaka: I enjoyed hearing Mori on the live radio show "Hatsuratsu Studio 505." I envy those who live in Tokyo who were able to be with him right there in the studio. As I listened to the live broadcast, I shouted along with the studio audience, "Mori-san!"

5/93, K.N. from Osaka: [While watching a televised singing appearance by Mori] without thinking, I called out "Nippon ichi!" (The best in all Japan!) and applauded right there in front of the TV.

These shouts, exhortations, and applause, even for mediated Mori, provide bodily evidence of the intimacy of fans' relationship with him.
Doing Mori fandom means performing large and small acts of worship, from joining his fan club to waving a penlight as a member of that fan club at a Mori concert. These penlight-waving activities, like Mori's move through the audience, are not spontaneous, but carefully planned by the production team that choreographs Mori's promotional activities as well as the fan club. Watching mediated Mori prompts fans to take up the penlight as proof of their affections.

8/93, T.T. from Osaka: [After watching Mori's performance on TV] I was so happy. I will be sure to bring my penlight to the next concert.

In the darkened rows of the concert hall, penlight waving becomes an act of solidarity, allowing fans to perform their devotion back to Mori. In fact, it is the one fan performance to which he, and he alone (theoretically), lays witness. The two performances face one another—he singing from the stage, they waving their penlights in unison to the rhythm of his song—and converge in a spectacle of intimacy. Penlight waving thus becomes more than a simple gesture, but an assertion of a fan's support of Mori, her identity as a Mori fan, and her relationship with Mori.

The act of singing Mori's songs in karaoke may be interpreted similarly. One letter writer explains:

> 8/93, M.S. from Tokyo: I am one who always shies away from karaoke, but yesterday my husband took me to the neighborhood *sunakku* [bar] and I chose Mori's new song to sing. The sunakku owners were the only ones to applaud, but I will try harder next time so that I can receive applause from other customers. I will support this song and help make it a hit.

Singing Mori's songs at karaoke becomes an act of intimacy through forming lips around his words and bodies around his gestures. This may be all the more meaningful if the fan is one who normally "shies away from karaoke." Here, she must overcome her natural inclinations to better serve Mori. The quality of her surrogate singing matters far less than the sincerity with which she pursues promoting Mori's new song. Her singing serves as an act of devotion (even as it may here devolve into an act of tolerance for those listening). Through *monomane* (imitation), she achieves the ultimate in staged intimacy and tribute, becoming nothing less than surrogate Mori.

[It is of little concern to these fans that their practices of fandom play so neatly into the hands of record companies] The commercial aspects of fandom find little criticism among fans to whom I have spoken.

> 9/93, Y.H. from Yamaguchi: Mori's newest song is a song that could be pegged as a sure hit from the first day of sales. As predicted, it has now climbed the enka charts. When it became a big hit this autumn, my heart beat fast. I can hear it played often on the radio and see it in the record stores lined up as part of the Top 10 songs, and it makes me so happy. Let's all try our best to permeate all of Japan with the melody of this song!

These fans willingly, even eagerly, act in accord with the record company's wishes, buying Mori's cassettes and CDs, peopling promotional events, sending in postcard requests to play Mori's songs on radio and television shows, singing Mori's songs at karaoke, ensuring that Mori's songs "enter the ears" of the general public.

If one is looking for a rationale, one may find it in the fact that what fans do enhances Mori's status, and thereby their own. Yet, fans themselves do not reconstruct their efforts to support Mori in this way. Rather, as one fan writes, "Supporting Mori gives my life meaning (*ikigai*)." In entering into a social relationship with Mori, however mediated, fans participate in a process of creating their own identities. As Skov and Moeran point out, "being a consumer is a form of self-reflection" (1995:5), to which I add that being a consuming fan is a form of self-constitution. Consuming Mori means consuming the emotions and sensitivities that he is made to represent. The shift from mere consumer to avid fan asserts a particular relationship based in loyalty, obligation, and responsibility. Requesting a song by postcard is a small price to pay for finding such meaning in life.

Concluding Intimacies

Examining these published fan letters inevitably raises the question of the letters that never get published. We never read of any threats to Mori, of what might be called "dangerous fanaticism," of overtly sexual letters, even letters critical of Mori or his performances. Yet, we must assume that Mori is no exception among public figures who may receive these types of letters. What is published is censored, sanitized fandom along cultural models that reinforce intimacy and charisma. I read these letters both as sincere expressions of fandom, as well as carefully screened parts of a constructed image.

In writing letters to Mori, fans lay claim to their involvement within a charismatic relationship. In publishing those letters, as well as Mori's replies, the kōenkai affirms that relationship. Here is virtual Mori in print, speaking with a kind of intimacy that a fan would never share otherwise. Through these letters, fans can make of Mori what she will—a confidante, a lover, but most important, a son. Unlike a face-to-face relationship, this relationship rests solely on her action, not in interaction. Within this model, Mori's charisma does not exist until one fan chooses to place herself within that relationship. Each letter, then, invokes participation within a charismatic relationship, and therefore authentication of Mori's appeal. In this sense, these fan letters are no less than foundational to the kōenkai organization, to Mori's stardom, and to the creation of fans as fans. Writing fan letters becomes a form of "textual and enunciative productivity," yielding declarations of membership within a fan–star relationship (Fiske 1992).

Like the female romance readers of Janice Radway's study, the women of Mori Shin'ichi's fan club may be interpreted as engaging in an oppositional, "combative and compensatory" practice in actively refusing, if momentarily, their "self-abnegating social role" and instead focusing on their own affective needs (1984:210–211). The time these fans spend and energies they exert—attending

Mori concerts, singing Mori songs at karaoke, writing Mori letters—may be considered time and energy spent away from their social roles as wives and mothers.

At the same time, at least part of Mori's appeal lies in his making available to his female fans the very role they abnegate by their actions—that of mother. He calls out to them, his pain whetting their appetite to amayakasu, to indulge another's dependency. In his neediness he becomes the son to which they devote their emotional lives. Moreover, that devotion becomes their ikigai. In a 1987 poll taken by Mori's kōenkai regarding what place Mori holds in their lives, among the most frequent responses were ikigai (18.4 percent), yasuragi (12.2 percent), and "as a son" (over 10 percent). Expressions of fandom follow gendered constructions and expectations. Fans portray themselves as passive recipients of Mori's charm, even if their actions belie no passivity. Their practices of fandom often revolve around maternal expressions of concern, making his needs their own.

Mori Shin'ichi is part of what may be called "women's culture" in Japan, or more specifically what I call "housewife culture" *(shufu bunka)*, reflecting the life stage of most of his fans. These women are far from rebels, although some of their actions may be interpreted as small acts of rebellion. In the minds of fans, theirs is not oppositional culture, and Mori is not an oppositional figure. Indeed, most of their lives are spent replicating the structures of the male-dominant society—marrying, having children, tending to the needs of others. However, in choosing not only to listen to Mori's songs and attend his concerts, but to become active letter-writing, penlight-waving members of his fan club, these women create subjectivities and identities wound around the constructed intimacies of a charismatic-based relationship.

These letters, selected by the record-company-controlled fan club, support the image of Mori as hardworking servant, as son to these women whose own biological children have, for the most part, grown and left home. More than erotically charged expressions, these letters form a web of maternal affection and concern. They cluck, even as they pant, selling an image of Mori based in warmth more than heat. They are careful not to disrupt (cf. Kelly, introduction, this volume). They draw a distinct line that preserves the social order of hearth and home. His is an image of a son–man who suffers, and in suffering draws on what is construed by enka's reputation as a national-cultural well of pain. It is Mori (or his image) as victim—of his own sensitivity, his lover who left him, his memories of a childhood long past. Mori the victim née son, calls on fans to invoke the maternal yoke, to raise what might be called—if one is to accept enka's moniker as "expressive of the heart–soul of Japanese"—the national Mother, even as he at times and in his own way mothers and nourishes them. Fandom in this vessel locks the charismatic relationship tight, fan to image, bound within the seeming simplicity of the womb where warmth and heat commingle. Mori's fans herald the position to which they lay claim, engaging in the practices of public motherhood that never end.

References Cited

Aoyagi Hiroshi
    1999   Islands of Eight Million Smiles: Pop-Idol Performances and the Field of Symbolic Production. Ph.D. dissertation, Department of Anthropology, University of British Columbia.

Buruma, Ian
    1984   Behind the Mask: On Sexual Demons, Sacred Mothers, Transvestites, Gangsters, Drifters and Other Japanese Cultural Heroes. New York: Pantheon Books.

de Certeau, Michel
    1984   The Practice of Everyday Life. Berkeley: University of California Press.

Dyer, Richard
    1993   Entertainment and Utopia. In The Cultural Studies Reader. Simon During, ed. Pp. 271–283. London: Routledge.

Fiske, John
    1992   The Cultural Economy of Fandom. In The Adoring Audience: Fan Culture and Popular Media. Linda Lewis, ed. Pp. 30-49. London: Routledge.

Gilmore, David D.
    1990   Manhood in the Making. New Haven: Yale University Press.

Grossberg, Lawrence
    1992   Is There a Fan in the House? The Affective Sensibility of Fandom. In The Adoring Audience: Fan Culture and Popular Media. Lisa Lewis, ed. Pp. 50-68. London: Routledge.

Hatfield, Elaine, John Cacioppo, and Richard Rapson
    1994   Emotional Contagion. Cambridge: Cambridge University Press.

Ivy, Marilyn
    1995   Discourses of the Vanishing: Modernity, Phantasm, Japan. Chicago: University of Chicago Press.

Jenkins, Henry
    1992   Textual Poachers: Television Fans and Participatory Culture. New York: Routledge.

Kasulis, Thomas
    1990   Intimacy: A General Orientation in Japanese Religious Values. Philosophy East and West 40(4):433-449.

Konfidensu
    1992   Ōen shitaku naru kashu no jōken to wa? (What are the conditions for a singer who wants to gain public support?). Konfidensu (Confidence) 26(1335):21-37.

Lebra, Takie Sugiyama
    1994   Migawari: The Cultural Idiom of Self-Other Exchange in Japan. In Self as Person in Asian Theory and Practice. Roger Ames, Wimal Dissanayake, and Thomas Kasulis, eds. Pp. 107-123. Albany: State University of New York Press.

Lindholm, Charles
   1990   Charisma. Oxford: Blackwell.

Painter, Andrew A.
   1996   Japanese Daytime Television, Popular Culture, and Ideology. *In* Contemporary Japan and Popular Culture. John Whittier Treat, ed. Pp. 197–234. Honolulu: University of Hawai'i Press.

Radway, Janice
   1984   Reading the Romance: Women, Patriarchy, and Popular Literature. Chapel Hill: University of North Carolina Press.

Skov, Lise and Brian Moeran
   1995   Introduction. Hiding in the Light: From Oshin to Yoshimoto Banana. *In* Women, Media, and Consumption in Japan. Lise Skov and Brian Moeran, eds. Pp. 1–74. Honolulu: University of Hawai'i Press.

Yano, Christine
   2001   Torching the Stage: Korean Singers in a Japanese Popular Music World. Hybridity: Journal of Cultures, Texts, and Identities 1(2):45-63.
   2002   Tears of Longing; Nostalgia and the Nation in Japanese Popular Song. Cambridge: Harvard University Press (for Harvard University Asia Center).
   2002   The Burning of Men: Masculinities and the Nation in Japanese Popular Song. *In* Masculinities in Japan: Dislocating the Salaryman Doxa. James Roberson and Nobue Suzuki, eds. Pp. 77–90. London: Routledge.

3

Buying Intimacy

Proximity and Exchange at a Japanese Rock Concert

Carolyn S. Stevens

Merry White notes that contemporary Japanese youth culture is characterized by "obsessions with goods and information" (1994:138), astutely linking the accumulation of objects with the acquisition of knowledge. This chapter is similarly concerned with consumer behavior and intellectual—and emotional—experience. Here, I examine the many loyal fans of one of Japan's longest-running rock groups, The Alfee (see Figure 3.1). The Alfee fans avidly consume not only the group's concerts and recordings but also purchase a range of objects that carry the band's name or image, produced by The Alfee's management company specifically for the fan market. Some products have intrinsic utility—a T-shirt with The Alfee logo is an article of clothing, for example—but more important, they are imbued with The Alfee's "spirit." These products are deliberately not sold through retail stores; only those who attend concerts or order directly from the management company can acquire these goods. There are no "intermediaries" who interrupt the connection between the fan-purchaser and the "insiders" who work directly with the stars.

Consumption does not merely involve material objects. Fans also consume information about the band, officially (for instance, through *The Alfee Mania* newsletter and the fan club controlled by The Alfee's management company) and unofficially (through amateur electronic mailing lists and websites). Information, though intangible, has specific value because it brings the fan closer to the star through the power of knowledge. The recent development of interactive websites means that band information is not only easily consumed but also circulated and even produced, and this affects the fans' perception of their proximity to each other and to the stars.

Figure 3.1
The Alfee: Sakurai Masaru (l), Sakazaki Kōnosuke (c), and
Takamizawa Toshihiko (r). Photograph by Sugiyama Yoshiaki. Used with the
permission of Baba Keisuke, Project III Company.

Fans pay for the goods and the music they receive, but a strong sense of "gift" (in an anthropological sense) underlies their experience of fandom. The "gifts" they believe they receive are those of pleasure, inspiration, and even nostalgia. Receiving this gift prompts some fans to return the favor by sending objects or letters to the stars, thanking them for their performances. This has created a circular movement of capital, objects, and affect between fans and stars (although we must remember that The Alfee's production company makes most of the monetary profits). Though both producers and consumers are operating in a capitalist system, these practices are more than mere economic exchange; rather, they are charged with emotion. These transactions reveal the dynamics of a perceived personal relationship and emotional bond between fan and rock star. Fans can gain proximity through the accumulation of objects, as a kind of emotional capital.

They acquire the opportunity to give through fandom, and exercise their power to give in order to create personal relationships with their idols and with other fans.

Fans are often attributed a passive role in the economic and psychological structures of consumerism. However, my argument here about the "obsessions" of The Alfee fans is that they are empowered rather than manipulated by their "capital accumulation" of artifacts and information. Objects and knowledge are constitutive of the relationships of fans and stars, and form the emotional framework of fandom.

This notion of fandom as a form of capital accumulation is drawn from John Fiske (1992:42–43), who posits that collecting paraphernalia is central to fan identity. This chapter examines two particular forms of material and emotional exchange: fans' purchase of "Alfee Goods" sold at concert arenas and fans' offerings of gifts and letters to the stars. In both cases, material objects symbolize and convey an emotion-charged relationship. Indeed, my premise here is that fans are those who establish physical or emotional "closeness" with the star.[1] Closeness, for them, is physical proximity to The Alfee, by regularly attending concerts or by frequenting places where they are known to be (the management office, the recording studio, or even their residences). Insider information is often necessary to obtain top tickets or the groups' schedules and travel plans, and some fans can get these through staff leaks. However, such fans appear to be few in number. In part this is because such information is difficult to come by, but also because most fans follow a conventional notion of propriety; they feel that certain lines must be drawn between fans and stars to maintain the two roles and their relationship.

My informants, who generally respected mutually determined lines of privacy, nonetheless relished leaked tidbits of Alfee gossip. Once, the electric guitarist allegedly made a slightly inebriated late-night appearance at a Tokyo fast-food restaurant, and a fan acquired the paper napkin on which he had doodled some cartoons. The woman photocopied the napkin and distributed it free to others at a subsequent Alfee concert. This small token of the informal social life of her idol was neither hoarded nor sold to other fans. It was shared openly among the community. At the same time, fans condemned others who "stalked" The Alfee for taking the game "too far." Netsuretsu na fuan (intense fans), who took unusual means to get close, were disparaged by my informants as having "personal problems."

Though separated physically from the stars, the fans I interviewed did feel an emotional closeness to the band in a range of ways. One Alfee fan explained:

> It's not a question of physical closeness, but a question of "distance of the heart" . . . fans have never even once met the members nor have they ever spoken directly to them, yet each fan, in his or her own way, thinks of The Alfee as his or her friends, teachers, brothers, lovers.[2]

For those fans who lack an empowering knowledge of the stars, emotional distance is foreclosed, and they experience intimacy by accumulating and exchanging objects. Endowing a material object with a subjective social relationship actualizes an intimacy with the star. Such an equation of distance and intimacy with material objects is not unusual among fans in other societies. A 16-year-old British rock-music fan admitted: "I really enjoy my collection because it feels like I have a piece of them in my possession" (Vermorel and Vermorel 1990:485). The possession of these goods marks the collector as a fan of the star, and this becomes crucial in creating a shared identity, another source of pleasure for fans.

Japanese fandoms have been explored historically in several contexts, including kabuki (Leupp 1995; Raz 1983) and Takarazuka (Robertson 1998). Leupp ventures that kabuki fans in Tokugawa, Japan (1600–1867) might have felt at home in the 21st century:

> Urban audiences expressed their enthusiasm for these actors in ways that would be familiar to fans of contemporary rock n' roll stars. They organized fan clubs, often on a ward basis; fiercely loyal, they would bar any member who patronized another actor's performances. They circulated posters bearing their . . . hero's image and attend his performances in groups, chorusing their devotion. They purchased "actor-techniques" that publicized not only his dramatic skills but his physical charms as well. . . . Most important, the devotees patronized the theatre often enough and paid sufficiently high ticket prices to make some actors very wealthy. [1995:130]

Even this brief citation shows how the kabuki fans' support of the stars (both emotional and economic) was so intense that competition between stars led to confrontations between the fans as well. Robertson writes that early critics of Takarazuka were concerned with fans' behavior, fearing that institutionalized fandom would be socially disruptive (1998:140–142, 146–149). Generally, fandom is viewed in an ambivalent manner in Japanese culture. Connoisseurship is valued and respected; obsessive fixation is not. But few seem to agree on where the line is drawn. The mass media claim that Alfee fans are renown for their intense fandom; an article in a weekly magazine described them cynically as *dai-nekkyō* (huge fanatics) (Arashiyama 1998: 165), suggesting that they would go to any extreme to get close to their idols. In fact, as we have seen, Alfee fans generally follow rather than transgress social norms of decorum. Their supposedly deviant behavior is actually quite conservative, suggesting that Alfee fans constitute a mainstream "mania," mediated by the fans' other cultural identities and capital.

"The Japanese Rolling Stones"

The Alfee, or "Arufii," are a pop–rock trio that was formed in 1973 by three Meiji Gakuin University students: Takamizawa Toshihiko (electric guitar),

Sakazaki Kōnosuke (acoustic guitar), and Sakurai Masaru (bass guitar) (see Figure 3.1). Their backgrounds were unremarkable, even mainstream: Takamizawa and Sakurai are from Tokyo suburbs in neighboring Saitama prefecture; Sakazaki is a native of the downtown section of Tokyo. All three are from middle-class families (Sakurai and Sakazaki are sons of liquor shop owners, while Takamizawa's father is a retired school principal). Like many other young Japanese of that era, they were greatly influenced by U.S. and U.K. rock and pop. Significantly, they are all second sons, which meant that the presence of an elder brother relieved them of parental pressure to follow in the family businesses. Sakurai and Takamizawa first met when they were classmates at the senior high school affiliated with Meiji Gakuin University. Later, Sakurai introduced his friend to Sakazaki, who had entered the university from a public high school.

From its start in 1973, The Alfee were active in the Meiji Gakuin student music scene. They released their first single in August 1974. Their early music was influenced by the Japanese folk music movement in the late 1960s and early 1970s. Folk music did not require a percussion section, so their trio of guitars (a bass and two acoustic guitars) was self-sufficient, and all contributed vocals.

Their first full-length album was released in 1975 by Victor Records under the name "Alfie." It did not find an appreciative audience, and their record contract was not renewed. They were later picked up by Canyon Records in 1979 and released a series of singles and their first album with the name "Alfee."[3] Two albums and seven singles later, success still eluded the trio, though their appearances in small "live houses" were gathering a following. They also worked as a back-up band to Ken Naoko and other established artists in the mainstream pop music scene.

In 1981, after years of recording and performing without a "big break," the band decided to rearrange itself. Until then, Sakazaki had acted as front man and made most of the artistic and business decisions. As this arrangement was not producing results, Takamizawa, the group's songwriter, took the position of leader and, like Dylan, exchanged his acoustic guitar for an electric one. He remains the creative and business leader of the band today. Sakazaki, ever faithful to the band's roots as a folk ensemble, remained on the acoustic guitar. Still a guitar-based trio, they hire other musicians to play drums and keyboards during recording sessions and concert tours, but only the three guitarists constitute official membership in the group.

The band released their first rock album in 1981 with Pony Canyon. In January 1983, The Alfee commenced their first national tour despite the fact they had not yet achieved a national hit single. In October 1983, The Alfee entered the Japanese charts at number 7 with "Marie-Anne," their first hit. It was their 15th single with Pony Canyon (and 16th in the history of the group), giving them the image of a band who had "paid their dues" in a highly competitive industry. They released another single, "Hoshizora no Distance," in 1985, and its success clinched their position as one of the premiere rock bands of the 1980s. From then on, The Alfee sustained their place in a competitive pop industry through steady touring and recording. From 1984 to 1986, they performed a total of 330 concerts (The Alfee, 1998). At the peak of their popularity, The Alfee performed an average of 94 shows a year; released 22 full-length albums, 28 singles, 21 concert videos; and presented 39 outdoor and special events (The Alfee 1995). Their concert tours remain well attended; in 1997, they ranked ninth nationally for concert attendance among all pop groups (Nikkei Entertainment 1998:39). When asked what concerts they had seen in the last year, a random sample of university students replied that The Alfee performances were the 11th most frequently attended concerts (Inamasu 1994:90).

Structurally, The Alfee's business activities are conducted through five organizations. Four of these are controlled by group members or those close to them; the fifth is their record company, a major corporation.[4] The first of these is Project III Co., Ltd., which is their artist management agency (or *jimusho*, literally, "office") that oversees the bulk of Alfee's business affairs. Although it also manages a handful of other artists, nearly all of its income derives from The Alfee. This is in contrast to other management agencies that handle hundreds of artists, such as Hori Productions, Watanabe Productions, Amūzu, Johnny's Junior (which specializes in young male idols), and the recently popular Being. While other artists come and go through these agency doors, Project III is identified with The Alfee, and without other major talent, the agency's survival depends on the group's existence. Project III was established by the band members and their manager, in cooperation with Tanabe Shōchi, of the well-established Tanabe agency. Tanabe put up the start-up money and remains a stockholder. Takamizawa, the leader of the band, makes nearly all of the artistic and business decisions, in consultation with the executive producer (the band's former manager) and the chief manager.

The second company, 8Days Co., Ltd. (after The Beatles' song "Eight Days a Week"), is a production company that concerns itself solely with concert tours and souvenir production. It provides concert direction, performer management, stage management, sound technicians and engineers, lighting designers, transportation, merchandising, photography, wardrobe, makeup, and general staff assistance. 8Days employs approximately forty people, full and part time. The third company, The Alfee fan club Alfee Mania, is attached to 8Days, which hires two women, originally fans, to operate the fan club. Finally, Time Spirit Co., Ltd. is a private company of Takamizawa Toshihiko, who has "incorporated" himself for tax purposes and because he requires extra staff to manage his affairs. He has also built his own recording studio, T's Studio.

The outside company extensively involved with The Alfee is Toshiba EMI. Project III represents the artists to the record company, with whom they hold a fixed-period contact. As is customary, their Toshiba recording contract specifies the number of albums and singles to be produced within the contract period. Beyond these recording obligations, The Alfee's activities are generally self-generated and self-managed through the smaller companies associated with the band.

The Alfee's situation is rather unusual in the Japanese world of *geinōkai* (entertainment). Relatively few Japanese artists have so much control over their material, and its presentation and marketing. However, this autonomy is consistent with some other artists, particularly in the genre known as *nyū myūjikku* (new music). The first new music performers were accomplished singer-songwriters, rather than "manufactured stars" such as idols (Aoyagi 1999). Singer-songwriters from the folk movement such as Yoshida Takurō and Minami Kōsetsu (of the group Kaguyahime) are credited with starting this genre in 1975. They wrote their own music and often produced themselves, making them independent from the long-established, strictly hierarchical talent agencies and music-publishing companies. These artists were seen as "authentic," similar to the original folk movement. A most important feature of "new music" artists was that they were not as vulnerable as manufactured stars to consumer trends. If and when they became successful, they were able to enjoy longer careers. Though the musical styles of the new music artists vary, they all have in common relative creative and business control and a consistent fan base.

The Alfee as a group have had, and continue to enjoy, a significant career in the Japanese music business. Other "super groups" such as Off-Course and Y.M.O. have disbanded; though members have established themselves as solo performers (Oda Kazumasa and Sakamoto Ryūichi, for example); except for The Alfee and the Southern All-Stars, all other bands have disintegrated over time.[5] Thus, The Alfee are often referred to as the longest-running Japanese rock band, or "The Japanese Rolling Stones." Like the Stones, they are always claiming in the media that they will be active into their fifties.

It is difficult to define The Alfee's musical genre, for definitions of *pop* and *rock* differ for Japanese and Western audiences. This is due to the comparatively over-representation of "idol" singers in the Japanese music industry. Japanese idols are carefully manufactured consumer products who do well for a few years before they retire to make room for the next rising star. According to Keith Cahoon, youth, looks, and "sentimentality" are the only requirements for a Japanese idol. Musical talent is of little consequence; television exposure is vital (1993:1286). In the early 1980s, like idols, The Alfee enjoyed high media coverage and their youthful good looks were used to promote their records. Furthermore, they benefited greatly from "tie-ups" with product companies and television studios (almost half of all Alfee singles released between 1983 and 1986 were television, film, or commercial campaign songs). Unlike the majority of idols, however, The Alfee performed their own material. Their long career and their commitment to live performance and musicianship are consistent with this distinction. A Western music critic might place The Alfee in a pop or idol category, in contrast to a Western definition of "serious" rock music. In the Japanese context, though, The Alfee are not idols and should be seen as "serious" performers in the field.

Nonetheless, most Western and even many Japanese music scholars and critics agree that The Alfee draw mainly on Western pop references. The group's music makes no strong political statements, contains no avant-garde expressions, and seldom deviates from the Beatlesque, pop–rock formula that they have employed since 1981.[6] They have developed a consistent and comfortable routine—one or two singles and videos released annually, an original album every other year, and two national tours and one summer event per year. Their music has changed somewhat over time (incorporating the songwriter's personal interests such as a reliance on classical arrangements in the late 1990s), but their songs from the late 1980s are their trademark sound. However, The Alfee are not a consciously "retro" band. Instead, they represent reassuring continuity.

The Alfee are an excellent example of mainstream rock, commercialized and marketed on a relatively large scale. Interestingly, the band has not been plagued by scandal in the way other Japanese celebrities are (Matsuda Seiko, for example). This, I believe, is partly because of their structural ability to control their image in the geinōkai, and partly because the band members work so hard grinding away at their annual routine that they have little time to get into trouble. The Alfee phenomenon throws into relief the organizational qualities of the roles of management, artists, and consumers, and illustrates the workings of the production side to fandom. Project III, 8Days, Time Spirit and Alfee Mania are essentially businesses to create profit. However much it gains financially, though, The Alfee must yield something in exchange. The following sections describe some of the ways in which fans claim their own means of control in this relationship.

The Alfee Concert as an Arena for Exchange

Of all fan activities, concert attendance is most valued because it places the fan in closest physical proximity to the star, and we see later that the concert arena is most frequently used as a venue for making connections with the band. Competition for tickets is great for highly populated, urban arenas because of the recent reduction in concerts they perform per year.[7] Outside the concert hall, fans without tickets look to buy them from other fans, not from *dafu-ya* (ticket scalpers). The band discourages fans from using scalpers and many fans appear to agree. This is because ticket scalpers interfere with the direct exchange between the band and the fans. The fans want their money directly channeled to The Alfee as a demonstration of their good faith: strong economic links make for strong emotional links.

In the lobby of the concert hall is the "Alfee Goods" area, where CDs, T-shirts, caps, and the like are sold. A 1996 Alfee Goods catalogue lists other items: pamphlets, towels, guitar picks, watches, toiletries, and jigsaw puzzles. Through such goods, The Alfee can be taken everywhere with the fan, and their presence can be felt in all spheres of life.

Also in the lobby is a table for depositing gifts, flowers, and letters for band members. Giving is "individuating"; the star reads their thoughts expressed in letters, reinforcing the fans' sense of identity as discrete individuals. The concert arena is not the only place where fans send letters and gifts; the fan club office, radio stations, and the management office also act as collection points for the fans' gifts.

These gifts and letters are the only objects that can overcome physical boundaries between star and fan. At a concert, fans are restricted to the lobby and their seats. The band members do not venture outside, nor are fans invited backstage. Despite this, I found gifts and letters in all the dressing rooms, so the fans' presence was felt in the forbidden areas. The gifts crossed the boundaries and made connections between the fans and the stars (see Figure 3.2). For this reason, gifts and letters are important as they make the trip that the fan cannot.

The band realizes the importance of this connection. A photograph from a 1996 pictorial collection (Iwaoka 1996) showing the members "casually" talking among themselves also prominently displays gifts from fans. The images evidence fan–star "contact" and represent the stars' recognition of the gifts. Imagine the rush felt by the fan upon seeing his or her gift, carefully chosen and wrapped, in the hands of her idol. This exchange acts as connection, physical as well as emotional, between the fan and the idol. The band members, by accepting these gifts, can foster a sense of connection without having to meet the fans personally.

Another path by which the band is promoting this kind of exchange is through the Internet. The electric guitarist of the band set up a website in 1996 (http://www.takamizawa.com). There, fans can send him e-mail through the "Send My Heart" page. Messages from fans may be divided into the following categories: "Send Your Question" (regarding fan *nayamigoto* [worries]); "Send Your Diary" (*anata no nichijō no dekigoto*); "Send Your Letter" (about the guitarist's radio program—"no fan letters" says the JAVA script); and "Send your Emotion." Interestingly, the title of the home page implies that if the fan sends in his or her message, the guitarist will reciprocate by sending his own "heart."

The website went further in creating virtual proximity with fans in November 1998 when Takamizawa set up his own virtual city—"T Com City"—of which he became "mayor." The cyber village is complete with housing and cultural spots such as museums, concert halls, an amusement park, and a radio station that transmits sound files of the mayor's speeches. A fan may become a "citizen" of this city by registering with the site; after paying an annual fee of 5,000 yen ($50), the "resident" is assigned a parcel of land, an address, and an alias by which to communicate with other "residents." He or she also receives general announcements from city hall, which are not personal communications but which do give the fan a sense of connection to the idol. Furthermore, the residents contact each

Figure 3.2.
Two sisters with homemade dolls of The Alfee for presentation to
the group. Photograph by Carolyn S. Stevens.

other through their residential aliases, creating a virtual community of fans. Distance and intimacy are completely redefined in the Internet world of The Alfee.[8]

The Business of Exchange: An Interview with the Merchandising Director of 8 Days Co., Ltd.

Exactly what, and how much do fans buy? The merchandising director of the band told me that production figures are based on calculations from past records. This formula is based on sales figures of concert pamphlets, which serve as an indicator of sales of other goods.[9] Pamphlets sell at a rate of one-half of ticket sales.

The director stated that female fans buy more than male fans. Items for male consumers are thus given lower priority, but in fact the basic set of goods is androgynous; both male and female fans can use or wear or display them without transgressing status quo gender boundaries. The items that sell best are copies of apparel that the band wears on stage or during television appearances; the director called them "artist goods" because of their close association with the stars (these too must be androgynous). Older fans buy less than younger fans, hinting at eventual market saturation. Fans at metropolitan venues buy about the same amount of goods as fans at regional concerts, showing that consumption is not merely an urban phenomenon.

When asked why he thought fans bought Alfee goods, the director first replied simply "Arufii ga suki da kara" [Because they like The Alfee]. He then elaborated on the fans' desire to mark the concert as a special event: "Sekkaku konsaato ni kita kara" [They've come all this way to the concert]. Part of the pleasure of attending a concert is not just listening to music or watching the show but also browsing among, choosing, and buying the souvenirs to create and sustain memories of the personal experience. He believes fans are caught in a cycle of wanting, which provokes the buying, which temporarily fulfills desire, but which also creates further wanting.

The merchandising director expanded his position at the management company in 1996 by also taking on the duties of artist manager. The artist manager has an all-purpose and often thankless role; he is schedule keeper, driver, go-for, and liaison between the star and the public, in both private and professional matters. When the director became the electric guitarist's manager, he became one of the primary means by which the public (including the anthropologist as well as the fans) makes contact with the star. I witnessed the director in this capacity as we walked through the lobby of NHK Hall after a concert. He was confronted by a number of female fans who pressed upon him envelopes to pass to the stars backstage. He accepted them silently but diplomatically avoided other questions and requests, cutting off the fans' utterances with the phrase, "I'm very busy right now." Backstage, I asked him about the number of gifts and letters delivered at concerts: "Back then, there were so many gifts and such . . . like a mountain. . . . These days the numbers of gifts are falling off. Of course Christmas, Valentine's Day, and birthdays still reap numbers but recently we don't get so much at other times. . . . Why? I guess the fans are growing up."

The director has been employed with company since 1988. However, his current position was facilitated by his membership in the fan club, Alfee Mania. He was active in the fan club for seven years before he was asked to join the company after his college graduation, illustrating the ultimate "cross-over" in status and distance. This has, of course, required that he leave his fan status behind, changing the way in which he dresses, speaks, and behaves. He also said that nearly every employee of the management company is a recruited fan because the hours are long and the pay is fairly low. "No one but fans who truly love The Alfee would do this job," he said.

Buying Goods: Fan Interviews

In several rounds of interviews with Alfee fans, they reported a surprisingly broad range of consuming habits, suggesting that they are rather more discriminating than passive consumers.[10] They report buying souvenirs to bring The Alfee into their own everyday lives, to impart special characteristics to their personalities, and to show their solidarity and support to the band and with each other. Moreover, fans offer gifts and letters to show appreciation for the band's hard work, especially in their live performances. They do not view these gifts in the classical anthropological terms of Marcel Mauss, by which giving creates an obligation to reciprocate with a return gift that itself demands a return, creating a perpetual cycle of giving–receiving–giving. Alfee fans never claim to expect such reciprocity, although, as we shall see, there is much that they do in fact seek and gain from their offerings.

Attending a concert can incur many costs beyond the ticket itself. One male fan claimed that 80 percent of his savings went to The Alfee—for tickets, of course, but also for concert programs and transportation and accommodations for out-of-town venues. Although he did not buy other Alfee souvenirs, he did buy the expensive guitars designed by the lead guitarist and produced by ESP. A female fan said she collected only concert pamphlets ("except I bought a key chain in 1995," she was quick to recall). Another woman stated that she not only bought souvenirs but also spent time and money on sewing clothing based on her idol's stage costumes to "get his power." One fan said he collected Alfee sheet music, which highlighted his connection to the band as a musician who learned his craft through imitation. Another told of her collection of old Alfee records (she also had all of their CDs). She also regularly bought the full range of tour goods each season (when interviewed, she was wearing an Alfee watch).

One interesting aspect of collecting is the practical storage problems it poses, especially in a society with limited per capita housing space. The average fan history of my informants was 12.5 years, and many had amassed ever-increasing piles of magazines, books, souvenirs, and CDs. This presents myriad challenges and dilemmas. A couple, both Alfee fans and planning to get married, was pondering over what to do with their combined collections as most of the items were redundant. Another female fan was distraught over her friend's offer to give her boxes of 1980s magazines about The Alfee. The friend was moving and had no storage space at her new house. The interviewee felt unable to refuse the material, but complained that her own burgeoning collection was outstripping her available requirements.

Fans tend to place their financial investment in following The Alfee within a cycle of support. The band performs because it has the resources to put on the concerts; the concerts earn them money, which allows them to perform again (and again and again . . .). If they didn't, the trio would stop touring; it would lose popularity and its record contract, and might well disband. The fans accept that it is their responsibility and in their own interest to keep the band financially solvent.

These interviews show that fans differentiate between products available and particular consumption practices. Only a small number of fans regularly bought all the items offered, yet all informants had collected pamphlets to commemorate their concertgoing. Pamphlets are clearly the top-ranked souvenirs—perhaps because of their ease of storage; ESP guitars are also highly desirable because they are expensive and because they are felt to transmit The Alfee's musical talent to the buyer. Goods produced and circulated beyond Alfee company control are also avidly collected, including "antique" items like vinyl records (see Hosokawa and Matsuoka, chapter 7, this volume). Alfee records constitute an informal second-hand market among the fans themselves. Here, fans engage in an autonomous sphere of material exchanges bound by mutual commitment to the band.

Fan Letter Writing and Gift Giving

Vermorel and Vermorel report a British fan's comments about his imaginings of Duran Duran:

> Usually what I think about is that they're human beings and they've got to be doing something this very moment. . . . 'Cos I know Duran Duran exists. I know Nick Rhodes exists and I like him and I'm spending money buying things for him and everything. . . . But he doesn't know I exist. (1990:487)

Sending letters and giving gifts to the star is one way of relieving this situation. The star theoretically acknowledges the fans' existence by accepting the letter or gift. It is a means by which the fan can be empowered by displaying his or her existence to the star.

Half of the fans I surveyed had given presents to band members. Most of them gave presents more than once; the mean was 4.15 times, and the most was 12 occasions. The gifts had been distributed equally among the three members. A fan might give more often to a favorite member but will generally send something to all three members at least once. Alcohol is the gift of choice (64 percent gave wine, beer, or sake) and the most popular context for gift giving at the concert arena (93 percent). One fan remarked that the motivation behind giving alcohol to the members at a concert was to communicate "O-tsukare sama! ippai demo!" [A job well done! Have one on us!]. This gesture is widespread in Japan, so much so that it cannot be taken as personal but rather as quite socially conventional. Only occasionally will a more personalized or "intimate" item be offered; one interviewee had sent sofa cushions and a neck massage machine to the acoustic guitarist.

The timing of gifts also tends to follow the o-tsukare sama custom. They are frequently given whenever the band gives a concert (their tours run from April to June and October to December); however, the physical closeness to the stars backstage must also be taken into account considering 40 percent of all gifts were given in this context. Emotional proximity is shown in the preference for Christmas, Valentine's Day, and birthday presents, customarily offered to people close to the giver. These holidays account for 36 percent of gifts given. Another Japanese social convention, the offering of *omiyage* (souvenirs) after the giver has traveled somewhere, is also observed (9 percent). Nearly all gifts were passed to staff members at concert arenas rather than sent to the fan club or management office. Not one respondent received acknowledgment of the gift, nor had they expected one.

Letters, which communicate a message more precisely than an abstract gesture transmitted through a gift, were less common. Compared to the 50 percent of fans interviewed who had given gifts, only 32 percent had written letters or sent faxes to their idols. As with gifts, the letters were evenly distributed among the three Alfee members, and the content was also generally consistent. Fans wrote messages of support, impressions of concerts or recordings, and details of their personal lives (e.g., work, romance, and dreams of the future). One fan claimed, "By talking to him [through letters], I feel as if I have organized my thoughts." One fan who had never written to the band did admit that "Sometimes I do feel the inclination to let the band members know what I am thinking." However, one fan was critical of the practice, objecting that "As a fellow musician, I believe that they should be able to produce music as they like without bending to the will of the audience, so I don't write them letters about their music."

Fans have low expectations about receiving acknowledgments of their gifts or letters. When asked if she received a reply, one fan retorted "Masaka!" [You've got to be kidding!] Another conceded, "I might sort of expect a reply but not receiving one is only natural." Another fan claimed that the offering of gifts and letters was a selfless act, a special form of devotion offered to the star; one cannot realistically expect to be loved back. Fandom to her is a "labor of love," a service performed without expectation of retribution. However, these fans all believe that in some way their "labors" are appreciated by the band and this brings them closer to them. "Fuan o daiji ni suru" [There is no other group which treats its fans so well], said her friend.

This feeling of closeness contrasts with the band's perception of their fans. Though I was not able to conduct in-depth interviews with these heavily scheduled celebrities, who value their privacy, I did have an opportunity to ask a few brief questions of one of them, including the following exchange:

"So what do you think of your fans?"

"I'm glad they like my music."

"But they don't just like your music, they say they like you."

"No, they just think they like me, but they don't. All they really like is the music."

"So what do you think of that?"

"Well. . . I'm happy they like my music but sometimes I [lose] my music to the fans *(jibun no mono ga mina no mono ni naru)*."

The artist does not acknowledge the fans' deep feelings for him personally. To him, it is his music that creates and mediates the relationship. One might even applaud his deflection of fan adoration. At the same time, he does recognize the fans' own power in his rueful claim that they "take over" his music. A song that had special meaning to him when he composed, recorded, or first performed it is appropriated and reinterpreted by fans who then make it part of their emotional lives, reminiscent of the British fan who "possesses" his idol through collection (Vermorel and Vermorel 1990:485). Ironically, fandom can distance a star musician from his music rather than strengthening the bond.

Conclusion

I have argued here that emotional distance can be measured and closeness experienced through the accumulation and distribution of material objects and information. The success of "artists' goods," the physical and psychic distances breached through gifts, the power gained through physical contact with guitars or costumes—these ideas evoke David Buxton's Foucaultian analysis of rock consumption: "The rock star mediates between . . . abstract enhanced use value[s] and the consumer in anthropomorphic form . . ." (1990:436). Here, the body is a site not only of discipline but also of "anti-discipline," the essential theme of rock and roll (p. 432). We are reminded not to overlook the physicality of that body—it is not just an ideological metaphor.

Alfee fans in Japan, we can conclude, enjoy their antidiscipline in disciplined ways. These fans are not social rebels. Their gifts to the stars cross firm, acknowledged boundaries, thus they are potentially dangerous gestures of rebellion. In reality, most gifts never threaten these status boundaries. Their contents are impersonal and conventional. They are given with no expectation of acknowledgment or return favor. Selfless action symbolizes the fans' feelings for the band. At the same time, this possessive love for the band may be what separates the band members from their music. Intimacy gained by the fans is that lost by the artists.

Thus, the artists can be seen as both winners and losers in this mutual relationship. Since most of the money flows from the fans to the stars and their management company, they are profiting in a very real sense from these circulations. However, with heavy touring, demanding recording schedules, and tight security, the musicians' lives have become highly regulated, so much so that even their music is "taken over" by their listeners. Although our topic in this volume is fandom, we must also understand stardom, its logical counterpoint, which shapes fandom. Stardom entails both individual profit and loss. The stars lose normal perspectives of physical distance. Much of their lives revolve around concert hall dressing rooms, backstage passages, the recording studio, hotel rooms, and limousines. Their movements are restricted and regulated to maximize their marketing potential. Ironically, the strategy most successful in increasing fan support—facilitating intimacy—is that which restricts them the most. They can never freely walk the streets of Tokyo precisely because a fan might be tempted to cross the predetermined boundaries and accost them. Yet, they must create an image of accessibility, presenting the fans with fantasies of the boys next door (Sakazaki is particularly portrayed as such a type). Fantasy, at first, requires distance; giving form to and deriving enjoyment from fantasy requires an imagined intimacy.

Fantasy is important in analyzing fandoms, but empirical data offer necessary grounding. By analyzing marketing techniques, we can see what and how much fans are actually buying. Interviews with these fans yield a portrait of discriminating rather than passive consumers. They do not buy products they do not need or desire. They see their money paid to The Alfee's tour company as an investment not only in the band's future but also in the fans' own future. Without concerts, the fans would have no arena for interaction, and they articulate a responsibility to maintain it. And much of the pleasure they receive is not just from The Alfee. It derives too from other fans. For example, one fan attending a concert close to her home spent additional money to take a hotel room with her out-of-town friends. "I live nearby . . . but I'd miss out on so much!" she claimed. As one sees with many other fandoms, Alfee fans value their friendships with each other as dearly as they cherish a felt connection to the stars.

The Alfee themselves, though colluding with their fans to sustain an image of mutual closeness, live in a world entirely separate from even their most faithful fans. What "real" closeness exists in Alfee fandom occurs among fans, constituted by their shared consumption practices. Cynics may wonder if the fans are not fooling themselves, but there may be more self-awareness than outsiders expect. As a David Bowie fan recognized, "It is a bit odd really, having devoted so much time to him and never having actually met him. But then again it's quite nice in a way. I don't have any regrets about not meeting him" (Vermorel and Vermorel 1990:489). Imagined intimacy can be more satisfying than real intimacy.

References Cited

Alfee, The
    1995   Progress Countdown 95 The Alfee. Tokyo: 8Days Co., Ltd.
    1996   1996 Autumn The Alfee Goods Mail Order Catalog. Tokyo: 8Days Co., Ltd.
    1998   Nouvelle Vague Countdown 98 The Alfee in NY. Tokyo: 8Days Co., Ltd.

Aoyagi Hiroshi
1999   Islands of Eight Million Smiles: Pop-Idol Performances and the Field of Symbolic Production. Ph.D. dissertation, Department of Anthropology, University of British Columbia.

Arashiyama Kōzaburō
1998   Konsento nuita ka! Ima Arufii ga yōchūi shirushi da" (Unplugged! The Alfee demand attention now!). Shūkan Asahi, September 4: 164–165.

Buxton, David
1990   Rock Music, the Star System and the Rise of Consumerism. In On Record: Rock, Pop and the Written Record. Simon Frith and Andrew Goodwin, eds. Pp. 427–440. New York: Pantheon Books.

Cahoon, Keith
1993   Popular Music in Japan. In Japan: An Illustrated Encyclopedia. Pp. 1284–1285. Tokyo: Kodansha.

Fiske, John
1992   The Cultural Economy of Fandom. In The Adoring Audience: Fan Culture and Popular Media. Lisa A. Lewis, ed. Pp. 30–49. London: Routledge.

Inamasu Tatsuo, coordinating ed.
1994   Gendai wakamono to ongaku: Wakamono ni okeru ongaku kōdō no kisoteki na jittai chōsa, 1989–90 chōsahōkoku (Today's youth and music: A basic survey of youth music trends, 1989–90). Tokyo: Gendai no wakamono to ongaku kenkyūkai.

Iwaoka Goro
1996   The Alfee Synchomesh. Tokyo: Tokyo FM Shuppan.

Leupp, Gary
1995   Male Colors: The Construction of Homosexuality in Tokugawa Japan. Berkeley: University of California Press.

Nikkei Entertainment
1998   Shijō saikyō no raibu a-teisuto o sagase! (Searching for the all-time greatest live performer!) Nikkei Entertainment, July, no. 16: 36–55.

Raz, Jacob
1983   Audience and Actors: A Study of their Interactions in the Japanese Traditional Theater. Leiden: E. J. Brill.

Robertson, Jennifer
1998   Takarazuka: Sexual Politics and Popular Culture in Modern Japan. Berkeley: University of California Press.

Stevens, Carolyn
1999   Rocking the Bomb: A Case Study in the Politicization of Popular Culture. Japanese Studies 18(1):49–67.

Vermorel, Fred, and Judy Vermorel
1990   Starlust. In On Record: Rock, Pop and the Written Word. Simon Frith and Andrew Goodwin, eds. Pp. 481–490. New York: Pantheon Books.

White, Merry
    1994   The Material Child: Coming of Age in Japan and America. Berkeley: University of California Press.

Interviews

Interview with Baba Keisuke (merchandising director and artist manager) at the offices of Project III Co., Ltd., Tokyo, November 19, 1996.

Group interviews with 13 Alfee fans. Tokyo, November 19, 1996, and June 14, 1998.

Questionnaire distributed to 30 Alfee fans, June 1998.

Notes

1. Kelly's introduction and Yano's chapter 2 in this volume further discuss intimacy and emotional closeness. Tierney's chapter 5 is a parallel analysis of gift giving and patronage in the world of professional sumo.

2. All translations from Japanese are mine. I should add a note here about my own relationship to the group, as employee, fan, and researcher. Most ethnographers choose their subjects; in this case, the subjects chose the investigator. Like many graduate students in Japan, I sought part-time translation work to help make ends meet while doing my fieldwork on volunteerism in a low-income area in Yokohama. From 1992 to 1994 I was a part-time employee of a subsidiary of The Alfee management company. I was first hired to write English copy for various products such as promotional posters, concert programs, and CD and video liner notes. Later I translated and interpreted English song lyrics (frequently used in Japanese pop songs) and directed vocal performances in the studio.

Because I started out as an employee and not a fan of the group, my "insider" status colors my interpretation of the public consumption of the band. It was only after years of wading through lyrics and paying my respects to the company officials by repeat concert attendance that I grew to appreciate The Alfee's music in ways that I might not have if I had come across their music by chance. Though no longer an employee, the management company still recognizes my former professional position, and this allows me some access to spheres of production which might have been cut off to an outsider.

3. The second record company changed the spelling of the name of the band to avoid copyright infringement. In 1986, the band began using the article "the" preceding the name "Alfee," in an attempt to anglicize their image (as in "The Beatles"). However, "The Alfee" (in roman letters) tends to be a written sign for the band and the Japanese term "Arufii" (in katakana) is used generally in speech. Canyon Records later became Pony Canyon.

4. In 1997, The Alfee signed with Toshiba EMI Japan after their contract with Pony Canyon expired.

5. The Southern All-Stars is another veteran band sometimes known by the initials SAS. Though SAS (led by Kuwada Keisuke and his classmates at Tokyo's Aoyama Gakuin

University) had an earlier professional debut and gained national fame more quickly, The Alfee had formed one year earlier. Thus The Alfee is the oldest continuous band in Japan while the SAS are the longest successfully recording band in Japan.

6. See Stevens 1999 for a discussion of political meaning in The Alfee's music.

7. This is due to the band members' choice to perform fewer, but higher quality, shows.

8. One fan told me that rumors had spread that one of the band members had actually entered an Alfee chat room under an alias, pretending to be a fan, to see what fans were saying in cyberspace. She and her friends were annoyed at this pretense; though they preserved their own anonymity by using nicknames, they thought that the star had crossed over an unacceptable boundary and invaded their privacy.

9. There is no fixed schedule for introducing products. Every year the company offers pamphlets, guitar picks, bags, key chains and badge pins. The director will introduce a new product when one comes to his attention, either through his own shopping trips or through producers who approach him. The sales table includes only items offered by 8Days for sale at concert arenas. It does not include the many other products sold elsewhere such as sheet music, books, and guitars, as well as outside product endorsements by the members (including, in 1996, life insurance).

10. Data were gathered in two stages. I conducted the interviews about souvenirs in late 1996 and most of the interviews on gift giving and letter writing in mid-1998. The same fans were interviewed in both stages, but the 1998 data were supplemented by a questionnaire that was circulated electronically among people on an Alfee fan mailing list.

4

Sense and Sensibility at the Ballpark

What Fans Make of Professional Baseball in Modern Japan

WILLIAM W. KELLY

It's like when your child is running in a foot race in kindergarten. Even more than winning a first-place ribbon, you cheer your kid on fervently hoping that she or he will at least do well and get through without an injury. That's what cheering the Tigers is all about!

—Anonymous "Tiger-crazy" fan

Whew! The season's over! We got through another year without incident! I can't tell you what a relief it is; I feel like a huge burden's been lifted from my shoulders!

—Comment by Fujita Kenji, executive officer of one of the outfield fan clubs, upon leaving Kōshien Stadium at the close of the final home game on September 30, 1997

"Omaera wa gomi ya" [You're all just trash]

—Comment by stadium official to officers of the Private Alliance of Hanshin Tiger Fan Clubs

Meeting the Fans: Kōshien Stadium and the Hanshin Tigers

About fifteen minutes by train west of the city center of Osaka is the most famous baseball stadium in Japan—Kōshien. To New York Yankee fans, Yankee Stadium has long been known as "the House that Ruth Built," but Japanese fans know Kōshien as "the House that Ruth Played In." It was the only real baseball stadium in Japan at the time of Babe Ruth's barnstorming tour of the country in 1934, and the two games he, Lou Gehrig, and the rest of the Branch Rickey All-Stars played at Kōshien are memorialized by a large plaque at the stadium entrance. Kōshien's origins go back ten years before that. It was built and opened in 1924 as Asia's largest stadium, a steel-and-concrete colossus that seated almost 50 thousand, nearly rivaling Yankee Stadium itself, which had opened the year before with a capacity of 62 thousand.

Amid the burgeoning metropolitan mass culture of the 1920s, Kōshien drew immediate national attention for its flush toilets, its vendor food, and the national middle school baseball tournaments held there each April and August. Flush toilets were still rare at the time, and they impressed and scared spectators and players coming from all parts of the country. Visitors were also immediately taken by what the concession stands sold as Kōshien "coffee and curry rice." Curry rice was made at home, but its preparations were lengthy, and there was a boom in this menu at the stadium and in restaurants. During the school tournaments, upwards of 15 thousand coffee and curry rice meals were sold daily.

Baseball was already the most popular spectator sport in Japan at the time of Kōshien's opening. It had first developed as a club sport in the late 19th century at the elite higher schools and early universities—of particular note were the clubs of First Higher School and of Waseda and Keio Universities. By the early 20th century it spread to middle schools across the country. National middle school tournaments were begun by the two major Osaka rival newspapers, Asahi and Mainichi, in 1915 and 1916, respectively, and it was their fast-growing popularity that encouraged the Hanshin Electric Railroad Company to join them in sponsoring the construction of Kōshien, midway along its single trunk line between Osaka and Kobe.[1]

Today the stadium is still owned by the Hanshin Company, and it remains the sacred site of amateur baseball as the home to the two national high school tournaments. However, Kōshien is also home to the company's professional baseball team, the Hanshin Tigers, which was organized for the inaugural professional season in 1936, two years after Babe Ruth's visit. The name was selected from a public competition and mimicked the Detroit Tigers, from another city built on manufacturing. For decades, the Hanshin Tigers and their arch rivals, the Yomiuri Giants in Tokyo, have been the twin poles defining the force field of the Central League.[2] For most of the post–World War II era, there were four professional teams in the Kansai region, all owned by private railroad companies—the Tigers, the Hankyū Braves, the Nankai Hawks, and the Kintetsu Buffaloes. In the late 1980s, Nankai's team was sold to Daiei and moved to Fukuoka, and Hankyū sold its Braves to Orient Leasing a year later; the latter team remains in Kobe as the Orix BlueWave. Kintetsu has a far larger rail network than Hanshin, and the BlueWave, with superstar Ichirō, enjoyed enormous success in the 1990s. However, despite their mediocre record (only one Japan Series victory in the postwar half century), the Tigers remain the overwhelming sentimental favorite in the region, for reasons that will become evident in this chapter.

Orix plays in the aptly named Green Stadium, a spacious suburban ballpark west of Kobe; and Kintetsu moved several years ago to Osaka Dome, a city center extravaganza ringed with shopping and entertainment arcades. Kōshien remains little changed over seven decades of use. Additional seating was added along the first and third base lines in 1929 to accommodate the school tournament throngs.[3] But otherwise, its ivy-covered brick walls, the still natural-grass outfield, the open wooden press box behind home plate, and the dingy locker rooms all sustain an aura of timelessness and keep vivid the memories of past contests, amateur and professional.

Getting off the Hanshin train at Kōshien Station and walking across the plaza, the stadium looms before you, impressive despite the construction of an elevated expressway that cuts some of your sight line. Immediately facing the ticket windows, you can pay from 2,200 yen to 3,500 yen (about $20–$35) to enter one of the several infield seating sections. But if, instead, you walk all the way around the outside of the stadium to a smaller shed in the back, you can buy a 1,400 yen (about $13) ticket to the unreserved outfield bleachers and make your way by a separate rear entrance to a very different part of the stadium.

This is the territory of the Hanshin Tiger fan clubs (which is how I render in English the term ōendan), which fill the right-field stands and spill over into the left-field stands and into the right-side infield "Alps" section (see Figure 4.1). Tiger paraphernalia and motifs are everywhere. It is a throbbing sea of yellow-and-black face paint, Tiger happi coats, Tiger uniform shirts, jerseys, and headbands. It seems as if everyone is wearing a Hanshin baseball cap and beating together a pair of miniature plastic baseball bats to accompany their lusty chants—"Kattobase Yamada!" "Kattobase Hiyama!" "Kattobase Wada!" Kattobase is the all-purpose cheer: "Let it rip, Yamada!" "Let it rip, Hiyama!" "Let it rip, Wada!"

Those who pay attention to some combination of Japan and sports have a fairly predictable set of understandings about the forms and feelings of baseball in that society. There is a constant circulation in journalist reports and academic literature of mutually reinforcing images about grueling overpractices, abject obedience to coaches and managers, timid strategies, and abiding prejudice against foreign players. There is enough truth to each of these to explain their durability and popularity, but like most exaggerated images, they poorly capture the variety in the game and its considerable changes over a long history in Japan. Our stereotypes even

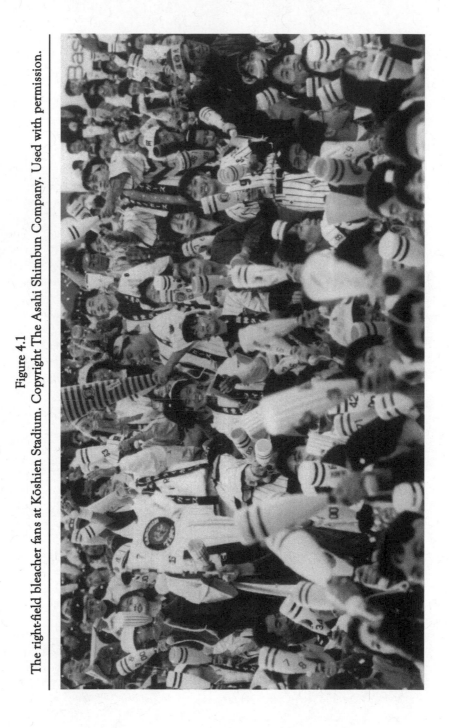

Figure 4.1

The right-field bleacher fans at Kōshien Stadium. Copyright The Asahi Shimbun Company. Used with permission.

extend to the fans as well, who tend to be dismissed as hysterical groupies, slavishly following their team through maniacal and monotonous collective cheering.

There may be no smoking gun for the ultimate source of such durable and popular imaginings, but there is a smoldering keyboard, belonging to Robert Whiting. Because of his long experience on the Japanese baseball scene, his prolific and astute writings in English and Japanese, and his impressive way with words, he has been consulted, quoted, misquoted, and plagiarized by two decades of reporting and commentary. Whiting has portrayed the Japanese fan coming out to the ballpark and quickly shedding his usual "restraint": "Spurred on by energetic cheerleaders, and the pounding rhythms of taiko drums, horns, whistles, and other noisemakers, he becomes a veritable wildman, yelling and screaming nonstop for nine solid innings" (1989:114).

This may be an understandable initial impression. The raucous noise and swaying bodies may well remind an American visitor less of New York Yankees baseball than of the frenzied student and alumni crowds at a Big Ten college football game. But we must be careful not to take this view too literally—not only because it can conform too neatly to certain stereotypes about an alleged Japanese character of mindless collectivism (their "undividualism" we might say), but also because it can quickly play into a more general dismissal of fans as undiscerning and overly emotional sports boors.

A more charitable appraisal supposes that fans emerge out of mass culture audiences in search of intensified meanings and pleasures through acts of social and aesthetic discrimination. Fans selectively appropriate from among the personalities, products, and productions of this mass culture, and creatively rework their selections into a stylized matrix of practices and identities. This is a theme I have developed in the introduction to this volume, and it is the basis of my own understanding of these Tiger baseball fans. Much time in the Kōshien bleachers over three seasons (1996–98) and extended conversations with fan club members, stadium personnel, and others in the baseball world have shown me that there is more to Kōshien cheering than first assaults the ears. Based on that fieldwork, this chapter analyzes aspects of the Kōshien fan experience that both illustrate more general characteristics of fandoms and distinguish these baseball fans from other cases in this volume.

The reader might properly wonder at this point why such Tiger fans are worth analytical attention and in what ways they are either instructively representative or strategically distinctive as sports fans. First, I readily acknowledge that passionate followers of other sports in Japan like the recently organized J.League professional soccer (Horne 1999; Takahashi Yoshio 1994:41–101; Taniguchi 1997) or sumo (Tierney, chapter 5, this volume) or Western-style professional wrestling (Thompson 1986) cannot be characterized in precisely the same terms as those of baseball. Nonetheless, there are several features of mass sporting spectatorship that set it apart from other consumer activities and that are common conditions of sports fandoms.[4]

Sports fans, for example, have a stronger oppositional identity than many other mass culture fans. Unlike a rock concert or a comic book fanzine fair, sports present spectators with a contest, which ends in victory or defeat. A baseball game is a continuous series of tests between pitchers and fielders versus batters and runners over several hours, and games themselves are units in seasons of struggles among leagues of teams. There are player rivalries and league rivalries and national rivalries, but most of all, there are enduring rivalries between teams. Certainly Hanshin's longest and bitterest rivalry is with the Tokyo-based Yomiuri Giants; to be a Hanshin Tiger fan is, and has been since the league's founding in 1936, to be an anti-Giants fan. As I will discuss later, the oppositional quality embedded in sports fan identity allows Tiger identity to symbolically condense broader rivalries, especially those between the national center and the second city.

Team rivalries and local identity are fostered by the home and away structure of games and the permanent location of teams in stadiums. Team support and local identity can be mutually affirming. Kōshien spectators may become Tiger fans because they are Ōsakans and the team is invested with Osaka pride, but as they become Tiger fans they may become more ardently and reflectively Ōsakans. Similarly, one may join a fan club because of previous connections to its members, but the club experience may create and sustain bonds among members as well.

Contestation has several other corollaries, including the ever-present possibility of violence—fighting with other fan groups and spectators, invading the field, accosting umpires and players. This is an issue I will consider. Equally important is the problem of self-esteem in the face of losing. As with any sport organized around league play, there is only a single victor at the end of the game and a single Japan Series champion at the end of the season; 11 of the 12 teams lose, year in and year out, and they and their fans must live with defeat. What does it mean to invest so much of one's identity in a frequently "losing" cause? This is another element of special relevance to the Hanshin case because the team has been woefully unsuccessful; since the two-league structure began 48 years ago, the team has only won the Central League title four times. It has won the Japan Series championship only once in the last half century, in 1985, and in the 17 seasons, 1986–2002, it finished in the league cellar ten times and in next-to-last place three times (it also finished in third place twice and in fourth place twice).

And within sports, certain characteristics of baseball lend distinctive qualities to cheering and supporting. First, all professional sports have proven to be highly quantifiable, but baseball in particular is densely calibrated and exhaustively recorded. The annual *Japanese Professional Baseball Official Record Book*, for example, records individual pitcher statistics in 22 categories and individual batting statistics in 19 categories. Such a continuously quantified and recorded sport deepens the knowledge possible, and perhaps necessary, to follow, interpret, and evaluate players' and teams' performances. Moreover, baseball is an interval sport, a game of pulsating oscillations of fast action and slow preparation. Its physical and mental rhythms are thus quite different from continuous flow sports like soccer and basketball, and this obviously influences spectators' modalities of engagement. In sum, these and other qualities distinctive to sports and particularly to professional baseball significantly shape the experiences of the Kōshien Stadium bleacher fans.

Yet I must also acknowledge that these fans are rather special even in the arena of baseball. Indeed, even at the stadium, the vocal and organized denizens of the outfield bleachers represent only one type of stadium experience. The larger numbers of spectators in the infield sections may follow the fan club cheers but are seldom as noisy or as organized. And, of course, those who come to the stadiums are only a small percentage of those who regularly follow baseball. Many self-described fans seldom get to the ballpark; instead, they keep up with their favorites by nightly television or radio, and by close reading of a daily sports paper, often as they commute by public transportation to and from work. There has been much theorization about how media (especially television and sports papers) interject themselves between the action and the audience, packaging the former as spectacle and creating the latter as indirect spectators (see, e.g., Whannel 1992). Fandom, it is argued, is largely eroded by such near-total mediation.

I doubt that, but clearly the husband who sprawls in the family room of his south Osaka apartment every evening at 7:30 after work with a cold beer taking in the Tigers' game on television or the company man packed in a crowded commuter train who avidly reads about the previous night's Tigers' contest in his favorite sports daily on his way to work are very different "fans" from those who come out to Kōshien every night. This is not because the stadium experience offers an intimacy, immediacy, and spontaneity that cannot be matched by the televisual and print mediums, but rather because these qualities are transmuted by these mediums. Sports on television create some of the same "quasi-intimacy" that Andrew Painter (1996) has argued for Japanese daytime variety shows; indeed, baseball televiewers peer right over the shoulder of the pitcher, are given multiple camera angles and replays on the action, and are privy to the authoritative commentary of announcers who speak directly to them. And the vivid color graphics, exploding font shapes and sizes, and multiple stories, stats boxes, and sidebars by which sports dailies dramatically report Tiger games make the experience more akin to reading a *manga* (comic art magazine) than a news story. Kōshien bleacher fans are not the only fans of Tigers baseball, then, but I would claim that the sociality and the organized influence of the bleacher fans are distinctive among baseball fandoms. I focus on them here because they usefully demonstrate the dynamics of collective appropriation also true for other arenas of leisure and entertainment.

It's Not All "Kattobase!" The Choreography of Cheering

It is certainly the case that one's first impression of the Kōshien bleacher sections is that all this constant cheering is not only excruciatingly loud but also exceedingly monotonous. All they do seem to be chanting, over and over, to a thumping percussive beat, is "Kattobase! Ya-ma-da" or "Kattobase! Hi-ya-ma," or Ma-ko-to, or whichever player is at bat. But there turns out to be more to Kōshien cheering than first assaults the ears. When one starts to listen a bit more closely, it is possible to discern small differences, in the lyrics and the beat. Each starting player and regular substitute has his own "hitting march," and the most fundamental cheering, then, is singing a version of the hitting march of whoever is up to bat with a kattobase refrain (there is a generic hitting march for others). Following are the 1997 hitting marches for rightfielder Hiyama Shinjirō and catcher Yamada Katsuhiko:[5]

この一打に賭けろ	The game rides on the swing of your bat
気合いで振り抜けよ	Hit it with all your might!
だれもおまえを止められぬ	Nobody can stop you;
桧山よ突っ走れ	Run, Hiyama, Run!
守り抜く	Home plate is all yours to defend;
ホームベースは俺のもの	Show us again your strong arm;
今日も見せるぞ鉄の肩	It's you, Yamada—
山田まかせたぞ	We're countin' on you.

The hitting march cheer begins when the batter steps into the box and continues until his at-bat is finished—no matter how many pitches or foul balls. Then, if he reaches base safely, either by hitting or being walked, he is rewarded with another quick chant. If Hiyama, for example, has singled in a run, he will be greeted with "taimurii, taimurii, Hi-ya-ma" (Timely, timely, Hiyama; "timely" being a fabricated term for a clutch hit).

The chants are accompanied by a noisy choreography of trumpets, bugles, whistles, Japanese *taiko* drums, Western bass drums, flags, and banners. Each has a distinct location and an orchestrated role. The taiko drummers (see Figure 4.2) are below in the first row of seats while the trumpeters and bass drummers play in the upper seats; huge flags are waved from the upper tier skillfully and precariously just above the heads of those seated below, and player banners are tied along the walkway between the lower and upper seating tiers. Rights to the banners, one per player, are held by individual fan clubs.

Figure 4.2
A Private Association drummer in the right-field bleachers at Kōshien
Stadium. Copyright The Asahi Shimbun Company. Used with permission.

Larger cheering routines create a game pace. For example, there are pregame chants and opening player name calls; when an opposing pitcher is removed from the game, he is serenaded with "Auld Lang Syne"; in the middle of the "Lucky seventh" inning, when the Tigers come to bat, a spirited rendition of the Tigers fight song concludes with the release of tens of thousands of balloons (tagged "condom balloons" for their distinctive shape); and at the end of victories, everyone stands to sing a cycle of the hitting marches and then the Tiger anthem, "Rokkō oroshi," with a bansai cheer.

There is, then, a variegated choreography, a structured flow to fan club cheering—from batter to batter, through the innings, over the stretch of the game. True, the lyrics are not inspired; they combine the exaggerated heroics of a praise song with the polite imperatives of an encouraging command. And I don't want to exaggerate the inventiveness or sophistication of this structured flow. It is not like following Bach's Goldberg Variations or the Paul Taylor Dance Company. But it does miss the intent and the effect of the outfield cheering to dismiss it as mindless, repetitive droning.

Rather, this constant, collective chanting is a way of claiming an active role in the game. Sitting in bleachers a distant 250–300 feet from the main action at home plate, it is nearly impossible for them to follow the subtleties of pitching, to judge the close umpire calls, to hear the dugout chatter, or otherwise share the intensity of the game as those in the infield seats can. Rather, with their cheering, the outfield fans participate as "mood makers." More precisely, they become mood "remakers," because this particular cheering pattern assertively layers the normally punctuated rhythms of the game on the field with the continuous rhythms of vocal chants and body sways. They convert (or perhaps divert) the game from interval to flow. This participatory intervention is a key dimension of their role and identity as fans.

Indeed, there may be an even deeper structure to cheering. Takahashi Hidesato (1995), a sociologist at the Nara University of Education, has studied both Hiroshima Carp and Hanshin Tiger fan club cheering and argues that the fundamental rhythmic pattern of these cheers is a three-seven beat that is reminiscent of agricultural song cycles that date to the medieval centuries. These songs were appeals to the gods for fertility and harvests, and he contrasts them structurally with two-beat patterns of other chants and songs that were messages from the gods to the human world, such as the fire warnings called out with clappers by the night watchmen who made the rounds of urban neighborhoods at night. If this is true, it implies that, symbolically at least, the fan club cheering is *for* the players but *to* divine agents. It is active supplication on behalf of the team, in particular, to the goddess of victory, the deity of outcomes being coded feminine in Japanese sports cosmology.

I find Takahashi's hypothesis implausible at face value; I have asked many fans and others in the stadium audience to whom they are cheering when they urge Hiyama to "let it rip," and not surprisingly all find my question rather silly. Of course, they are directing their support to Hiyama. At the same time, though, the goddess of victory is a folk belief of wide salience, and it is equally unsurprising that chanting patterns should bear symbolic association, however unrecognized, with such rhythms.

They Haven't Been Sitting There Forever— A Brief Organizational History of Kōshien Fan Clubs

It may also strike a first-time observer that apart from a few yellow-jacketed, white-gloved leaders down in front, there is an anonymous uniformity to the bleacher crowds. It turns out, however, that there is a rather elaborate structuring of the fans, which has both deep historical resonance and some fairly recent organizational initiatives.

Well-known in the urban commoner society of the Edo period, especially from Genroku on, were the *teuchi renjū* (hand-clapping clubs) from commoner neighborhoods or fire squads or guild workers who organized around particular kabuki actors and sumo wrestlers and who exhibited their loyalties with color-coded scarves and seat cushions. These claques were celebrated for their precisely timed shouts and elaborate and distinctive hand-clapping routines whenever their actor or wrestler appeared—and castigated for their often violent encounters with rival clubs in the theaters, in the temple grounds on sumo days, or in the streets (Kelly 1994; Raz 1983).

Baseball cheerleading origins, however, are as foreign as the sport. When the Waseda and Keio baseball clubs toured the United States in the early 20th century, they were so impressed with American collegiate cheering (especially football) that they made extensive notes of the patterns and instruments, which they then introduced back home. Cheerleading became its own club activity, a flamboyant and disciplined display of school spirit that remains prominent today at the high school and university levels.

Professional teams, from the start of the first league in 1936, were sponsored and owned by major corporations. They faced a skeptical public, wary that playing for pay would sully the amateur ideal that it associated with school baseball. Thus the teams adopted a number of elements of school baseball in an effort to allay these suspicions. For promotion and support, most of the early clubs organized kōenkai (fan supporter groups), which were often just groups of their own employees given free tickets and encouraged to lend their voices to the company team. Flags, megaphones, and cheer songs were used for color and cohesion, although records of the early decades indicate that most spectators were not part of organized groups.

Thus the lineage of fan support is long, but the current structure of Kōshien fan clubs emerged in the mid-1970s after a decade in which professional baseball's appeal greatly broadened to a national audience of viewers and readers. This was precisely the period, as the introduction to this volume argues, when defusing political strife, double-digit economic growth, the spread of television, and other factors combined to accelerate and "massify" metropolitan consumption. Of particular stimulus to baseball were the proliferation of sports dailies, the popularity of several series of baseball comic books, and especially the Yomiuri Giants' nine-year run as Japan Series champions from 1965 to 1973 (earning them the title, the "V-9 Giants"). Television, and Yomiuri's ownership of a national network, made the Giants organization and its success emblematic of corporate nationalism and economic resurgence (Kelly 1998). Polls identified its star third baseman, Nagashima Shigeo, as the most popular public figure in Japan.

However, the stadiums themselves, especially the outfield bleachers frequented by the working class, remained rowdy places, not quite fit for prime-time television. Small clubs of ordinary fans shared the bleachers with bookies and gangsters. Betting was still common, and at least some fan support—and anger—focused on whether the team was making or not making the betting spread. Inebriation and fights were common, often between rival gambler groups. Incidents of spectators jumping out onto the field to accost umpires and players were not uncommon. I interviewed a number of people, now in their seventies and eighties, who were involved in initial efforts from 1974 on to create some regular cooperation among the ordinary fan groups at Kōshien, in what amounted to an effort to take back the stands from rowdies and gamblers, to widen the base of spectators, and to alter the participatory spirit.

This gentling of spectator behavior can be related to larger societal trends in law and order. The early postwar period was marked, of course, with considerable turbulence. Labor union strife in the 1950s, massive demonstrations against the U.S.–Japan Security Treaty renewal in 1960, anti-Vietnam protests and the large-scale student unrest of the 1960s, and consumer movements, youth motorcycle gangs, and the Narita Airport agitations in the 1970s were among the public expressions of constant social discontent. I do not believe—and have found no one who has argued—that there were direct connections of these to the (quite apolitical) sports rowdiness of the era. At the same time, the rowdiness was one more anxiety for corporate and official Japan. What is remarkable here, however, is that it was the ordinary spectators themselves who acted independently of the stadium and ball team to redirect the energies and attentions of the crowd.

Throughout the seasons that I observed, in the front row of the outfield bleachers, near the foul line pole in the lower extreme right corner of the stands, sat an elderly gentleman in the yellow jacket of a fan club official. This was Moritani Kazuo, who was 77 in 1998, and the fan clubs' evening performances began only when he stood to shout "Ikee!" [Let's go!], and initiated their pregame chants. By then, Moritani had had overall charge of outfield cheering for 12 years. He was a Waseda University graduate and with his wife ran a small bar, Ta'ichi, near one of the Hanshin stations about a ten-minute ride from the stadium. The bar, with just one long counter, celebrated its 25th anniversary in 1997 and has long been an information center for Hanshin fans. Mrs. Moritani ran the bar during all of the season's home games when her husband was at the ballpark.

It was Mr. Moritani and several others who worked for a number of years to build what is now called Hanshin Taigaasu shisetsu ōendan (the Private Alliance of Hanshin Tiger Fan Clubs). The alliance's origins date to 1973, when Moritani, Fujiwara Katsumi, and Matsubayashi Noboru (who also remain as top officers) began talking with the hundreds of small fan clubs about creating an umbrella organization to try to bring an end to the fighting that constantly erupted and which gave Kōshien a "scandalous" name (*fushōji* was the term Moritani used). They met with little initial success because many fans did not want to give up their own styles of cheering. In February 1975, the Fierce Tiger Club, the Young Tiger Club, and two others merged into what they called optimistically the Private Alliance, but which only totaled 120 members. It was not until 1980 that a large enough number of clubs joined to give it a presence in the left-field bleachers. In that year, the association was legally constituted with an 11-clause "club regulations" and a 28-clause "rules of conduct."

One serious difficulty for the organized fan groups was that all outfield and Alps seats were unreserved; club members had to line up with everyone else for every game. Often club members and nonmembers were mixed together, and that led to squabbling and fighting, especially when drinking and during key contests. Older club and stadium officials recall that *yakuza* (organized crime) groups were prominent and constant troublemakers. They simply displaced ticket holders from choice spots, including the seats at the walkways and the railings for hanging banners.

The major impetus in alliance growth was the Tigers' championship year of 1985, the only time in team history that it captured the Japan Series. The region was engulfed in Tiger pride, demand for tickets was far beyond capacity, and the exuberance of the spectators greatly concerned stadium officials as the season progressed. This apparently convinced them to create large blocs of season ticket seats in the right outfield and to give the association some advance preference in requests. This, in turn, made fan club membership and alliance participation immediately attractive for individuals and clubs.

The Private Alliance has now grown into a quite elaborate association. Its constituent Tiger fan clubs stretch from Hokkaido to Okinawa and claim over 10 thousand members in four branches and 40 clubs. There are over one hundred officers in parallel administrative and stadium hierarchies. The former handle alliance organizational matters and the latter orchestrate the cheering at the stadium itself. Moritani's title is general head of stadium affairs, and as the title suggests, he has overall authority for everything that happens at the stadium. He is assisted by two vice heads. Under them are a club head and five vice heads, below which is a chief of cheerleaders, who in turn has 11 vice chiefs, who finally supervise and evaluate the 66 "leaders" who do the actual cheerleading. There are also officers and instrumentalists for the trumpet and drum brigades. Club membership is surprisingly diverse in age, class, and gender, but the club and association leadership is overwhelmingly male. Even at the lowest levels, there were only two women among the 66 cheerleaders.

The Private Alliance, complex as it is, does not exhaust the organizational map of the right-field stands. There are a great many small fan clubs that remain outside this Private Alliance, 24 of whom joined together in 1989 as a second association, the Middle Tiger Clubs Association. Relations with the Private Alliance are generally cordial, and Moritani and several others sit on the advisory board of the Middle Tiger Clubs Association. And there are an estimated two hundred other fan clubs throughout the country who belong to neither, although usually cooperate with their efforts.

All of this has created a well-defined, albeit historically shallow, social ecology and procedural order. Cheerleading initiative is retained by the Private Alliance officers, the so-called *ki-jyaaji kumi* (yellow jackets) because of their yellow-and-black uniform waist jackets, who occupy the seats across the bottom rows. Officers serve for two-year terms, and there is constant movement up, down, and across the organizational charts. Cheerleaders and instrumentalists are licensed by the alliance officers, and they all must meet and practice before each game in the grounds of the temple adjacent to Kōshien.[6] Composition of the hitting marches is also a Private Alliance prerogative. They are usually drafted by several of its music consultants, who are music professors at local universities, and vetted and approved at the several levels of meetings that are held throughout the year—of the general membership, of all leaders, and of the top officials.

Clubs in the Middle Association occupy many of the seats along the walkway between the lower and upper tiers and certain left-field bleachers and Alps sections. They and some Private Alliance clubs control the support banners for all regular players and the large club flags that are waved from the upper tier. The flag waving and all other elements of cheering comportment are worked out in meetings between the two associations and stadium officials. For example, until 1992 or so, clubs were waving their flags during much of the games; this not only obstructed the view of many of the spectators, but also meant that individual clubs could not stand out. Thus, it was agreed in one of the negotiation sessions to restrict flag waving to the hitting songs of players the club supports and certain other moments in the game.

Thus, in looking around the right-field bleachers, one must be aware that there is a rather complicated two-decade history of organizing that has created the complex social structuring of this time–space. It is notably ironic that while they are often criticized for a perceived rowdiness, the clubs were organized for precisely the opposite reason: to bring some order and decorum to the outfield stands. Its own charter announces that the purpose of the Private Alliance is "to love the Hanshin Tigers and to support the team in a decorous and orderly fashion." Like the "red beret" resident patrols in minority neighborhoods in New York City in the 1980s, this self-policing carries an ambiguous political charge. It is an initiative to stake out and regulate a zone within the private corporate space of the most famous stadium in all of Japan. And yet they are regulating—shaping the spectator experience toward a proper metropolitan sensibility.

It's Not All Cheering—The Sociality of Ōendan

At the same time, however, what goes on in the right-field stands is not nonstop chanting, but a pulsating rhythm of frenzy and calm. That is, a cardinal tenet of cheering is that you cheer when your team is at bat, but not while it is in the field. There are hitting marches but no "fielding marches." Of course a good play is applauded, and groans and jeers can be elicited by an opposing team's home run.

But when the visiting team is at bat, the cheering initiative shifts to the visiting team fans in the left-field stands.

So what does go on when one's team is in the field? Drinking and eating, of course; almost all games now are at night, beginning at Kōshien at 6 p.m., and most people come right from work. There is also some prepping for the next at bats. But mostly what goes on is schmoozing. Half the game—the top half of each inning—is spent talking, sharing news, chatting up fellow club members, visiting with other fan clubs, flirting, gossiping, pushing deals, and so on. For many of the denizens of the bleachers—especially those from the small-business sector—fan clubs and base-ball games are substitute activities for the hostess clubs and quasi-obligatory drink-ing that fill the watery evening zone between workplace and home. It is the layering of another, quieter flow over the interval action on the field.

Consider the Namitora-kai (Roving Tigers Club), a representative club in the Middle Tiger Clubs Association. The Roving Tigers Club currently has about two hundred members, mostly in its headquarters Kobe club but also in five branches in Kyoto, Okayama, Nagoya, Tokyo, and Toyama. These are all places where the Tigers play a couple of times during the season; this allows reciprocal hospitality and guar-anteed seats. At Kōshien, the club purchases a ten-seat block of season tickets in ad-dition to the seats purchased by individual members. Club officers occupy the seats and railings along a section of the middle walkway, where they have designated cheering responsibility for two players, Hiyama and Yamada, and have two trumpet players and a drummer. Also from a walkway perch, one of the experienced mem-bers waves the large club flag precariously low over the heads of spectators seated in the seats below.

The club's executive officer through the 1990s was Fujita Kenji, who turned 50 in 1996 and is president of a small Kobe marine trading company that sup-plies repair parts to ocean ships. Several of his ten employees come to the game at his expense, and everyone piles into his minivan for the one-hour drive to the stadium. Before entering, they stock up on food and drinks at their favorite local shops to carry in for their evening dinner and refreshment. Fujita pays for all of the purchases, about 10,000 yen ($100) per game, out of his own pocket.

Among the club members are a number of Fujita's business associates—from the air freight and trucking companies he uses and from other ship parts companies. Like many other fan clubs, the Roving Tigers Club is a venue for maintaining busi-ness ties. This is especially so for the medium and small businesses that are the bulk of the Kansai economy, but large workplaces are also in evidence. Adjacent to the Roving Tigers is a block of seats for Love the Tigers Club from the labor union of the Central Osaka Post Office, and to their side is group seating for the Tiger Crazy Alliance, a club from the giant Mitsubishi Heavy Industry and Mitsubishi Electric, and another block for the Strong Tiger Guys from Nittō Electric.

For businessmen of small companies and corporate managers, the fan clubs offer an alternative to business socializing that is at once easier and more burdensome than more customary expense-account entertainment in bars. The season and each game set a predictable framework to such obligations that limits both drinking and expenses. At the same time, there are considerable costs of this club fandom on the efficiency of small companies like that of Mr. Fujita. To arrive at the ballpark requires his closing the office around 5 p.m., in order to drive the hour to Kōshien and then stock up on supplies; he and the other Kobe members get home around midnight, making it difficult, they acknowledged, to come to work the next morning at peak effort. It is only 65 nights a year, and he says they work until 7 p.m. on nongame nights to make up for lost time, but, year after year, that is a lot of travel and drinking. And pressure—both the sense of obligation out of which some employees participate and the very heavy responsibility that Fujita himself frequently expressed for insuring, game after game, a safe and enjoyable experience for members and those around him. No wonder he was so visibly relieved at the end of the final game of the season, when I went with him and other officers for a long celebratory night of drinking in the Osaka bar district—at an establishment managed by a Roving Tiger club member. When he exclaimed it was a season "without incident," in the quote at this essay's opening, he was referring to his fan club's fortunes and not those of the ball team.

However, not all Roving Tiger members are business related. In the late 1990s, there was a young woman who worked as a Yamaha electric organ teacher, a fellow who worked for a janitorial service, a JR railroad conductor, some Osaka college kids (who usually played the club's two trumpets and bass drum), and others. But all showed up, and were expected to show up, regularly. Miss 30 games or so in a season, and they would find themselves dropped from the rolls—and from the access to the club's reserved seating, trips to away games, and the several social events and club assemblies held throughout the year away from Kōshien.

While workplace groups predominate, neighborhood and other kinds of social networks are also bases for Tiger fan clubs. There is, for example, the Tiger Ladies Club of about thirty-two middle-aged women and the Fierce Tiger Club of the Civil Engineering Department of Kyoto University. And the association network fosters social ties among the clubs as well. To the right of the Roving Tiger Club is a club whose members are predominantly *tekiya* (itinerant stall operators and hucksters at markets and carnivals). Given their peripatetic schedule, the club is often shorthanded and Fujita and his members lend a hand in hoisting the banners and flag. Fujita is also generous in providing beer and food to younger adult members of adjacent clubs "because they just don't have the pocket money." And during a game one evening in late 1997, a club director accompanied two of his members, a father and son, around the bleachers; introducing them to officers of various other clubs, they distributed invitations to the son's upcoming wedding reception. More substantially, following the devastating 1996 Kobe earthquake, the Private Alliance and constituent clubs provided much logistical and financial assistance to those many clubs and members who had suffered (often enormous) losses.[7]

But whatever the principle of formation, I have come to appreciate that, for these outfield fans, of equal importance to the coordinated high-energy emotion is the quieter, routinized sociability of a time and place that is somewhere between work and home. It may not be immediately obvious that schmoozing is an appropriate dimension of baseball fan conduct. Here at Kōshien, however, it is central to what Grossberg (1992) calls the "affective sensibility" of the fans' space–time, whose rhythms are both distinct from and intimately attuned to the field of play it overlooks.

Neither Insiders nor Outsiders— Whose Side Are the Fan Clubs On?

Fans are by definition "fanatics," maniacs, and mania is a schizoid condition. It expresses itself, on the one hand, in abiding devotion to their object of loyalty, even the most hapless of teams. A Tigers' fan is *tora-kichi* (Tiger-crazy), with the same depth of feeling that English football fans are "supporters" and Italian fans compose *la fede calcistica* (the football faithful), as suggested by the Tiger-crazy fan quoted at the outset of this chapter (from Rokusai-sha 1996:60).

At the same time, and in apparent contradiction, Tiger fans are ever vigilant for any slip or mistake by the objects of their adulation, quick to criticize for any expectations not met. Tiger players, managers, and club officers have all been vulnerable to sudden swings of fan support. At several moments in games during the recent seasons of dismal Tiger teams, the fan clubs have even boycotted the team by refusing to cheer.

The audiences at Kōshien are famous for their *yaji* (jeers), and even in the midst of the fan club cheering, one can hear heckling and catcalls. Heckling ranges widely, from boorish catcalls ("Yoshida, you idiot!" or "Get the bum out of here!") to more witty satirical barbs, phrased in Osaka dialect and thrown out with the timing and pitch that recalls the *kakegoe* (audience interjections) from kabuki aficionados. In fact, a group styling itself the "Crazy-About-the-Tigers Heckling Research Group" published a collection of jeers heard during the 1994 season at the stadium (Hanshin Taigāsu ni nekkyō suru yaji kenkyūkai 1994). Like an annotated poetry volume, each was identified by date and moment, given in original dialect, and the circumstances and substance were explained. Interestingly, when I asked players and front-office people why so few of the player wives attended Hanshin games, they very often voiced concern that the wives would be upset by the booing and jeering. (This is questionable because most heckling cannot be heard from the backstop box seats in which wives and other favored guests sit and because the wives themselves more often cited the difficulties of bringing young children to night games. Still, I do not doubt the sensitivity of the team to jeering.)

Fandom in sports, then, like other fandoms, is a peculiar combination of attachment and fickleness, of long-suffering patience and a demand for instant gratification. Just whose side the fans are on is never entirely clear—or at least never stable. First, one must realize that what one sees in the right-field stands of Kōshien is not only solidly organized but also resolutely independent of the Hanshin team—hence the "private" *(shisetsu)* in its title. This is not always true of fan organizations of other teams. The Yomiuri Giants, among others, rather tightly control the association of Giants fan clubs, and in 1989 a number of the fan organizations of Pacific League teams, embarrassed by the rowdy image of Hanshin and other fans, came together in an Association of Pacific League Fan Clubs that is recognized by the league office.[7]

But at Kōshien, the years have witnessed considerable mutual antagonism between the fan clubs, stadium officials, and the Tigers club. To be sure, there are some obvious converging interests. The fan clubs have sought and benefited from certain concessions by the stadium, especially in shifting of the 6,000 right-field seats to a season-ticket basis, to which fan club members have special access. For their part, the fan clubs provide intangible but essential color and background for stadium ambiance and television and radio broadcasts.

Nonetheless, their colorful, constant presence is a mixed boon to the Hanshin club, and fan club practices do not always reinforce the stadium company's and the club's own marketing efforts to attract and appeal to audiences. The official promotion days, team mascots, and scoreboard-led cheers are only lukewarmly met by the fan clubs. In a real sense, the outfield sections are a separate territory, largely self-disciplined by the fan club alliance with only circumspect oversight by stadium guards. As I have mentioned, there are periodic meetings between fan club alliance leaders and stadium officials to discuss rules for banners, seating, flag waving, drinking, and concessions. The baseball club, for its part, refuses to get involved in any way with the fan clubs. When I made my initial introductions to the Hanshin front office in 1996, for example, I expressed an interest in contacting the fan club officials. I was quickly informed that the team had no relationship to the fan organizations, and I would have to approach them on my own. An even less guarded front-office opinion is quoted at this chapter's outset.

The small issue of beer coolers is illustrative of this tension. They are not allowed in the stadium. And yet, packed with cans of beer (and cans are not allowed either, their usefulness as projectiles having been demonstrated on more than one occasion), cooler after cooler is carried through the turnstiles right past the stadium guards and left in open display on the walkways filled with beer and whiskey to quench the thirst and lubricate the hospitality of the fan club officers and their guests. But as long as the association officials can control their members' drinking behavior, the stadium company silently concedes them the right. It even sends around a senior employee at the end of every game to bow and offer words of thanks to the head of each and every fan club "for their cooperation" that evening.

The fan clubs also harbor skeptical, even hostile, attitudes toward the media as well. Modern sports are "spectator sports," opening up a distinction between those who do and those who watch; this is reflected in stadiums that create barriers and arenas and also in the media (radio, television, print) that do just that—inter-mediate, transmit, interpret the doers to the watchers. Actually, though, media do not simply passively report the play, but intervene more actively than their name suggests to frame and dramatize the sporting event (see, e.g., Ariyama 1997; Nagai 1997; Sugimoto 1997; and Taniguchi 1997). Radio and television, especially, often need and encourage spectators as animated participants in the drama presented; the cameras pan the stadium crowds and microphones are fixed in locations throughout to pick up the cheers and groans and catcalls. The organized fan clubs obviously offer the most desirable camera shots, and the clubs take some pride in the show they provide. At the same time, many members feel misused and misrepresented because those broadcasts associate the clubs with the more zany and sometimes violent behavior of fans who are often not even members. An article in the Private Alliance regulations requires members to channel all media requests through association officers, who even object to pictures taken of them and their clubs in the stands without their permission.

Given these tensions, the potential for fan violence is never far below the surface, although its extent is difficult to gauge. On the one hand, sitting in the right field bleachers in over fifty games over three seasons, I only saw three fights erupt among bleacher fans (and they were quickly broken up by club officers). The general level of fighting and posturing is well below an average Sunday afternoon National Football League crowd. Nonetheless, there are enough occasional incidents to keep team and stadium officials and fan club officers anxious. On June 1, 1996, for example, during my first year of observation, a slump in May angered Hanshin supporters, about fifty of whom surrounded the hotel in Chiba where the team was staying; they accosted several players leaving the hotel to go to dinner and surrounded another in a threatening manner in the hotel elevator. Then in August, a drunken fan club member beat up a stadium guard outside the ticket entrance after another loss. And throughout the disappointing season, constant fan jeering and grumbling was directed at the manager and the front office. Midway through my fieldwork, in June 1998, the Tigers again fell into last place and the sports papers began reporting and railing against Tiger fan "hooligan behavior." In Shizuoka on May 16, a scoreless game with Yokohama was interrupted in the eighth inning by Hanshin fans who pelted the outfield with trash and bottles; after the game, five fans jumped the fence and ran around the outfield trying to stir up the spectators. Two days later, against Yokohama in that city, angry Hanshin fans threw their megaphones at the team bus as it left the stadium. This prompted the stadium to add 50 extra guards to the normal complement of 200 for the crucial Giants series on June 19–21 (two of the games were rained out and the third was a close victory for Hanshin, with no reported incidents).[8]

Much more common, of course, are the moments of exuberance that could, but seldom, become ugly. For example, returning to Osaka's central Umeda Station from a game at Kōshien against the Yakult Swallows on a sweltering August night in 1997, I happened to ride in a packed train car into which, at the last moment, spilled a spirited fan club of young males. They drew worried looks from the other passengers as they moved through the car, aggressively although not threateningly demanding expressions of Tiger support. However, they soon had most passengers entertained and involved in a nonstop series of chants for the 20-minute ride. They began with the fan club chants for each Hanshin player before shifting to a series of insult chants against Yakult. Then they announced that "Because the wave is banned at Kōshien, let's do it here," and they got most of the passengers in the car to bob up and down three or four times in a back-to-front wave, before launching into another series of insult chants against arch rival Yomiuri Giants—attacking the players, Giants manager Nagashima, Yomiuri's sports daily *Hōchi shimbun* ("only good as toilet paper"), and the Yomiuri television network NTV ("idiot-TV"). They then sang some insult verses directed to Hanshin's next opponent, Yokohama BayStars, by which time the train was pulling into the station to their pulsating chant of "Umeda, Umeda, Umeda." The group poured out of the car, rushed down the platform, and reassembled in the main foyer for a final round of chants and songs before disbanding. Station personnel and fan club officers who happened to be riding the train looked on with a skeptical bemusement, ready to gently intervene.

These and many other incidents sustain a wary standoff between the fan clubs, the rest of the stadium audience, the Kōshien stadium company, and the Tigers baseball club. The fan clubs do not officially condone violence or even rude displays against the team or its opponents; indeed, they actively patrol and monitor. And most of the serious reported incidents appear not to involve association members. Nonetheless, members can be quite vocal in their dissatisfaction with the team and its performance and occasionally express this in gestures and demeanor. In short, the fan clubs are neither *uchi* nor *soto* (neither insiders nor outsiders). Like fans everywhere (and like some anthropologists), they are participants and observers in an ambivalent zone, more passionate and partisan than ordinary spectators, but quick to assert their independence from the team itself.

Fanning the Flames of Mass Culture

The noisy and colorful presence of fan clubs is certainly one of the key features distinguishing professional baseball in Japan from its older sibling in the United States. Yet in appreciating this difference, we must be careful to avoid orientalist exaggerations and essentialist explanations. For example, while organized fan cheering is absent from professional baseball in the United States, it is certainly a crucial and occasionally disruptive element of other Western sports, including American football and European and South American soccer.[9] And in highlighting the outfield fan clubs, I have neglected the more numerous infield spectators, who may add their voices at suspenseful moments and important games but which by and large behave rather like crowds at American ballparks. To them, indeed, the fans clubs are a curious spectacle and something of a mystery.

Surely, then, we cannot dismiss the Japanese fan as "a veritable wildman, yelling and screaming nonstop for nine solid innings." The Kōshien fan clubs have created and sustain a distinctive and discriminating time–space in the right-field bleachers—and this chapter has attempted to explicate ethnographically the historical conditions and social processes and cultural elements by which they have, for a time at least, been able to do this.

First, we have seen that it was not an inevitable Japanese collectivist urge but some historically particular circumstances that prompted the Private Alliance at Kōshien. These and other organized fan clubs for professional baseball in Japan owe something to the sport's early development there in schools, whose cheerleading squads offered a model of fan support and whose prestige (as the spirit of "amateurism") was inducement to borrow. More recently, as the professional leagues' strove for respectability and television share in the national markets of the 1960s and 1970s, some teams sponsored fan organizations to exert control over stadium crowds. Now, for public relations, marketing, and managing the stadium show, all teams pay some attention to "fan service."

Nonetheless, great differences remain among the Central and Pacific League teams in the fan clubs' scale, showmanship, volubility, internal organization, and relations to the ball club. The Tiger fan associations reflect the determinedly autonomous efforts of certain fans to convince a great many others to create and to elaborate organized and self regulated routines of cheering that invest enthusiasm and commitment in the fortunes of the team and in the pleasure of their own company while claiming both the space and the voice to do that amid the sometimes heavy-handed corporate interests of the team and its parent corporation.

I have suggested that the particular structure and style of the Kōshien clubs are, in part, a function of the medium- and small-business character of the local economy—a significant working class with a taste for spectator and gambling sports (there is a horse track and a speedboat stadium nearby Kōshien); a direct, even blunt, style of business dealings; and patterns of business socializing beyond the upscale, expense-account hostess bars that cater to white-collar management and upper civil servants.

Consequential also is the enormous emotional charge given the Tigers for symbolically bearing the pride and determination of the Kansai region in its intense rivalry with the formidable concentrations of the Kantō capital. The other two area teams have both done better than the Tigers in recent years, but they play in the Pacific League and do not confront the Yomiuri Giants 26 times a season like the Tigers. One of the grand themes of 20th-century Japanese state making has been the dramatic shift in the Kantō–Kansai balance of power, especially Osaka's loss of economic parity with Tokyo and its postwar subordination in the Tokyo-centrism of the present political economy. In a circulation of rhetoric, local media commentators and ordinary fans alike are quick to recite a litany of contrast pairs (Tokyo versus Osaka, national bureaucrats versus local businesspeople, national imperviousness versus regional pride, and big powerful big corporations versus vulnerable small business) that are symbolically condensed in the Giants–Tigers rivalry.

This helps us understand, too, the local resolution of the universal sports challenge of coping with losing—for half of each game's participants and their followers, for all but a single team in any league in every season. Hanshin's baseball success came in pro baseball's early years, in the 1930s and 1940s, when Osaka itself was the rough equal of Tokyo. In the postwar decades, as Osaka's power ebbed, so did the fortunes of the Tigers. Many fans feel inevitability—and injustice—in the declining success of the Tigers. This does not incline them toward passive resignation but rather toward a certain arch cynicism about Giants (i.e., Tokyo) domination, which can veer menacingly toward the Hanshin company when it is suspected of failing to fight with proper resolve and resources, despite the odds. Again, the distinctive and defended autonomy of the Tiger fan club associations derives from this freighted sensibility.

In the end, though, perhaps the most striking contradiction may well be the contrast of an initial impression of the outfield fans' wild abandon and the later realization that there is an authoritative order that quietly but effectively imposes itself on these fans. This might well lead the reader to think I am, finally, reaffirming the crush of the collective in this as in other areas of Japanese life. If the screaming fans are not veritable wildmen, are they not then obedient automatons, mindlessly chanting the choreographed lyrics?

I think that this too would be mistaken because it neglects both the pleasures of these fans and the perplexities they present to the media and the baseball world. Despite the gendered and age-graded administrative hierarchies of the clubs and their determined orchestration of fan sentiment, the mood among the thousands who nightly fill the right-field stands is not as militaristic and routinized as the structures suggest. People pay close attention to batting (having to cheer constantly focuses attention) and some attention to the other team's at bats. However, rather than the regimented mass spectator formations of the Chinese National Games that Brownell (1995) describes, Kōshien games remind me much more of the delicately balanced "mood" of festivals I have attended, with their mix of the choreographed and the spontaneous, of knowledge and passion (e.g., the Kurokawa Festival; see Kelly 1990). There are wide swings of deeply felt emotion at the ever-changing fortunes of the team and great evident enjoyment in sharing a summer evening with friends (and strangers). It is simply fun to be out there, although both exhilarating and exhausting. The highly conventionalized forms of expressing such emotions less compromise than enable the sharing of feeling. It is perhaps one more illustration of a cultural presumption (which is not a national character) that social forms can enable as effectively as restrain personal feeling.

Fan club cheering is also about Moritani's thrill of shouting "Ikee!" to start the evening; the head leader proudly waving his tasseled baton to start the inning; the syncopated, white-gloved clapping of the leaders stationed throughout the stands; the drummers and the trumpeters putting their all into the beat; and so on. The right-field crowd, then, can easily feel a sense of participating, of "losing" oneself in the mass cheering, but all down the line one can also have a sense of leading—Moritani opens the proceedings, the baton starts the cheers, the drum leads the trumpet, the trumpet leads the chants, and everyone's chants lead and motivate the players.

To see the fans as automatons also belies the constant anxiety and perplexity of stadium and team officials and even fan club officers at the unpredictable course that such high emotion and deep knowledge can take. Thus, rather than treating baseball fans in Japan as some noisome aberration of proper sports spectatorship, we should instead understand them as bearing witness to the central role of fandom in mass culture everywhere today. It is a commonplace observation that modern societies offer highly commercialized and "massified" forms of entertainment and leisure, and profit motives rather than performance standards more typically motivate the culture industries that produce what we watch and listen to. Japan, with its manga and *pachinko* (pinball) and karaoke, is an exemplar and not an exception.

Clearly too, the old "bread and circuses" complaint that mass culture only induces passivity and stultification ignores the many ways that some viewers and readers and spectators creatively consume and actively reproduce. Out of audiences, whether at stadiums or theaters or video arcades, emerge some "fanatics" seeking to intensify their experience. It is these fans who are the unstable center of this commodified culture, because they are so poised between the forces of production and the sites of reception. Fans, here in the form of the Kōshien outfield fan clubs, are paragons of exemplary consumption, embodying with their money and time and energy a commitment to the professionalized spectacle of sport. And yet they are also creative agents, interrupting the spectacle and diverting its messages with their own appropriations of meaning and interventions of energies within the space and time of the sport.

It would be wrong to exaggerate the disruptive and oppositional potential of fans, especially in a sport that has come to be so imbricated in the institutions of mainstream postwar society. Yet to a significant degree, the outcomes of games, the careers of individuals, and the profits of corporations are dependent on the barely manageable sensibilities of those segments of the audience who insist on cheering on and jeering at their own terms and to their own beat.

Acknowledgments

I appreciate especially the comments of Ian Condry on a draft of this chapter.

Notes

1. For the development of the school baseball tournaments and Kōshien Stadium in the context of the Osaka metropolitan economy, see Ariyama 1997, Kelly 2000, and Kiku 1993, 1994.

2. Until 1950 there was a single professional league; that year professional baseball was reorganized into two leagues, the Central and the Pacific Leagues, each now with six teams. The 135-game regular season is somewhat shorter than U.S. Major League Baseball's 162-game schedule, but is played over the same seasonal calendar, from the beginning of April through early October. In mid-October, the winners of the two leagues meet in the championship Japan Series.

3. This expanded seating in the outer infields along the right and left sides were soon tagged the "Alps" sections by a newspaper journalist. This was not just because of their steep pitch but because the home and visiting team supporters were seated there during school tournament games, and the sea of white blouses worn by the girl students reminded him of the snowy upper slopes of the Matterhorn.

4. The most comprehensive treatment of Japanese sports fans is the 1997 volume by members of the Kansai Sports Sociology Research Group (Sugimoto 1997).

5. Audio recordings of player hitting marches, the Tiger anthem "Rokkō oroshi," and other fan songs from Kōshien Stadium may be sampled at http://research.yale.edu/wwkelly/ ht/audio_sampler.htm. *Rokkō oroshi* refers to the famous winds that blow down off the slopes of the Rokkō Mountains that are the backdrop to the Osaka–Kobe corridor and which can be seen from the stadium. A library of hitting march lyrics can be found at http://research. yale.edu/wwkelly/ht/ht_lyrics_catalog.htm.

6. Ordinary membership requires recommendation by one officer of at least assistant club leader rank and two leaders; club regulations stipulate that all responsibility for the conduct of the new member shall be borne by his or her sponsors.

7. Indeed, one very common complaint of Hanshin fans has been the way that the Kobe-based Orix BlueWave seized the public relations initiative after the earthquake. The Orix club sponsored numerous benefits and dedicated its 1996 season to reviving the civic spirit of the city; its players still wore a "Gambarō, Kobe!" (Let's Fight On, Kobe!) patch on their uniform sleeve. However, the working-class and small-business neighborhoods of downtown Kobe that were the hardest hit by the quake and subsequent fires have long been strong supporters of the Hanshin Tigers, and the Hanshin railroad sustained the most serious damages among regional transport companies.

8. Despite the borrowed term, these "hooligans" bear little resemblance to their English football namesakes, about which there are now some fascinating anthropological accounts (especially Armstrong 1998; Giulianotti 1997, 1999:39–65; Hognestad 1997; Robson 2000) as well as sociological-historical studies (Dunning et al. 1988, 1991) and literary portraits (particularly Hornby 1992).

9. Indeed, there are intriguing parallels between the Private Alliance and certain supporter associations of Italian soccer clubs, as suggested by the ethnographic research of Bromberger 1993, Dal Lago and De Biasi 1999, Lanfranchi 1995, Portelli 1993, and others.

References Cited

Ariyama Teruo
1997   Kōshien to Nihonjin: media no tsukutta ibento (Kōshien and the Japanese: An event constructed by the media). Tokyo: Yoshikawa Kobundō.

Armstrong, Gary
1998   Football Hooligans: Knowing the Score. Oxford: Berg.

Bromberger, Christian
1993   "Allez l'O.M., forza Juve": The Passion of Football in Marseille and Turin. In The Passion and the Fashion: Football Fandom in the New Europe. Steve Redhead, ed. Pp. 103-152. Aldershot: Avebury.

Brownell, Susan
1995   Training the Body for China: Sports in the Moral Order of the People's Republic. Chicago: University of Chicago Press.

Dal Lago, A., and Rocco De Biasi
1999   Italian Football Fans: Culture and Organization. In Football, Violence and Social Identity. Richard Giulianotti, Nick Bonney, and Mike Hepworth, eds. Pp. 73-89. London: Routledge.

Dunning, Eric, Patrick Murphy, and John Williams
1988   The Roots of Football Hooliganism: An Historical and Sociological Study. London: Routledge and Kegan Paul.

Dunning, Eric, Patrick Murphy, and Ian Waddington
1991   Anthropological versus Sociological Approaches to the Study of Soccer Hooligans: Some Critical Notes. Sociological Review 39(3):459-478.

Giulianotti, Richard
1997   Enlightening the North: Aberdeen Fanzines and Local Football Identity. In Entering the Field: New Perspectives on World Football. Gary Armstrong and Richard Giulianotti, eds. Pp. 211-238. Oxford: Berg.
1999   Football: A Sociology of the Global Game. Oxford: Polity Press.

Grossberg, Lawrence
1992   Is There a Fan in the House? The Affective Sensibility of Fandom. In The Adoring Audience: Fan Culture and Popular Media. Lisa A. Lewis, ed. Pp. 50-65. London: Routledge.

Hanshin Taigāsu ni nekkyō suru yaji kenkyūkai, ed.
1994   Kōshien no yaji (Jeering at Kōshien Stadium). Tokyo: Dōbun shoin.

Hognestad, Hans Kristian
1997   The Jambo Experience: An Anthropological Study of Hearts Fans. In Entering the Field: New Perspectives on World Football. Gary Armstrong and Richard Giulianotti, eds. Pp. 193-210. Oxford: Berg.

Hornby, Nick
1992   Fever Pitch: A Fan's Life. New York: Penguin Books.

Horne, John
  1999   Soccer in Japan: Is Wa All You Need? *In* Football Culture: Local Contests,
           Global Visions. Gerry P. T. Finn and Richard Giulianotti, eds. Pp. 212–229.
           London: Frank Cass.

Kelly, William W.
  1990   Japanese No-Noh: The Crosstalk of Public Culture in a Rural Festivity. Public
           Culture 2(2):65–81.
  1994   Incendiary Actions: Fires and Firefighting in the Shogun's Capital and the Peo-
           ple's City. *In* Edo and Paris: Urban Life and the State in the Early Modern Era.
           James L. McClain, John M. Merriman, and Ugawa Kaoru, eds. Pp. 310–331.
           Ithaca: Cornell University Press.
  1998   Blood and Guts in Japanese Professional Baseball. *In* The Culture of Japan as
           Seen through Its Leisure. Sepp Linhart and Sabine Frühstück, eds. Pp. 95–112.
           Albany: State University of New York Press.
  2000   The Spirit and Spectacle of School Baseball: Mass Media, Statemaking, and
           'Edu-tainment' in Japan, 1905–1935. *In* Japanese Civilization in the Modern
           World XIV: Information and Communication. Umesao Tadao, William Kelly,
           and Kubo Masatoshi, eds. Pp. 105–116. Senri Ethnological Studies Number
           52. Osaka: National Museum of Ethnology.

Kiku Koichi
  1993   "Kindai puro supōtsu" no rekishi shakaigaku: Nihon puro yakyū no seiritsu o
           chūshin (The historical sociology of "modern professional sports": Focusing
           on the emergence of Japanese professional baseball). Tokyo: Fumaidō.
  1994   Butteki bunka sōchi to shite no Kōshien Sutajiamu (Kōshien Stadium as ma-
           terial culture). *In* Kōkō yakyū no shakaigaku: Koshien wo yomu (The sociology
           of high school baseball: Reading Kōshien Stadium). Esashi Shōgo and
           Komuku Hiroshi, eds. Pp. 83–111. Tokyo: Sekai shisō-sha.

Lanfranchi, Pierre
  1995   Cathedrals in Concrete: Football in Southern European Society. *In* Giving the
           Game Away: Football, Politics and Culture on Five Continents. Stephen Wagg,
           ed. Pp. 125–137. Leicester: Leicester University Press.

Nagai Yoshikazu
  1997   Tsukurareru supōtsu fan: Kigyō no keiei senryoku to puro yakyū (Making
           sports fans: Professional baseball and the economic strategies of business). *In*
           Supōtsu fuan no shakaigaku (The sociology of sports fans). Sugimoto Atsuo,
           ed. Pp. 51–70. Tokyo: Sekai shisō-sha.

Painter, Andrew A.
  1996   Japanese Daytime Television, Popular Culture, and Ideology. *In* Contemporary
           Japan and Popular Culture. John Whittier Treat, ed. Pp. 197–234. Honolulu:
           University of Hawai'i Press.

Portelli, Alessandro
  1993   The Rich and Poor in the Culture of Football. *In* The Passion and the Fashion:
           Football Fandom in the New Europe. Steve Redhead, ed. Pp. 77–88. Aldershot:
           Avebury.

Raz, Jacob
1983 Audience and Actors: A Study of Their Interactions in the Japanese Traditional Theater. Leiden: E. J. Brill.

Robson, Garry
2000 No One Likes Us, We Don't Care: The Myth and Reality of Millwall Fandom. Oxford: Berg.

Rokusai-sha henshūbu, ed.
1996 Nan to ka sen kai Taigaasu!! (What about them Tigers!!). Nishinomiya: Rokusai-sha.

Sugimoto Atsuo, ed.
1997 Supōtsu fan no shakaigaku (The sociology of sports fans). Tokyo: Sekai shisō-sha.

Takahashi Hidesato
1995 Hiroshima shimin kyūjō ni okeru puro yakyū no shūgōteki ōen ni kansuru kenkyū (Research on the collective cheering at professional baseball games in Hiroshima Civic Stadium). Supōtsu shakaigaku kenkyū 2:54–66.

Takahashi Yoshio
1994 Sakkaa no shakaigaku (The sociology of soccer). NHK Books No. 717. Tokyo: NHK.

Taniguchi Masako
1997 Supōtsu fan no ittaikan (Sports fans' feeling of oneness). In Supōtsu fan no shakaigaku (The sociology of sports fans). Sugimoto Atsuo, ed. Pp. 173–190. Tokyo: Sekai shisō-sha.

Thompson, Lee Austin
1986 Professional Wrestling in Japan—Media and Message. International Review for the Sociology of Sport 21(1):65–82.

Whannel, Gary
1992 Fields in Vision: Television Sport and Cultural Transformation. London: Routledge.

Whiting, Robert
1989 You've Gotta Have Wa: When Two Cultures Collide on the Baseball Diamond. New York: Macmillan.

5

It's a "Gottsan" World

The Role of the Patron in Sumo

R. KENJI TIERNEY

While I was watching sumo at a tournament near the end of my fieldwork, I received a gift from an important patron of the sumo stable that I was researching. He had been sitting alone at the base of the sumo ring and periodically returned to his four-person *masu-seki* (box) to relax, talk, eat, and drink. I had been spending time in his box with the other three guests—his wife, the stablemaster's daughter, and a former wrestler of the stable who was the brother of its top wrestler. During one of his trips back, the patron, exclaiming that he had grown tired sitting up front, asked if I would like his prized *suna-kaburi* (sand-covered seat). These seats are the best—and most dangerous—seats in the stadium. Composed of a half dozen rows of cushions immediately surrounding the sumo ring, they get their name—and their dusting of sand—from the wrestlers who inevitably come crashing down from the elevated ring. To prevent injuries, those seated on the cushions need to be able duck out of the way and are forbidden to eat or drink. Public decorum also encourages ticket holders to sit properly, rather than spreading out their legs and relaxing (see Figure 5.1).

While uncomfortable and lacking amenities, the seat holders are but a few feet from the sumo ring and often appear on television. Thus, the tickets are coveted for both the ticket-holder's ability to see and to be seen. To obtain one of these tickets is complicated. They are not for general sale and can only be acquired by those with connections to the sumo world.

In an age when sports and athletes constitute a multibillion dollar global industry, it is crucial to understand how these athletes and their activities "represent" a nation on an international stage.[1] It is equally important to examine the fans and supporters whose backing, financial and otherwise, sustains these sports and allows the athletes to flourish.

Figure 5.1

The raised sumo ring surrounded by the front-row "sand-covered" seats. Photograph by R. Kenji Tierney.

While most professional sports depend heavily on the willingness of fans to pay to attend, sumo offers a more complicated situation. While sumo is Japan's feted "national sport," neither its popularity nor its national status pays the bills or feeds the wrestlers. The bimonthly sumo tournaments are broadcast exclusively on public television (NHK), which prohibits direct corporate advertising. Given sumo's unusual ticketing structure the vast majority of Japanese viewers never pay to see live tournaments, and few people buy the sumo products that the Nihon ōzumo kyōkai (Japan Sumo Association) sells at the tournaments. Finally, and significantly, the formal financial sponsorship by major corporations is small when compared to other professional sports in Japan. Therefore, the world of the sumo fan is particularly interesting because of the separation between the relatively unconnected television viewer and the critically important patron.

As a physical contest, sumo is deceptively simple: Two men in a clay ring grapple to force the opponent to the ground or outside the ring.[2] However, it has been much transformed over its centuries-long history, and the political, economic, and cultural spaces occupied by today's professional sumo are not those of previous historical eras. It was during the late 19th century and the early 20th century that consciousness of a national "public" or "mass" emerged, and the abstract concept and specific forms of "sport" were introduced. It was at this time that sumo shifted from a performance–spectacle to both a sport and a tradition. The national discourse on sumo during these decades reinterpreted sumo to become more sportlike (Thompson 1989) while recreating it as *kokugi* (the Japanese national sport). The objective of this chapter is to understand sumo's current status as *the* national sport and to delineate the specific roles and functions of the patrons whose contributions of time, effort, and money allow generations of young men to step into the ring.

In sharp contrast to other professional sports, professional sumo exists in a world of its own. As a nonprofit organization, the Japan Sumo Association (hereafter referred to as the JSA) does not have strong formal ties to either amateur sumo leagues or large corporations, nor must it adhere to international standards as with baseball and soccer.[3] Traditionally, professional sumo has not recruited from the ranks of amateur sumo. Instead it has relied on its networks of scouts (often patrons and ex-wrestlers) to "tap the shoulders" of large boys (generally around 15 years of age) and entice them with dreams of becoming grand champions. Finally, few of the "average" fans ever attend a sumo tournament more than a handful of times in their lives.[4]

Despite this "otherworldliness" of sumo from the perspective of the Japanese themselves, these "topknots and loincloths" are often chosen to represent Japan to the outside world; the wrestlers are regularly dispatched as *hadaka taishi* (naked ambassadors).[5] In Japan, the emperor and the imperial family, as well as national and local politicians, regularly appear at the tournaments. Intense debates about sumo's status as national sport *(kokugi sumō)* occupy a perennial space in the public discourse, be it in the Diet or in the mass media, further signifying sumo's importance for Japan and the Japanese people.

In addition to its traditionalization as Japan's national sport, sumo differs from other sports in another crucial way: in its continued dependence on an extensive network of patrons. Their intimate and sustained involvement with over one thousand wrestlers and support people and more than fifty *heya* connects sumo to the larger Japanese society.[6]

Patrons have been indispensable in sumo since the Edo period, when feudal lords kept wrestlers, known as "*kakae rikishi*," to compete against each other and enhance the glory of the feudal domain. Wealthy merchants were also important as patrons of *kanjin-zumō* (charity sumo), which was a popular entertainment in the flourishing plebian culture of the shogun's capital of Edo. Famous are the stories of articles of clothing thrown on the ring that wrestlers later returned to their owners in exchange for money and gifts.

The end of the Tokugawa shogunate in 1868 left these wrestlers "unemployed" in the new Meiji nation. They sought out rich families, nobility, and others to replace their lost benefactors, while seeking political patrons to protect them from the backlash against sumo by the political modernizers. Still, sumo's popularity plummeted in the last two decades of the 19th century when Japan was actively Westernizing. Laws were passed banning wearing the topknot and appearing naked (in a loincloth) in public, and sumo was shunned as a symbol of Japan's backwardness.

Sumo's fortunes revived only when the Tokyo ōsumō kyōkai (Tokyo Sumo Association; forerunner of the JSA) successfully reconnected sumo to the emperor, stressing a long history of *tenran-zumō* (sumo performed in front of the emperor) and associating sumo with the emerging notion of *kokutai* (national polity). Sumo was first labeled Japan's kokugi in 1909 upon the completion of the Kokugikan, a sumo stadium hall designed by the most influential architect of the Meiji period, Tatsuno Kingo. This development, achieved through effectively using political patrons and supporters like the powerful politician Itagaki Taisuke (Itagaki 1906), transformed sumo into a grand spectacle. It was during this period of rising nationalism when the Tokyo Sumo Association, later the Dai-Nippon ōzumō kyōkai (Greater Japan Sumo Association), actively supported the war effort and aligned itself with Japanese imperialism.

While sumo was busy raising itself to the level of national discourse, sports, especially baseball, were becoming extremely popular in Japan. At the same time, international stages were created for sports competitions, especially the quadrennial Olympics that were begun in 1896. This international context was decisive in the shifting of sumo from a marginal form of entertainment into the national sport. Soon sumo's checkered past as a contest of strong men on street corners and riverbanks was transformed into an incarnation of *bushidō* (the way of the warrior) that became *sumō-dō* (the way of the wrestler): an activity for training body and spirit and a compulsory form of exercise in schools. Sumo publications soon shifted from reports on events in professional sumo to articles on the nascent amateur movement. Thus, sumo changed from a spectacle to watch into an activity to be performed. Numerous publications advocated sumo as a way to strengthen the nation, both physically and spiritually. Thus began the discourse stating that sumo exists for the good of the kokumin (national subjects). Since this transformation, popular support by fans has been welcomed and sought after, but professional sumo's financial survival continued to be in the hands of patrons.

In the postwar period, the JSA has gradually increased its schedule to hold six 15-day national tournaments a year. Now, millions of spectators in Japan and throughout the world follow the fortunes of champions, aging veterans, rising stars, and determined journeymen via television and radio broadcasts along with the gaudy sports papers and regular newspapers. Beyond the daily coverage, fans can avidly follow numerous sumo magazines or the JSA website or numerous other websites devoted to individual wrestlers, stables, or sumo in general.

A television viewer of the tournaments will see a packed arena—several front rows of sand-covered seats and then several tiers of seating where slightly raised rectangular frames create the box seats in which groups of four are packed into a space overloaded with gift bags, boxed lunches, and beer and sake bottles. Behind them are the stands, extending up to the rafters and equally crowded (see Figure 5.2). However, sumo's great paradox is that while it has a multitude of fans, access to the sumo tournaments themselves is quite circumscribed. Because the six tournaments are held in only four cities (three in Tokyo, and one each in Osaka, Nagoya, and Fukuoka), and all of the heya are based near Tokyo, tournament attendance is convenient only for those in these metropolitan areas. Moreover, only a few thousand tickets are distributed through public sale, and all the best seats and much of the remainder are distributed through the heya and through the official guide services, the Ryōgoku Service Companies.[7]

This distribution system provides an important source of income for the heya while favoring their patrons access to the tournaments. The guide service companies are better known by the age-old term chaya (teahouses). Even today the chaya stalls line the entrance hall, employing dekata (guides) in period outfits to lead their customers to their seats. Their services are not cheap, and the teahouses add commissions and gratuities to the already high face value of tickets; four tickets can easily require 100,000 yen or more (about $950 at present).

Up to 90 percent of the tickets at five of the six tournaments are sold through the teahouses, and they are thus integral to both the presentation of sumo and the finances of the JSA. Given the exorbitant ticket cost and the daytime scheduling, only the very rich or well connected, such as high corporate executives, can afford to attend.[8] Not surprisingly, many of them do not pay for the experience themselves because many corporations maintain their own boxes at the Kokugikan for entertaining clients.

Figure 5.2

A view of the Kokugikan Hall in Tokyo during a sumo tournament. Photograph by R. Kenji Tierney

Thus, although nominally separate, the teahouses are closely connected to both the heya and the JSA. Many of the owners are relatives or direct descendents of current or former *oyakata* (stable master) and these close ties preclude the reforms that many critics have proposed. Although the chaya justified their place as providing the JSA with a stable source of customers, this also has given them a near monopoly on tournament tickets.

Patrons

The general public sees patrons as occupying spaces at the edges of the sumo world. Their names are on the bottoms of the showy aprons worn by the top wrestlers; their faces surround the victorious champion posing at his heya; and their behind-the-scenes influence is imagined, questioned, and criticized in the tabloids. The concept of the "patron" is a broad and unstable category, and it overlaps with that of a "fan." I distinguish the former, though, by his reciprocal relationship—personal, social, financial—to the sumo world. Patrons can be supporters of a heya, a single wrestler, an oyakata, and even a *gyōji* (referee) or *yobidashi* (name announcer). Most commonly, though, patrons support a heya as a unit. In this sense, patrons range from the local grocer who occasionally donates some vegetables to help out a heya to the wealthy businessman who spends millions of yen every year and whose approval and influence is essential for all the major decisions at the heya.

The patron, of course, is not unique to sumo.[9] Other terms, such as *hiiki* (fan) and *kankeisha* (associate), are also commonly used. However, probably due to their long-standing importance, sumo patrons are known by a special term, *tanimachi*. One explanation claims this is taken from the name of the Tanimachi district in Osaka, which was the home of a well-known sumo aficionado of the early 20th century, a dentist who gave free dental services to wrestlers. Another explanation connects the term to *tanemochi* (having seed).

The main organizations for patronage are the *kōenkai* (supporter groups) typically based around a heya, wrestler(s), or an area (e.g., Waka-Taka Kōenkai, Kansai Kōenkai, and Jimoto Kōenkai). Every heya has supporter groups in the four tournament cities, and there are others located either in the hometowns of current or former wrestlers or simply where fans of a wrestler live. Because all heya are headquartered in or near Tokyo, the Tokyo supporter group is usually the largest and most influential. During the other three tournaments, when the heya all relocate to Osaka (March), Nagoya (July), and Fukuoka (November), the local kōenkai becomes central for what is usually a six-week stay (the heya move about a month before the tournament to acclimate and train for the two-week tournament). The heya or individual wrestlers may make special trips to supporter groups in other cities for parties or rituals (e.g., end-of-the-year parties, weddings, funerals), and their members come to Tokyo to visit the heya, watch practice, and be treated to a meal.

It is important to note that while the majority of kōenkai members are keen fans of sumo, not all are. Because the kōenkaichō (kōenkai president) gains personal prestige and influence in the heya in proportion to the size of his group and its contributions, he often uses his position to induce friends, associates, employees, and others to join. Since annual dues are quite low (often between 5,000 to 10,000 yen [$50–$100] for basic membership), one of my informants said that it was easier to pay than to say no.

Relationships between patrons and the heya are often complex and personal, since many of the patrons have been connected to a heya for decades and even for generations.[10] As such, the structural ties between patron and heya are often longer than most of the individuals involved. The role of the patron may be handed down from parent to child. The wrestlers themselves are the focus of heya patronage, but their time there is often the shortest. Most wrestlers enter sumo in their mid-teens and stay anywhere from a few weeks to a few decades. Less than one percent of these young men are successful enough to stay on as oyakata, who alone are assured of spending the rest of their lives in sumo.[11]

As an example of the iemoto (stem family system) that structures many craft and artistic schools (Hsu 1975; Noguchi 1990), the heya and its title are passed down from the oyakata to a successful deshi (apprentice). While there are famous examples of sons succeeding their fathers as oyakata, the most common mode of succession is through the marriage of the most successful wrestler to the daughter of the oyakata.[12] According to my informants, an oyakata makes sure to establish a good relationship between his best wrestlers and his best patrons, thus passing the patron down from master to apprentice. This can be the greatest gift to the apprentice.

"It's a Gottsan World"

The term gottsan is a crucial window into understanding the patron–wrestler relationship. The word is unique to sumo and is written in nonstandard Japanese, likely deriving from an Osaka dialect term for gochisōsama (a formal expression of gratitude). In a language with extensive status markers for politeness, gottsan (desu) can be used for arigatō gozaimasu (thank you), onegai itashimasu (please favor me), itadakimasu (to humbly receive), gochisōsama (thank you for the good food), and other polite phrases. Thus it is a broad cover for expressing thanks when receiving money, when sitting down to eat, after eating, when asking to have one's hair made up, when receiving a gift, when being complimented, and a host of other situations. For example, omiyage, gottsan desu (thank you for the present) is the proper way of gratefully receiving a gift.

Many patrons remarked to me that sumo is a "gottsan world" where the wrestlers constantly receive—from the oyakata, the okamisan, the patrons, and others—but are rarely expected to reciprocate in kind. As many commentators on sumo have remarked, the oyakata and the okamisan take the place of the wrestler's parents, and a similar relationship exists between the patrons and the wrestler. The relationship is often characterized as the "parents" doing all of the giving and the wrestlers simply receiving. More precisely, however, the wrestlers clearly do give something valuable in return: the expressions of deference and demonstrations of effort and success in the ring that bring satisfaction and prestige to the heya and the patrons. Wrestlers are socialized to be respectful to both the oyakata and the patrons and to seek their permission in any major decision, especially marriage. Thus despite popular representations, the gottsan world is a world of exchanges—unbalanced, delayed perhaps, but give-and-take nonetheless among patrons, stable masters, and wrestlers.

The "parental" relationship of the patrons is expressed in many ways. Once I was at the public bath that was made available especially for the wrestlers. The owner and his wife, who were patrons of the heya, started to chide the top wrestler, saying that he was no good and that he did not put in enough effort. They asked my opinion about what he should do and I answered that I thought him a very fine wrestler. They laughed at me and said that if I did not chide him, he would never advance up the ranks. Patrons often see themselves as parents trying to nurse potential out of the wrestlers. Many patrons worry that their relationship to a wrestler will ultimately prove detrimental to the wrestler. One patron remarked to me that the disposition learned in sumo of always receiving could prove detrimental when they leave the sumo world. He hoped that the lesson wrestlers learn would be the rewards of hard work.

More concretely, how does this gottsan world operate? Following a rich tradition in anthropology (from Marcel Mauss to Claude Lévi-Strauss and to more contemporary contributions) that studies social relationships through the flow of goods, signs, and people, I divide gifts in sumo into four major categories: commemoration, maintenance, subsistence, and emblem. The differences in the nature of these goods reveal much about the imbalanced exchanges and relationships between the wrestler, the stable master, and the patron.

Gifts of the first two types—commemorative and maintenance—flow to patrons from either the heya or an individual wrestler. Commemorative gifts include *tegata* (handprints), *yukata* (summer cotton kimono), and wrestlers' autographs and photos.[13] Such gifts are expressions of oneself, symbolically inalienable from the wrestler in the Maussian sense (1954; see also Weiner 1992), and they are not meant to have exchange or use value. Similarly, the JSA produces special envelopes called *oiribukuro* that are given to people associated with sumo on the days that the tournament sells out. Five- or 50-yen coins are put in the envelopes; the five-yen coin *(go-en)* puns its homonym which means an auspicious and predestined relationship.

These envelopes are supposed to bring good luck to the recipient. Oyakata will often have the envelopes specially printed with a patron's name. These are often displayed at the patron's business, advertising its connection to sumo. The oiribukuro are signs that convey the close relationship of the patron to the wrestler, the heya, or both.

Important also are nonmaterial "gifts" such as the time and presence requested of the wrestlers by heya patrons for attending gatherings with or hosted by the patron, thus letting the patron display his relationship with the wrestler. Similarly, patrons bring friends and associates to the heya either to watch morning practice or to attend other heya functions such as the end of the tournament parties. One patron remarked to me that she was not really interested in sumo, but she felt that the opportunity to take foreign friends to watch sumo practice served as an effective way to entertain them.

The maintenance gift is that which serves to remind the patron of his relationship to the stable and also obliges the patron with a return gift. Such gifts function to maintain regular contact with the patron. The sumo world constantly produces items that serve in this capacity, including *banzuke* (tournament ranking sheets), sumo calendars, and newsletters. Importantly, these are not commodities that are sold or purchased, and this endows them as special gifts that embody the relationship between the giver and the receiver. For example, two weeks before each tournament, a new banzuke is released with the current rankings of all the current wrestlers. On the day of its announcement, each heya buys from the JSA thousands of copies onto which the name of the heya or that of the oyakata is stamped and then sent to all of their patrons. Similarly, at the end of the year, many heya and the JSA itself produce calendars to distribute to patrons. The heya allows its associated wrestlers, referees, and name announcers to send calendars to their own family, friends, and personal patrons. While the banzuke and calendars are relatively inexpensive items, they are valued highly because they represent a patron's relationship to a heya or its personnel. Often a heya will use the banzuke announcements to attempt to establish new relationships, and thus hopefully enlist new patrons. The handing over of a business card to an oyakata often results in a banzuke arriving in the mail when the next tournament rolls around. These gifts are institutionalized in the sumo world rather than initiated by an individual wrestler or heya. It is through this regular cycle of gifts that the heya and the wrestlers attempt to invoke and maintain their relationships with the patrons.

Included in the category of maintenance gifts from the heya or the wrestlers are invitations to the regular functions of the heya. Besides the end-of-the-tournament parties, the patrons are also often invited to watch practice at the heya and to attend (and participate in) retirement ceremonies,[14] promotion ceremonies, weddings, pretournament parties, and a variety of other rituals and events. These ceremonies are enormously important in the sumo world where participation is exclusive. The scale of these events depends a great deal on both the status of the wrestler and his heya. They range from small, intimate events held at the heya or community center to posh parties held at luxury hotels and broadcast live throughout the country.

I was fortunate enough to be able to participate in the haircutting retirement ceremony of a lower ranked wrestler at a local community center and later to attend the famous Hawaiian wrestler Konishiki's retirement ceremony in the Kokugikan, filled with over 11 thousand people, which was followed by a nationally televised postceremony party. The ceremonies for the lower-ranking wrestlers held at the heya or a local community center are much more intimate and sometimes do away with many of the rules (such as the taboo on women's participation) that characterize the elaborate pageantry of the famous wrestlers' ceremonies.

The most common among the four types of gifts from patrons are subsistence gifts items. The most common gift is money,[15] but items useful for the daily operations of the heya such as rice, vegetables, shampoo, alcohol, and fish are also given. Some heya receive such a sufficient supply that they do not need to purchase much on their own. Although these are subsistence items as they are necessary for daily life, they can be luxury goods, as when patrons send expensive fish and fruits and other specialty foods. Similarly, patrons will often give expensive, brand-name items of clothing, shoes, and bags to the wrestlers. On occasions such as the end of a tournament, promotions, weddings, or retirements, the patron often gives a sizable amount of money to the heya or the wrestler, again depending on rank. Thus, patrons tend to give alienable gifts, that is, gifts that do not symbolize himself or herself. Although some of these items may be from the patrons' own businesses, the items are essentially, although not altogether, commodities.[16]

The second type of gift from the patron signifies, often in a most conspicuous and public way, the patron's relationship with the wrestler. I call them "emblem gifts." The most obvious is the *keshō mawashi*, the decorative apron that top wrestlers wear during their ring-entering ceremony. Starting at around 1,000,000 yen ($10,000) with some costing ten times or more, these aprons are of two main types: those with embroidery that symbolize the wrestler and those with designs that signify the patron or supporting organization. If a keshō mawashi is given by a support group, it is often financed by annual membership dues. In that case, the design is often agreed on by the support group and the wrestler. If the donor is the wrestler's hometown support group, then the picture is often of a famous landmark or an activity from that area, such as a mountain, bullfighting, or even the local space center. If a support group is giving a second apron to a wrestler, it will usually allow him to choose a design that he likes. On the other hand, keshō mawashi of individual donors often feature the logo of the company with which the patron is associated. For example, the recently-retired grand champion Akebono had a Coca-Cola ceremonial apron, while his nemesis Takatōriki, by chance or design, had one featuring the Pepsi logo. Others include the Canadian national flag and logos of golf resorts and universities. Corporate logos usually indicate that someone, such as the company president, is personally interested in sumo, rather than signify an official advertising campaign. Many of the patrons actually ask for the keshō mawashi back when the wrestler retires so that they can display it at their companies, community centers, or the like. Functioning similarly (but costing far less) are the *nobori* (banners)[17] that announce either the name of the heya or the wrestler. Displayed outside of the heya or tournament hall, these nobori are provided by patrons whose names are prominently dyed into them.

It is well recognized in anthropology that gift exchange is behavior that encodes and enacts social relationships. It is also recognized that gift exchange is everywhere governed by principles of hierarchy between the donor and the receiver. Pierre Bourdieu (1977:4–6) adopted from Jacques Lacan the term *méconnaissance* (the temporal structure of gift exchange whereby the countergift must be deferred as well as be different in kind), and he identified this as the mechanism whereby the reversibility of an exchange is misrecognized as irreversible. This is quite evident in the hierarchical gottsan relationship, which is structured so that the heya or the wrestler is categorically denied any chance of squaring the debt (or "clearing the abacus" as the Japanese say) and restoring equality to the relationship.

The power inequality between the patron and the heya or the wrestler is objectified in the types of gifts given by the patrons. Above all, subsistence gifts are seldom acceptable as gift items in ordinary circumstances (not only in Japan but elsewhere). Subsistence items, when given as gifts, indicate (1) an intimate relationship between the donor and the receiver; (2) the presence of an extreme difference in status between the two, as in the case of the sumo world; or (3) simple lack of common sense on the part of the giver. The emblem gifts too are expressive of an unequal relationship. This is less because of the objects themselves and more because these items, crucial to the heya and the wrestlers, may not be acquired otherwise; without the patron, for instance, there would be no keshō mawashi, the essential item for the ring-entering ceremony.

The keshō mawashi and nobori are symbolic essentials, but they are only two of the most prominent items received, as a variety of other items such as the *mon-tsuki hakama* (family crested formal clothing), *irotsuki mawashi* (tournament silk loincloth), and *akeni* (traditional luggage) also come from patrons. It is unheard of for a wrestler or a heya to buy these items. Thus, in this way, sumo is structured to provide a place for patrons and for the wrestlers and the heya to be indebted to them.

Patrons also function importantly in using their financial power and connections to help the heya, the wrestler, or the JSA. For example, a common duty of the patron is to secure the lodgings for the heya at the regional tournaments.[18] Oyakata try to have a range of patrons who can provide different services (e.g., railroad employees for discount tickets, doctors, farmers, realtors, construction company presidents). Thus, while the patrons expect and demand that they be consulted on important matters concerning the heya, often it is impossible to do otherwise because they are the ones who will be asked to carry them out.

These transactions create lasting yet shifting power relations. The lower wrestlers are socialized from the time they enter to be polite and obedient to their seniors (which is everyone else at that stage). To start their education, they are given responsibilities such as sending banzuke and calendars to personal and heya patrons. At times, the patrons will call up and scold the wrestlers if they are late in sending them. They become angered in part because patrons often redistribute them to their customers and friends. A wrestler's tardiness thus puts them behind in their own gift-giving cycles. As the wrestlers advance up the ranks, the power relations naturally shift as more patrons are vying for the top wrestlers' attention. Even so, as the presents from patrons become more valuable and more frequent, the top wrestlers must increasingly seek and receive permission for major personal decisions. As personal decisions of the top wrestlers affect the whole future of the heya, personal choices, especially marriage, are never really "personal."

Marriage is one of the most important decisions in a wrestler's career, and few would-be oyakata have the luxury of marrying whomever they please. To remain in sumo after retiring, the wrestler needs an elder's license, which he receives, typically by marrying the daughter of an oyakata, or must purchase at an exorbitant price (thus having the previous owner retire from sumo). Marrying the daughter of one's oyakata means that the heya–patron structure remains relatively intact. Purchasing a different license requires borrowing large sums of money from a patron or patrons, and thus being indebted to him or them. Thus the patron gains a voice in whom the wrestler marries because that woman will become the okamisan, the person principally in charge of interacting with the patrons. To the patrons, the wife of the oyakata holds the key to the balance of their investment in the wrestler and the heya. It is she who is typically in charge of every aspect of the seamless flow of tangible and intangible gift exchange. In fact in the apparently all-male world of sumo, the role of the oyakata's wife is crucial and her role cannot be underestimated. All patrons are keenly aware of this, and there are thus many well-known cases of patrons arranging marriages. Marriage without the permission of the patron or kōenkaichō is a stark violation of the unwritten code in the sumo world.

Sumo as a World of Exchanges

It is significant that sumo was recategorized as a sport at the historical moment that introduced not only an abstract concept of sports but also the notions of taishū (the masses) and kokumin. This reclassification led to an idealization of kokugi sumō as "a sport for the citizens," with all the trappings of the national sport: the title kokugi, nonprofit status for the JSA, and performances in front of the emperor. Early 20th-century nationalism was significant in elevating sumo's cultural and political position. Subsequent radio broadcasting (from

1928) and television broadcasting (from 1953) of sumo made it even more sportlike, with *shikiri-sen* (starting lines), time limits, championship systems, the elimination of draws, and so forth. Sumo gained enormous popularity from this increased exposure, but it has had little effect on its structure of patronage. Kōenkai and patrons still support sumo in ways that have changed little from the late 19th century.

As its popularity waxes and wanes and scandals come and go, sumo attempts to maintain its prestige as the country's national sport. While contemporary public discussion about sport insists the "democratic principle" that a national sport should be for the "average" fan and that it must be equally accessible to all, sumo remains tied to the patrons because their support is still essential to the structure and business of the sport. It is tempting to conclude that sumo has managed to become an exemplar of mass culture without the masses, but perhaps what we must reassess are the claims that any modern sport can exist for and by the public. Professional baseball, professional soccer, and sumo are all broadcast nationally; do the regionally based and corporate-owned baseball and soccer leagues have greater claim on the title of "popular" over the patron-based sumo? Is the average baseball or soccer fan really brought closer to the athletes by being able to attend the events instead of watching them on television? How precisely can professional sports and athletes represent a nation and its people? While this chapter cannot resolve these questions, it does suggest the need to reexamine the assumptions surrounding popular sports.

Sumo's patron–client system is not simply a premodern residue of an otherwise fully modernized sport. This system and what I call its "gottsan principle" are central to the continued existence of sumo and to any understanding of its place in contemporary Japan. My argument here has focused on two points: First, the patron–wrestler and patron–heya relationships can be understood in the terms of an anthropological theory of gifts and commodities, and, second, the patron system and the sumo world, in general, should be understood from the perspective of historical periodicity. To recapitulate these points, wrestlers and heya offer their performances, selves, and symbols of the self. In turn, patrons offer money and commodities—the modalities of transaction in modern capitalistic societies. Overtly, their relationship is characterized by power inequality, governed by the economic power of the patrons—again, the dominant force of modern societies. In other words, the wrestlers live in the Maussian world of "gift as self," while the modus operandi of the patron is the commodity transaction of the alienable commodities of the market economy.

To continue, for a moment, to examine the gottsan world as a system, rather than as practice, the transactions between the two do not "fit" in the classical modes. Most important, the gottsan transactions are of commodities between interdependent actors in intimate social relationships. This defies the classical distinction of gift exchange as between interdependent actors and commodity exchange as between independent actors with no social relationship. In sumo, though, the flow of commodities and money from the patron is predicated on a long-term relationship between the two and also on the premise of continuing relationship—the modus operandi considered to characterize gift exchange. The commodities given by the patron to the wrestler or to the heya, therefore, are not commodities in the classical sense.

One might speculate that the commodities given by the patrons are investments for the return gifts from the wrestlers in the form of symbolic capital—prestige and fame (Bourdieu 1977:180). Perhaps, but if so, these investments by patrons are enormously risky and unpredictable ventures. There are legendary cases of wealthy individuals who lost their fortunes by becoming patrons. Today, with sumo's prestige increasingly circumscribed, even the prestige a patron may accrue in nurturing a wrestler who fortunately rises to the top is not easily convertible into material gains. In fact, it is often said that to be a patron of sumo is *saigo no zeitaku* (the last luxury), as so many have gone broke trying to please their favorites. From the point of economic rationality, it is a bad investment, far from an act based on negative reciprocity. The patron's action thus defies all other principles of the market economy, except that it is commodities and money—alienable objects—that are transacted. We have already seen many excellent publications that point out that the dichotomy between commodity–money and gift is simplistic. Furthermore, it is the actors who assign meaning to objects and actions, sometimes giving the meaning of gifts to money. This leads to an even more complex issue of transactions and the resultant relationships between the patrons and the wrestler and the patrons and the heya in practice. Did a patron buy out Akebono who wears his keshō mawashi? But, then, Akebono "revolted" by choosing his own mate, incurring anger by the patron and the sumo establishment in general. A number of past revolts by top wrestlers offer evidence of individuals negotiating within this system. Such "scandals" result from breaches of taboos in the patron–wrestler relationship and reflect the constant maneuverings by the wrestlers, who are seldom passive puppets reproducing the system.

The patrons' relationships and their motivations are also varied and complex. Some patrons are far more personally involved than others in the affairs of the wrestlers and the heya. Since this is not a wise investment strategy, there are other motivations than simply economic gains or even the feel of power over the wrestlers. There always is room for méconnaissance in gift exchange, as suggested by Bourdieu (1977:4–6), by which the wrestlers are "tricked" to "misrecognize" the reversibility of the transaction as irreversible. Perhaps such misrecognition occurs. However, agents in economic transactions are humans with feelings, not economic robots in human disguise.

Notes

1. Because modern sports originated outside of Japan, the discourse on sports in Japan has always been framed in an international context. Examples of this are the prewar attempts to "domesticate" baseball through changing the game's vocabulary and the Meiji introduction of Western sports as a way to introduce "civilization" in Japan (see Roden 1980). This has continued through the second half of the 20th century. Well-known examples include the first postwar foreign baseball stars recruited to play for Japanese professional baseball teams (see Kelly 1998). Recently, the trend toward "internationalization" of Japanese sports and Japanese athletes has increased. Similarly in sumo, foreign-born participants have made noticeable achievements such as occupying the top ranks and becoming the head of a heya (see Tierney 2002).

2. Sumo consists of two competitors in a circular ring 4.55 meters in diameter. The first person to touch the ground with any part of the body besides the bottoms of the feet or to touch the ground outside of the ring is declared the loser.

3. The JSA was granted nonprofit status in 1925 and retains the status today. This has contributed to sumo's strong ties to the government (officially under the Ministry of Education) and has limited sumo's ability to establish formal ties to corporations.

4. In a recent survey, only one and one-half percent had seen sumo live in the previous year. This compares to 15.3 percent who had seen professional baseball (Mainichi Daily News 2002).

5. In the postwar period, the first of these trips abroad was the 1964 trip to Hawaii, quickly followed by the next year's trip to Moscow, and then to China in 1973. Since the initial trips, sumo has gone to various countries including the USA, Brazil, Mexico, Hong Kong, France, Germany, among others.

6. A heya is commonly translated as stable and is both the place where wrestlers live and practice and the local unit itself. An oyakata (stable master) and okamisan (stable master's wife) run the heya; many heya have other oyakata who serve in an advisory capacity. There is no limit to the number of wrestlers who can belong to a heya. Some heya have as few as two or three wrestlers, while others have as many as fifty. The gyōji (referees), yobidashi (name announcers), and tokoyama (hairdressers) can also belong to heya, but not every stable is required to have them. The total number of wrestlers continually fluctuates, but in July 1998 there were 840 wrestlers officially registered.

7. There are several ways to obtain sumo tickets. About a month before each tournament, a percentage of the tickets go on sale to the general public; recently, they were made available through a nationwide chain of convenience stores, in addition to those sold through regular ticket chains like Pia and Ticket Saison.

8. A full set of matches runs from 8 a.m. to 6 p.m. each day. Because the top wrestlers appear at the end of the day, most spectators arrive between 3 p.m. and 4 p.m.

9. The kōensha (supporter) or the kōenkai (support group) is a common presence in the political (see Bestor 1989), art (Havens 1982), and entertainment worlds (Brau, chapter 6, this volume).

10. While many smaller heya come and go depending on the success of the oyakata, there are numerous heya that have long histories, some dating back to the Edo period. The family of one patron I met has supported the same heya for four generations and over 100 years, each generation passing the role down from father to son. Because the length of time spent in a support group is extremely important in establishing influence within a stable, sometimes new rich patrons start their own support group to try to gain quick and immediate access to the heya, and hence, its wrestler(s).

11. To remain in sumo, a retired wrestler must own one of the 100 or so *toshiyori-kabu* (elders' stocks). This gives him the right to open up his own heya or to attach himself to an existing heya. Because these stocks are limited and many wrestlers want to stay in the sumo world, the prices have gone up tremendously. As the Japan Sumo Association is a nonprofit organization, it is illegal to sell the shares openly. It is rare for a wrestler to have saved up this amount of money by the time he retires; it is often one of the patrons who lends the money to him.

12. The *mukoyōshi* system (adopting a husband into the wife's family) is an effective way to accommodate individual ability into a system based on acquired status and has been commonly practiced outside the sumo world, especially in the corporate world and in politics.

13. The tegata is the autograph of the wrestler signed over a print of a wrestler's hand on the *shikishi* (standard autograph board) made of rice paper. Only wrestlers in the top two ranks (*jūryō* and above) are allowed to produce these tegata. Although the wrestler will produce hundreds at one time, when presenting the tegata, many times the wrestler will personalize it by including the date and the recipient's name.

Yukata are designed with the heya's name or crest and given to the more important patrons. The top wrestlers distribute their yukata with their personal name on it. Interestingly, it is the patrons who finance the production of these yukata that they, in turn, receive. The yukata are symbolic of the heya or the wrestler and thus are inalienable goods.

In the course of my fieldwork, I often combined my desire to take ethnographic photos with the needs of the heya to give commemorative photos of the different functions held by the heya. This role as the "heya's photographer" helped me become useful to the heya and also document what constitutes important events at the heya. In this way, I was able to improve my relationship with the heya and have access to the patrons.

14. It is during the public retirement ceremony when the relationship between the wrestler or the heya and the patron is publicly acknowledged. For the top wrestlers, ceremonies are held in the Kokugikan. There is a day of entertainment followed by a haircutting ceremony. During this ceremony, all of the important men in the wrestler's life go up on the *dohyō* where the wrestler is seated and cut a few strands of his hair (women are not allowed on the dohyō). All of the patrons of the wrestler and his heya participate in this ritual. The participation fee can be 100,000 yen ($1,000) or more for each person.

15. The amounts given to the wrestler and the stable are quite substantial. It has been reported that a popular top wrestler, who is now a stable master, stated, "During the time when I was an active wrestler, I never touched my salary" (Maishi 2000:44–45). Apparently, the *gorei* (tips or favors) that he received from patrons were enough to support him.

Even for lower-ranked wrestlers, the money received from the patrons can constitute much of their income.

16. This point is brought out again in the special language of sumo in which the term for money is *okome* (rice) because food must be bought if not received.

17. The nobori is a large banner hoisted on a long bamboo pole that has both the name of the wrestler written in large characters and the name of the patron or support group written at the bottom in smaller characters.

18. One young patron I met said that he wanted to use his job connections to bring success to the heya he was supporting. He wants to help raise the next grand champion and he is looking 20 years into the future when he is more powerful in his company. It is important to note that kōensha at a certain point think of the wrestler almost as a family.

References Cited

Bestor, Theodore
    1989   Neighborhood Tokyo. Stanford: Stanford University Press.

Bourdieu, Pierre
    1977   Outline of a Theory of Practice. Richard Nice, trans. Cambridge: Cambridge University Press.

Havens, Thomas R. H.
    1982   Artist and Patron in Postwar Japan. Princeton: Princeton University Press.

Hsu, Francis L. K.
    1975   Iemoto: The Heart of Japan. Cambridge: Schenkman.

Itagaki Taisuke
    1906   Sumō no shōrai (The future of sumo). Taiyō, May 1:182–184.

Kelly, William W.
    1998   Blood and Guts in Japanese Professional Baseball. In The Culture of Japan as Seen through Its Leisure. Sepp Linhart and Sabine Frühstück, eds. Pp. 95–112. Albany: State University of New York Press.

Mainichi Daily News
    2002   Ichiro Voted Fan Favorite. November 14.

Maishi Hiroyuki
    2000   "Utchari" wa naze kieta noka? (Why has the sumo technique "utchari" disappeared?). Tokyo: Nihon Keizai Shimbun.

Mauss, Marcel
    1954   The Gift: Forms and Functions of Exchange in Archaic Societies. Glencoe, IL: Free Press.

Noguchi, Paul H.
    1990   Delayed Departures, Overdue Arrivals: Industrial Familialism and the Japanese National Railways. Honolulu: University of Hawai'i Press.

Roden, Donald
1980   Baseball and the Quest for National Dignity in Meiji Japan. American Historical Review 15:511–534.

Thompson, Lee Austin
1989   The Modernization of Sumo as a Sport: A Study in the Sociology of Sport. Ph.D. dissertation, Department of Sociology, Osaka National University.

Tierney, R. Kenji
2002   Wrestling with Tradition: Sumo, National Identity and Trans/National Popular Culture. Ph.D. dissertation, Department of Anthropology, University of California at Berkeley.

Weiner, Annette
1992   Inalienable Possessions: The Paradox of Keeping-While-Giving. Berkeley: University of California Press.

6

Rakugo Fans at Play

Promoting the Art, Creating Community, Inventing Selves

LORIE BRAU

On a rare sunny Sunday during the rainy season I joined about a dozen members of the Tokyo *rakugo* circle "Sharaku" for their monthly meeting (see Figure 6.1). The main purpose of these gatherings is to exchange copies of tapes and information on rakugo, which means traditional comic storytelling. Sharaku met that day, as usual, in a drab conference room at Asahi Broadcasting Studios, where one member formerly worked. When this room is not available, the group has been known to convene on the second floor of a Roppongi McDonald's, a scene as remote as can be imagined from the old-fashioned setting of rakugo tales. After exchanging a few homemade rakugo recordings, the middle-aged men sat around the table drinking canned coffee and hashed over some unfamiliar software.[1] Later, they discussed the newly released CD collection of the late storytelling master Katsura Bunraku VIII.

A popular diversion for urban Japanese in the 19th century, rakugo lost much of its audience in the 20th century to mediated entertainments, but it thrives today on a smaller scale. Rakugo storytellers, called *hanashika*, appear in Tokyo and Osaka at theaters called *yose* and at rented halls and restaurants.[2] Seated on a cushion on a stage or raised platform, these kimono-clad raconteurs usually draw their material from a canon of tales that evoke a bygone world populated by stock characters. Rakugo is known for its comedy. Performers aim to make their audiences laugh through wordplay, one-liners, and gesture. The storyteller's art consists as well in his ability to depict a scene so that it materializes in the mind's eye. He acts out stories in the voices of the characters, and uses a hand towel and a fan to aid in representing their actions. While audiences may no longer be able to identify with

Figure 6.1
A meeting of the rakugo circle "Sharaku." Photograph by Lorie Brau.

the context of many of these stories, hearing them over and over makes them familiar. Fans savor the differences in how individual hanashika bring the traditional
tales to life. They also take pleasure in the storytellers themselves, both in their
own personas as performers and in their assumed roles, which include carpenters,
bossy wives, neighborhood know-it-alls, samurai, geisha, and fools.

Sharaku colleagues and even a few rakugo storytellers themselves jokingly describe one another as "rakugo *otaku*." An honorific word for *house*, or *you*, otaku
began to supplement *mania* to mean "hard-core aficionados" in the early 1980s
(Schodt 1996:43–44; Condry, chapter 2, this volume; Thorn, chapter 8, this volume). The term evokes an image of nerdy youths comparing comic book collections or reeling off trivia about a favorite singing star. Given the traditional image
of rakugo, the term *rakugo otaku* sounds like an oxymoron. Rakugo fans seem to
enjoy the irony.

While the rakugo world boasts its otaku, it also embraces *hiiki*, a term that means
"patron" or "favor." Before Japanese adopted the English word *fan* to describe devotees of sports, music, or theater they relied on this word to convey the idea of support. The commonly used ideograms for hiiki include four shells, symbolizing
money; fundamentally, hiiki provided financial support (Koyama 1985:82).

Not all contemporary rakugo fans fall into the two categories of otaku and
hiiki. They are as varied as teenage boys who commit to memory published vol-

umes of rakugo jokes, elderly women in kimonos who faithfully follow their favorite stars from venue to venue, and teeny-boppers who loiter at television studios to hand over gifts to young hanashika emerging from a taping. What is it that distinguishes these rakugo fans from fans of movie stars or rock musicians? Fans of all performance genres may be equally captivated by a performer's charisma. But perhaps this comedic narrative art that is neither elite nor truly popular today offers something else to its fans. It might even be rakugo's marginality that draws fans in that it endows them with a distinctive identity.

Like fans of other genres of performance, rakugo fans acquire cultural capital in what Fiske describes as an "economy of fandom" through their display of knowledge, their accumulation of performance documentation, and their patronage of and association with performers (1992:33). Bootleg tapes of obscure performances make up the currency of this economy, as does insider information about the rakugo world, obtained during drinking sessions with hanashika. Wit, as well as talent for mimicking the voices of the storytellers and the rhythms of rakugo, enhances fans' reputations among their peers.

This chapter discusses several styles of rakugo fandom in exploring how fans use rakugo to play and enrich their lives. It inquires into fans' affection for rakugo's jokes, clever wordplay, social commentary, pathos, and evocation of the past. And it explores how rakugo's diverse fan practices not only shape personal identity but also forge social relationships.

Before analyzing rakugo's importance to its fans, it is important to note fans' importance to rakugo. In Japan, fans have long been regarded as proactive contributors to all the performing arts, not only to rakugo. In his study of audience and actors in Japanese theater, Jacob Raz proposes the term *professional spectator* to illuminate the audience role in Japanese theater (1983:4). He cites Nō playwright Zeami as well as kabuki actors and Edo period writers such as Shikitei Samba, who wrote that an actor "cannot last 'even a single day, a single moment without his fans' support" (Raz 1983:190). The professional spectator boasts an impressive knowledge of the art to which she or he is devoted, and is aware of and abides by an established code of audience etiquette. It is possible to be a fan of a performer and know little about an art form. But fans do often end up becoming professional spectators. Indeed, they sometimes become scholars or even performers of the art.

Rakugo's origins have been traced back to before the 16th century, but the art of comic storytelling developed into what has come to be known as "rakugo" in the urban areas of Edo (Tokyo) and Osaka–Kyoto in the Edo period, around the end of the 18th century. Rakugo humor relies heavily on wordplay. Stories usually end in a punch line (called *ochi* or *sage*), often a pun. Indeed the contemporary name for the genre is derived from the word for punch line: rakugo, or *otoshibanashi* as the stories are also called, means "punch-line story."

From the beginning of the 19th century, a would-be professional storyteller apprenticed himself to a master. The development of artistic families encouraged the codification of the repertoire and performance style. However, the traditionalism inherent in art forms passed down from master to disciple has not precluded flexibility in the case of rakugo; to some degree, as a comic, solo performing art, it constantly reinvents itself. While most performers cherish the *koten* (classical) repertoire and strive to maintain the integrity of performance practices as passed down to them by their teachers, they acknowledge the need to adapt to contemporary taste in order to entertain audiences and attract fans. Performers of classical rakugo today strive to maintain a balance between fidelity to the text of the past and responsiveness to the performance context of the present.

In adapting to the performance context, storytellers sometimes dispense with the punch lines that give the genre its name. Many punch lines, as well as much of the vocabulary scattered throughout the narratives that precede them, have become obscure and must be explained in advance, thereby deflating their punch. Even without the punch line, audiences find much to appreciate in storytellers' representations of rakugo's beloved stock characters, and the humor and pathos of the stories.

To clarify the plot and flesh out the characters, the storyteller narrates in their voices. The story is acted out from a seated position in a conventionalized code of gestures. With fan and hand towel as props, the storyteller may pretend to be fishing, lighting a pipe, sipping sake, or even teaching a dance. Even a child (or a foreigner who speaks little Japanese) can enjoy a rakugo performance on some levels.

Despite these colorful, often humorous dramatizations, however, rakugo remains a minimalist performance in which gestures suggest rather than represent fully. Spectators must learn the code. In a sense, they collaborate with the hanashika to complete the performance in their mind's eye. Insofar as rakugo is a verbal art, it may be the spectator with knowledge of the archaic language and rakugo rhetoric who can most fully appreciate it.

Historically, *hanashi* (a broader term for rakugo) encompassed a variety of storytelling genres. It has evolved into an art that has been identified with otoshibanashi, punch-line stories that emphasize humor. Audience laughter has become the measure of a performer's communicative success. The fact that conservative rakugo fans and storytellers comment that rakugo should evoke smiles rather than guffaws suggests that, originally, laughter may not have been as central to the art, even for expressly comic tales. But rakugo and comic styles have changed. In an era when sight gags reign on television, storytellers pick up the pace and exaggerate visual elements to engage uninitiated audiences. One might argue that a comic performance today is not complete without the "laugh track."

Most hanashika are well aware that any sense of accomplishment they might derive from their faithfulness to traditional texts and performance practice does not make up for the disappointment of performing before an unresponsive audience. They approach the dilemma of "tradition versus adaptation" through a variety of strategies. This variety, along with the uniqueness of their stage personas and performance styles, ensures a diversity of audiences and fans who use rakugo in different ways.

Rakugo Fans and Professional Spectators in Historical Context

As a popular entertainment predating modern mass culture, the performance culture of rakugo included a strong fan component. In the late 18th century, it was fans of kabuki, the major popular theater of Edo (both the city and the era), who played a significant role in the engendering of what was to become professional rakugo. Utei Enba, credited with reviving and fostering comic storytelling in Edo, was a devotee of kabuki actor Ichikawa Danjūrō. He engraved all his carpentry tools with Danjūrō's *mimasu* (a "three measure" small drinking box) crest and established an official fan club for the actor called the Mimasu Ren. Members of this fan club were the mainstay of Enba's *hanashi no kai* (comic storytelling assemblies [contests]), which he initiated in 1786. Ichikawa Danjūrō himself joined in the sessions (Nobuhiro 1986:23). Through Enba's Mimasu Ren, the conventions of fandom associated with kabuki may have influenced the development of rakugo fan culture.

Given the historical association of rakugo and kabuki, kabuki fandom merits some attention here. Edo-period kabuki featured much greater actor–audience communication than it does today. Indeed, early forms such as *yūjo kabuki* (prostitute kabuki) endeavored to maximize actor–audience fraternization: The performance consisted of dances and skits enacting dalliance with prostitutes—direct invitations to the audience to purchase the performers' services for more intimate postperformance entertainment. Edo kabuki never entirely lost its early aura of eroticism. Actors frequently drank with patrons in their boxes at the theater. Rakugo storytellers today joke about their lack of sex appeal compared to kabuki actors, though they too frequently drink with fans, as I will discuss.

Edo-period fans short of the cash necessary to socialize with their favorites read up on them in *hyōbanki* (guides to actors). These booklets ranked actors, and provided mostly laudatory critiques and gossip about the stars (Raz 1983:156). Fanzines and webpages might be considered 21st-century counterparts to hyōbanki. In Edo kabuki, critiques were more immediately interactive than a webpage. Fans sometimes interrupted plays to make speeches in praise of actors, or interjected *kakegoe* (shouts applauding a well-executed pose or delivery of a line). Kakegoe have become so integral to kabuki that today actors hire "professionals" to shout them. Rakugo narratives are not structured to accommodate such interruptions, but occasionally fans exclaim "Matte 'mashita" [I was waiting for you] or a hanashika's nickname when he takes the stage.

Ancestors of the colorfully costumed cheering sections dotting the bleachers at a Japanese baseball game today—*teuchi renjū* (hand-clapping groups)—came to the kabuki theater in identical outfits and clapped, struck wooden clappers, or rhythmically sang to cheer their favorites. Well-respected members of the business community supplied props, stage curtains, and financial support for productions that featured the actors they revered (Shively 1978:21). Some of the renchū became so powerful that they demanded that theater management consult them on artistic and financial matters (Raz 1983:191–192). Rakugo fans never achieved this kind of power, but they did have some voice in the yose, the traditional rakugo storytelling venue, and they continue to offer substantial support to performers.

It was the yose that transformed rakugo into a professional performance genre in the late 18th century. By the middle of the 19th century, one of the most common leisure activities for urban Japanese was listening to stories at this cozy neighborhood storytelling house. At the height of rakugo's popularity, almost every neighborhood had its own yose. Men and women, young and old, people from all walks of life came to hear the recitations of the storytellers.

For many Edoites, the yose was, like the baths and the barbershop, an informal gathering place to hear not only news and stories from the stage, but also the latest gossip from their neighbors. The price of a yose ticket was within reach of most of the working class. This accessibility encouraged the establishment of a *jōren* (regular audience), who became "professional" spectators and leaders of an audience community with a power to influence the art. Storytellers began telling serialized stories to keep the regulars coming back night after night.

Hierarchical relationships among audience members evolved, with the more experienced passing on their wisdom. They taught newcomers about the performers, the stories, and the art of listening. They functioned as a kind of live "earphone guide," similar to those which explain kabuki to inexperienced kabuki goers today (Koyama 1985:103). Audience members' ranks were based not only on their knowledge or length of experience, but also on their contributions and service to the theater, as well as their *goshūgi* (tips) to performers. The theater would reward these higher-ranking audience members by lending them an umbrella or by placing their footwear in a more convenient spot at the entrance to the theater (Koyama 1985:103). A regular often had his own seat, and if someone unwittingly sat in it, an usher would direct him elsewhere (Koyama 1985:102). The hierarchical structure of the audience almost rivaled that of the performers.

Such local audience communities began to weaken during the years of Japan's modernization in the Meiji period (1868–1911) and after. The yose changed from a neighborhood hangout into a citywide venue, losing its character as an intimate, convenient place to visit in everyday dress. Horse-drawn carriages and trains transported fans all over the city to attend the larger, more famous yose. Better known yose thrived, while many of the smaller, local theaters lost their regulars. Some yose relocated to the entertainment zones of the city. A more anonymous, somewhat less stable audience replaced the jōren (Katō 1971:268).

Modern media changed audiences further. Motion picture viewing behavior, for example, influenced rakugo's reception. Katō Hidetoshi characterized this trend as a "minshū geijutsu no hijinkakuka" [depersonalization of popular arts] (1971:269). Broadcasting exacerbated the depersonalization process. Radio (and later television, phonograph records, cassette tapes, and CDs) expanded the number of listeners, and indeed increased the number of rakugo fans. But fans of mediated rakugo tend to be isolated from one another. The face-to-face solidarity and sense of community that existed among fans at the intimate yose would seem likely to disintegrate when mediated rakugo predominates.

Or does it? In the remainder of the chapter I describe rakugo fan cultures that give evidence to the contrary. One product of the cultural economy of rakugo fandom has been social: Fandom indeed produces communities. I now turn to a few of the many fan communities that make up contemporary rakugo performance culture.

A Typology of Rakugo Fans

Satirist Shikitei Sanba poked fun at kabuki fans in his 1811 parody of guides to actors, *Kyakusha hyōbanki* (Critique of Patrons).[3] He grouped patrons into such categories as the *shibai-zuki* (theater fan), who was addicted to the theater itself, and the *shibai tsū* (theater expert), who possessed a detailed knowledge of everything connected with the theater, theater history, and actors (Raz 1983:202). The *mukashi-buki* (the "good-old-days" fan), who waxed nostalgic for the theater of the past, had no interest in young stars. Sanba rated most highly the *hiiki jōren* (regular fan of a particular actor), who supported that actor and the theater with his unconditional love, without self-interest (Raz 1983:204). Sanba's parody attests to the fact that, just as it does today, 200 years ago fandom assumed many forms.

Satirical intent aside, some contemporary rakugo fans compare to a few of the types that Sanba identifies. The rakugo world includes his good-old-days fans, and *tsū* experts in their modern guises as history buffs, otaku and collectors, as well as patrons, "steady" fans, "chasers" *(okkake)*, and amateur performers. Many of these fans engage in multiple fan activities, from attending performances to performing themselves, and thus fall into more than one category.

Romanticizing the Past: History Buffs and Good-Old-Days Fans

Some rakugo fans take pleasure in the genre's evocation of the past, and in their own ability to understand it. Their knowledge of how to decipher not only rakugo's sophisticated wordplay but also its reference to archaic practices and ways of speaking brings them distinction. It is not simply to experience a sense of superiority that history buffs become this type of rakugo fan, however. They appear to take pleasure in reliving the past through rakugo.

One activity, a kind of "heritage" tourism, gives history buffs a chance to deepen their knowledge of the history of the genre and to apply what they know to play. After touring rakugo's historical sites in downtown Tokyo, one group of rakugo aficionados met at a restaurant to partake of local cuisine and engage in what the tour organizer described as *Edomae no asobi* (true Edo-style play). Rakugo fan and Sharaku member Hosoda Minoru arranged two tours that transported the present-day rakugo fan into a fictional past. His tours traced the itineraries recited in the rakugo stories "Koganemochi" and "Tomikyū." In Tomikyū, the entertainer Kyūzō rushes to his patron's house on the other side of Edo in the dead of a winter's night when he hears that a fire is ravaging that sector of the city. By scheduling his Tomikyū tour on a chilly December evening, Hosoda vividly recreated Kyūzō's experience for his participants. As they walked along the route once traveled by Kyūzō, fans on the tour may have been inspired to fantasize what it would have been like to be this fictional rakugo character. The tour provided a "time-out-of-time" experience and, in addition to the escape into fiction, an escape from the limitations of everyday identities.

Pilgrimages to rakugo sites highlight a central theme in rakugo fandom: nostalgia. They evidence a desire to recapture the past. There is an ideological component to this nostalgia, as the evocation implies an approval of past experience and culture. Jensen suggests that fandom may embody a critique of modernity (1992:9). The rakugo fan's idealization of an "authentic" world evoked by "traditional" storytellers might be conceived as such a critique. It may thus be said that for some fans, rakugo represents an arena of resistance to the rapid changes in Japanese language and culture. Rakugo symbolizes some ideal image of human relations, an essence of Japanese character considered lacking in contemporary life. One fan remarked that in rakugo "the way of life of the people in the Edo and Meiji period survives, just as it was. In the old days, in the tenement row houses *(nagaya)*, people helped one another. Japanese today cannot understand this."

Some hardcore history buffs regard themselves as guardians of rakugo authenticity and, by extension, traditional Tokyo culture. A few of these fans (and some storytellers) express concern about the genre changing beyond recognition to cater to contemporary tastes. They lament the fading of memories of Edo-period life. One fan and patron of rakugo, who claimed to love the art because it requires the listener to think, compared hanashika to the *kataribe* (storytellers of ancient times). He entrusted rakugo with the responsibility of preserving the language and mores of the Edo period.

To the mukashi biiki–type rakugo fan, rakugo of old seems more authentic—and better—than contemporary rakugo. Some of the older rakugo fans have heard Kokontei Shinshō (1890–1973) and Katsura Bunraku VIII (1892–1971) perform live. Others know this generation only through tapes, yet they still insist that their era was the good old days and that the art has since declined. Though some listen to contemporary performers and acknowledge their talents, they continue to insist that things used to be better. Next to Bunraku, present-day rakugo bores them. Rakugo today, they claim, is not the "real thing." The advent of electronic recording technology may have increased the number of these good-old-days fans over the past fifty years or so. Many respondents to a newspaper query that I submitted to the *Asahi shimbun* (February 29, 1992) rarely, if ever, went to see rakugo live. They knew the art largely from listening to it on the radio or on tape.

Collectors and Otaku

One fan response to a perception that rakugo is in decline is to gather memorabilia—that is, make recordings. In a sense, the good-old-days fan who converts a preference for the old masters into a passion for the recordings that preserve their voices leaves the good old days behind and becomes a kind of otaku. Collecting tapes is a preoccupation of many types of rakugo fan, even those who favor younger, maverick performers. And they do not only buy readily available commercial rakugo tapes and CDs. Fans produce artifacts for exchange within fan networks. Those with the equipment and the guts secretly record live performances, creating for themselves a source of capital in a cultural economy of rakugo fans. What they lack in clarity, these surreptitiously made tapes of live performances make up for in aura, which increases their value in the fan economy (Hosokawa and Matsuoka, chapter 7, this volume).

Some fans who record performances may be only vaguely aware of the illegality of their activities, and storytellers seem to look the other way. But one veteran of the practice, who sits in the first row at performances with a tiny Sony hidden in a small tote bag on his lap, commented that his less discreet colleagues should at least hide their tape recorders. Their lack of subtlety might send the message to other fans that taping is permitted.

There are hanashika who allow and sometimes even request fans to videotape their recitals (although they might be surprised at the number of dubbed copies circulated as a result). Perhaps these storytellers accommodate their fans' desire for records of live performances because they recognize that commercial recordings often lack the immediacy of a performance not intended for sale. Additionally, it is hard for fans to find recordings of all their favorite storytellers and stories. Big recording companies take an interest in only the most famous performers. Rakugo devotees seek to document storytellers in training, storytellers without the big names to attract a record label. As records of personal experience, bootleg tapes possess a value that exceeds that of recordings that can be purchased. The act of recording a performance endows the fan with a more active role in rakugo's performance culture.

Unlike a live performance, which is ephemeral and cannot be possessed except in memory, a recording, whether it is homemade or commercial, is an object that a rakugo fan can own and manipulate in ways not imagined or intended at the time of the performance. A recording creates the possibility for endless new listening contexts for the performance. For would-be amateur performers (and indeed even for professional hanashika) it becomes the basis for a script. Accompanied by a whiskey, it serves as a sleeping aid for the overstressed salaryman. Fans can achieve an intimacy with a performance that is impossible to attain during a transient, live show.

Although listening to a rakugo recording may be a solitary diversion, some collectors, such as the Sharaku members described earlier, form associations to exchange items in their collections. This club, in existence since 1986, joins individuals with a passion for technology and collecting as well as rakugo and differs from the more traditional type of fan club centered around individual performers. A hanashika stage name, as well as the name of a woodblock print artist famous for his portraits of actors, *sharaku* also means unconventional, free, unconstrained. The circle's hundred or so members include a printer, a retired flooring salesman, a high school English teacher, the chef–owner of a high-class restaurant, a university professor, a postal worker, and a retired television producer. Sharaku members pay modest dues toward the publication of a journal, issued a few times a year. Although the group as a whole does not meet frequently, those members who follow contemporary performers occasionally run into one another at recitals and meet afterward to discuss the performance. The circle convenes an annual end-of-the-year party where, as a highlight, some of the members perform rakugo and other verbal art genres.

Some members of Sharaku see themselves as archivists. One wrote, "I think it is our duty to bequeath these tapes to the younger generation of rakugo fans" (Nakano 1991). Another member once lamented the fact that there were two other recitals that he wished to attend on the same evening as a monthly recital that he has been secretly taping since its inception twenty-odd years ago. Even though the other programs appealed to him more, he felt obliged to document the less interesting performance: He could not bear the idea of breaking his continuity. Not all collectors maintain their collections with the intent of passing them on to the younger generation. One member wanted to preserve his tapes for posterity, but he also admitted that he just liked having them. Accumulation in itself gives pleasure and creates cultural capital. Tape collections serve as catalysts for social relationships among fans.

It is not only the artifact that is collectible. Many rakugo otaku are also obsessed with information about the repertory, the performers, and their performances. Otaku might be considered a variation of "professional spectator." But among many contemporary otaku, there seems to be more of an interest in information for its own sake, and in the technology of acquiring and maintaining that information, than would be the case among the more traditional professional spectator.

Entertaining a "mania" (or otaku) audience can be a harrowing experience for a hanashika. They know so much that it is difficult to make them laugh (see Kelly, introduction, this volume). While fan mania may unnerve performers, knowledge provides satisfaction and boosts self-esteem for otaku. Displaying knowledge can even become a kind of game. A few younger hanashika reclaimed the upper hand with the demanding otaku audience, playfully exploiting the otaku's taste for trivia at an experimental event called the Pokkuri Rakugo Kai (Drop Dead Rakugo Recital). They created a rakugo version of a popular television game show, *Karuto Q*, which featured panelists with extensive knowledge of very limited subjects. The questions asked at the Pokkuri recital included How many centimeters was hanashika Kokontei Shinchō's scar in his recent appendix operation? The contestants (who included an usherette from one of the yose theaters) were also asked to "name that tale" on a few recordings of the late Shinshō V. Some of the participants knew the recordings so well that they could identify the story in a few seconds, just by listening to how the theme music was played and how Shinshō uttered his initial "ee."

The Pokkuri Rakugo Kai trivia game demonstrates how intimately a fan can know a performance, thanks to technology. But the ability to memorize a recording does not necessarily amount to an understanding of rakugo. Fans today who acquire knowledge through recordings may have a more limited understanding of the art than the 19th-century professional spectator at the yose, who learned to appreciate rakugo through intensive exposure to live performances as members of a fan community.

Fans as Friends and Patrons

In yose audiences of the 19th century, patronage of a hanashika offered one means of establishing one's position in the fan hierarchy. Even the language used to describe the audience betokens the importance of patronage, or at least the interpersonal nature of performer–audience relations in the performing arts. When hanashika and Japanese critics talk about the rakugo audience they rarely use the Japanese terms that correspond to *spectator* or *audience* in the sense of *viewer* or *listener*. They instead call the audience *kyaku* or *okyakusan* (the more polite form), which mean both "guest" and "customer" and are widely employed in everyday speech. These words can refer to one or more persons, in contrast to the English term *audience*, which implies a mass of people, and plays down the individuality of the listener. The audience in rakugo is thus defined not in terms of their role as listeners but in terms of their social relationship to the performer. The expression "kyaku" may suggest the potential for a one-on-one relationship beyond the staged event.

Some audience members do achieve personal relationships with hanashika, as patrons or as friends. Hanashika generally make themselves more accessible to fans than do mass-media celebrities. They sometimes socialize with fans at post-performance parties called *uchiage*, which provide opportunities for developing friendships or even patronage.

San'yūtei Hōraku follows every one of his monthly solo recitals with a reception with his fans at a nearby restaurant. Almost the entire audience attended the uchiage that followed a small rakugo recital produced by Sharaku member Odashima Masashi on June 13, 1998. This recital featured three hanashika especially favored by mania-type fans. About 20–30 of these fans ate and drank with the performers for a few hours in a private room at a nearby tavern, circulating around the long table to pour one another beer and sake.

Hanashika Yanagiya Sankyō explained that formerly people of means who served as patrons took pleasure in nurturing the performer, making him into something. These days, he claims, people just want to be friends with entertainers: "Japanese people think that hanashika are funny and interesting. They believe that if they are with a hanashika he will make them laugh, and they will have fun" (interview with author in Tokyo, March 12, 1992). In some respects, hanashika compare with *taikomochi* (male geisha who entertained at parties in the old licensed quarters). As teahouse patrons paid for the company of a taikomochi, rakugo fans foot the bill for a night of drinking with a hanashika.

Despite Sankyō's assessment of fans as patronizing hanashika in order to be entertained, even today there are altruistic fans who evoke the image of the hiiki jōren praised by Sanba in *Kyakusha hyōbanki*. Not only do they support a performer throughout his lifetime; they remain true after his death as well, by supporting his disciples. Pharmacist Unemoto Itaru was a passionate fan of San'yūtei Enshō until the latter's death in 1979. Mr. Unemoto actively supports Enshō's artistic family today. He organizes small recitals throughout the Tokyo area featuring up-and-coming performers and buys and distributes blocks of tickets. He frequently wines and dines young performers and uses his connections to get them tickets to kabuki. Although he is particularly devoted to the San'yūtei family, he also lends a hand to many other young hanashika.

Steady fans recognize the limitations of less experienced young performers and they take special pleasure in identifying their promise and following them through their careers. Fans at the previously mentioned recital sponsored by Mr. Odashima waited patiently as a talented apprentice storyteller struggled to work his way out of a memory lapse in the middle of his recitation. "Start again, don't rush," they encouraged him. They did not expect perfection from an apprentice. As unnerving as a mistake may be for a storyteller, for a fan it may actually represent a welcome opportunity to communicate directly with the storyteller as the frame of the story is temporarily broken.

In any event, the true fan does not judge a hanashika by a single performance, but considers the complete performer—his past performances and the projected trajectory of his career. Tachibana Mayuko wrote about one performer in the

December 1984 issue of the fanzine *Yose suzume* stating that she thought he would "fill out and get more interesting." True fans' long-term loyalty explains story-tellers' jokes about playing to the children in the audience. Children, they say, will be around longer to support them.

The difference between the traditional hiiki and the more contemporary fan lies in the issue of social obligation, according to rakugo and kabuki commentator Koyama Kan'ō (1985:82). Obligations unrelated to reverence for a particular performer might compel one's support (hiiki). For example, one might have to support the performer whom one's boss supports. Fans, in contrast, follow their hearts.

The hiiki not only enacts obligations within his social network, but also toward the performer, through unfailing loyalty. Ideally, the hiiki feels a responsibility to cultivate a performer's artistry by buying tickets, giving goshūgi, helping out at recitals, and perhaps even offering constructive criticism to a performer over drinks. Koyama notes that *fan* in Japanese is almost a homonym for the word *fuan* (uncertainty). He regards the fan as less reliable than the old-fashioned hiiki (Koyama 1985:83). Perhaps because they practice a traditional art, hanashika tend to use the word *hiiki* to describe their supporters, rather than the word *fan*.

If a fan has the means and the desire to commit further to a particular performer, he can become his *odan* (patron). Full-fledged patrons sponsor performances, provide cash, and sometimes even furnish performers with expensive kimonos (at times inscribed with their own family crest). Koyama outlines one method for becoming an odan.[4] The first step, he explains, involves going to the yose where the favored hanashika is appearing. You inform one of the theater staff that you wish to send some sushi to the performer backstage. You leave your business card and enough cash to pay the check. The theater makes the arrangements. If the performer is courteous, he will send one of his disciples to the auditorium to thank you. After you have treated this performer to sushi two or three times at different yose, he will probably invite you backstage. During this first visit you should not stay too long, but invite him to dinner at a time convenient for him. From there on, your charm and finances determine your success in becoming one of his patrons (1985:80–81).

Patronage offers fans an opportunity to "display face." But there may be extra benefits to becoming the odan of a hanashika, as opposed to the patron of a singing star. Hanashika acknowledge patronage during their recitations, both in the prologues they compose and in the traditional tales they perform about entertainers and their benefactors. Rakugo's reflexivity effects a public affirmation of the patron–performer relationship.

Ochiken: Rakugo Clubs for Study and Pleasure

Hanashika distinguish themselves from amateurs by affiliating with an established professional and undergoing a three- or four-year trial-by-fire apprenticeship. The majority of professionals begin their careers in their late teens or early twenties, after a period as rakugo fans. Sometimes they have had experience performing as amateurs in school rakugo clubs called *ochiken*.

Ochiken (also called *rakken*) is an abbreviation for *rakugo kenkyūkai* (rakugo research association). The first university to sponsor such a club devoted to the study and appreciation of rakugo was Waseda, where eminent scholars of Edo-period literature (and rakugo fans) Teruoka Yasutaka and Okitsu Kaname started the club in the mid-1950s to raise awareness of rakugo's cultural value. Until then, the art had been ranked among the lowlier of Japan's cultural products.

Ochiken teach rakugo appreciation both through listening and performing. Hanashika are often invited to serve as teachers, through their recitals at clubs, question-and-answer sessions, and coaching of members in their performance efforts. Club activities include volunteering to perform at senior citizen centers. Though a few ochiken members quit college to become professional storytellers, not all members can truly be called rakugo fans. Some students sign up for reasons other than an interest in rakugo, though their choice of the ochiken at least reflects an attraction to comedy, performing, or both. The clubs as a whole may function as fan clubs and sometimes as patrons. For example, they may donate a backdrop stage curtain when a hanashika who has coached them advances to headliner status.

Their professional coaches notwithstanding, members learn stories from their seniors in the club, by listening to video or cassette tapes, or by memorizing them from collections of published texts. The heavy reliance on books and tapes distinguishes the ochiken approach from professional rakugo study. Although professional hanashika these days tape their lessons, and some revive old stories that they discover in published texts, their rakugo differs from that of amateurs. Professional performance is based on years of experience absorbing the techniques of one's teachers from the wings of the stage, day in and day out, from the time of one's apprenticeship. "Big" stories are generally proscribed for less experienced professionals. In contrast, amateur performers have no limitations on what they perform.

Just as some passionate fans of anime engage in "costume presentation," ochiken members enjoy dressing up as hanashika when they perform on such occasions as their university's annual student cultural festival. Both male and female students perform in kimonos, in imitation of professional hanashika. The women make a neat and pretty appearance in out-of-season *yukata* (a light cotton kimono) or in kimonos borrowed from their mothers. Few of the male students have experience in wearing a kimono and consequently they often look a bit sloppy. Western socks substitute for crisp white cotton *tabi* (Japanese-style socks), and obis are limply tied. To get laughs (and perhaps to save money), some students wear garish polyester tourist kimonos.

Ochiken stage names, which parody real rakugo stage names, reinforce the members' alternative identities. Although some students make up their own, others assume names passed down through the club and assigned to them by their seniors. One of the names available at Waseda was Erizabesu-tei Ra (Elizabeth Taylor). The *tei* suffix (meaning pavilion) is frequently used in hanashika family names (e.g., Kokontei, San'yūtei). Some Musashino University ochiken names were sexual or scatological puns.

Ochiken originally began as a way for students to learn about rakugo, both as performers and as spectators. Today, the social objective predominates in many clubs. In addition, ochiken are considered a place to develop one's sense of humor. For most students who join the ochiken for a chance to perform rakugo, authenticity is far less important than making a hit with one's peers. Performances tend to be geared to the in-group. Ochiken groups develop their own traditions of performance, which may or may not be related to professional traditions. Ochiken members include creative writers and natural comedians, but technical competence is rare. Just because one belongs to an ochiken does not necessarily mean that one is a rakugo fan; usually, only the mania types regularly go to hear live rakugo.

Performer Worship: Fan Clubs, Okkake, and Groupies

Fan clubs and cheering sections may not be as organized in rakugo as they are in kabuki or baseball, but they do exist. Towns and neighborhoods sometimes put together a fan club for a native son. A production office may organize a club for hanashika with media connections. Shunpūtei Koasa's management office, which includes performers in his artistic family, sponsors a fan club called Haruharudō. Members pay a small fee to belong. When I was a member in 1991, in addition to a newsletter that gave advance notice of performances, the main service that the club offered its members was the opportunity to buy tickets before the rest of the public, a boon in the case of Koasa's recitals, which sell out early. A good number of storytellers send out newsletters to their fans chronicling their activities. Fans finance some of the bulletins. These days many hanashika maintain webpages that not only announce their upcoming performances, but also offer biographical data and even advice.

Newsletters no doubt help the passionate fan keep abreast of where her or his favorite storyteller is performing. The fan who follows a particular performer, and makes an effort to catch all of his appearances is referred to as an "okkake," after *oikakeru* (to chase). I met such a fan at Koasa's 30-day run at the Hakuhinkan Theatre in the fall of 1990. A bit of a Koasa maniac myself, I had bought tickets for the entire run. The woman who sat next to me at every performance over those 30 days was hardly what we might identify as a groupie. She was in her early seventies but claimed to never miss a Koasa appearance within a day's journey from Tokyo.

Such a relentless fan used to trail the late Kokontei Shinchō. This fan may have seemed to be "stalking," but rakugo okkake usually maintain their distance. The Shinchō fan eventually moved to the back of the auditorium when he learned that his ubiquitous presence in the front was allegedly distracting his idol. He was so in awe of Shinchō that he remained silent when the two were once caught in an elevator. One young woman who ran after Yanagiya Kosanji (and other younger hanashika including Kosanji's disciples, one of whom she married) used to stand outside the stage door and wait for him to emerge after a performance. When he appeared, she bowed and thanked him for the performance. Though Kosanji served as the go-between at her wedding, mania fans joked that Kosanji would probably not mind if she divorced the disciple to make herself available to him.

Okkake include young women and girls comparable to rock "groupies." The late-night television show *Yotarō*, which was broadcast around 1990–91, created a new audience for rakugo or, to be more accurate, for young hanashika. Many *Yotarō* fans were high school girls. Although the content of the program had little or nothing in common with rakugo (except humor), the performers were all young hanashika from various Tokyo rakugo organizations.

Yotarō generated a mass media spillover. Fervent fans sought out their idols wherever they could be found, even at the traditional yose. When young women start chasing a performer, the media are never far behind. A new term was coined for the hanashika to whom *Yotarō*'s contingent of young female fans were devoted: *rakudoru*, a combination of rakugo and the Japanese–English word *aidoru* (idol).

A hierarchy exists among contemporary rakugo fans as it did among 19th-century fans. Some storytellers acknowledge the importance of young women because they attract the attention of the media. But teenage girls get low marks from older male fans, who deride them for their ignorance of rakugo, their overriding interest in a performer's physical attraction, and their poor audience etiquette. Even I found their behavior irritating. At one recital, a group of young women fans in front of me chatted or dozed off during most of the performers' sets but squealed and laughed continuously for their idols.[5]

Some of the young women fans who are initially infatuated with a performer end up coming to love rakugo for other reasons. One such group of women, which included my friends Koshina Masako and Tachibana Mayuko, met in the mid-1980s as participants at the National Theatre's special training program for women in *gidayū* (the declaimed narrative accompaniment to the Bunraku puppet theater). They parlayed their passion for rakugo into a clique they called the "Nedoko Gyaruzu" (Nedoko Gals).[6] The group's extensive knowledge of and deep interest in the traditional arts, including classical rakugo, distinguished them from the poorly mannered Yotarō groupies.

Fan Writing

Groupies, of course, write fan mail. Some fans, however, seek a broader audience for their writing. They may develop literary personae in the comic spirit of rakugo in their writings. They may support the art not only with tributes but also with critiques in fanzines. Rakugo fans produce various types of newsletters. Even *Tokyo kawaraban*, the monthly magazine covering popular yose entertainment in Tokyo, might be considered a kind of fanzine in that it is a side business subsidized by a rakugo fan. The magazine's editor, too, is a passionate rakugo devotee. The newsletter, *Jiyū rakugo* (Free Rakugo), published by a fan and comedy writer, solicits new rakugo stories from the general public. The newsletter of the Sharaku club introduced earlier features performance reviews and opinion columns along with annotated discographies and stories of carousing with performers. The journal provides a context for the fashioning of a rakugo fan identity: new members publish brief autobiographies.

In 1984–85, the Nedoko Gals put out a fanzine called *Yose suzume* (Yose Sparrow) to write about their favorite performers (see Figure 6.2). Their critiques display a sincere devotion to their favorites, generosity with their shortcomings, and delight in watching them develop, a common motif in rakugo fan discourse. Sometimes, one of the Nedoko Gals served as a scribe and recorded comments made during postperformance critiquing sessions. In their writings, they not only consider a performer's technique or his material, they react to the whole person. They construct their picture of the hanashika's character in myriad ways, some of them seemingly superficial—how he dresses, how he talks about himself, even what brand of overnight bag he carries. Some of them appreciate *sābisu seishin* (a performer's "spirit of service"). Others prefer a hanashika who holds himself more aloof.

In *Yose suzume*, observations about all aspects of the performances—performers' taste in kimonos, snatches of conversation leaked from backstage, flubs, and audience response—are presented uncut and jumbled together. At one postperformance critiquing session, a member inferred from storyteller Kingyō's presentation that he seemed like a "good person"; someone else critiqued his method of getting into the story. One fan liked Dankō's smooth, expressionless face. Another fan followed this comment by comparing his skillful way of playing a scene in "Toki soba" (the time-noodle con game) to that of another performer. While there was praise for his insertion of a contemporary reference to hay fever, there was also criticism of his noodle-eating gestures that "sounded like snoring." One woman commented on the way another performer's kimono harmonized with the color of the cushion on which he sat (Nedoko Gyaruzu 1985:4–5).

The group compared different performers' interpretations of one story and reflected on whether the differences had to do with their individual personalities offstage. Rakugo is interesting and fun, one remarked, because audiences can savor the variety of flavors of different performers doing the same story (pp. 7–8). On another occasion, one woman, in professing her adoration for Gontarō, explained that "with him, no matter what story he does, I can relax (Nedoko Gyaruzu 1984:4). She did not have to worry that he would make a mistake. She appreciated the fact that he took account of his audience. He was always "kankyaku

Figure 6.2

Front page of an issue of the fanzine *Yose suzume* (Yose Sparrow). Used with permission.

no ikizukai to tomo ni aru" [in synch with their breathing] (p. 4). These sorts of critiques reveal the degree to which audience–performer communication is held in esteem, and suggest the high level of involvement of some Japanese fans.

While most of their comments were positive and supportive, at times the Nedoko Gals' honesty could be cutting. *Yose suzume* was meant for their eyes only. Eventually, however, word about the publication got out and others started reading it. Some outside readers were critical of the women's frankness and questioned their right to write as they did. Koshina Masako speculates that perhaps without this criticism, the group might have continued to publish the fanzine for a longer time.

Writing critiques empowered these young women. The handwritten format and chatty style of the newsletters exuded confidence and personality. Their individual rakugo-inspired pen names may not only have afforded them the protection of anonymity but the excitement of alternative identities. The newsletters provided a context for self-fashioning.

Amateur Rakugo: Merging with the Performer

We have already seen how students turn to rakugo as a resource for trying on new identities in their school rakugo clubs, or ochiken. But one does not need an ochiken pedigree to adopt stage names or nicknames from a rakugo story to create an alternative identity. For example, one young man appended "*go-inkyo*" to his name, after the know-it-all retiree who appears as a stock character. For many fans, the play extends beyond a rakugo name. Hanashika Harusameya Raizō capitalizes on his fans' interest in having a rakugo identity. At his uchiage, he accepts fans as "disciples." In 1991, for a fee of 1,000 yen (about $8), Raizō legitimated his fans' stage names (which they chose themselves) and taught them a joke or two. Fans often engage in rakugo-related performance behaviors, impersonating storytellers, and retelling rakugo jokes and stories. One rakugo fan skilled in such vocal impersonation even taught his two-year-old daughter to imitate the trademark gesture of a legendary storyteller.

The assumption of hanashika identity may sometimes be unintentional. One fan claimed that after a few hours of listening to recordings of Shinshōhe he started talking like him. Even fans who lack skill in impersonation may season their speech with lines from rakugo stories. By speaking in a kind of rakugo-inspired code, they mark off the secret, insider's realm typical of play (Huizinga 1950:12). This code binds them to a closed society composed of other fans and enhances their sense of belonging.

Fans may express a familiarity with the insiders' code through parody. Mania fans who perform (including ochiken members) and even professional hanashika with an otaku streak sometimes create quasi-parodic, overdetermined versions of rakugo stories, full of allusions to past professional performances. Storyteller Tatekawa Danshi inserts these sorts of references. His performances reveal a detailed knowledge of his predecessors, acquired and polished by years of listening to his large tape collection.

It is possible for ochiken graduates to continue to indulge their love of the spotlight by joining the ranks of the *tengu-ren* (serious amateur performers who consider themselves on a par with professionals). People who think highly of their own abilities (in the arts or other fields) are sometimes referred to derogatorily as *tengu* (a long-nosed, birdlike mythical creature known as a boaster). Despite the "amateur" label, some tengu-ren performers are extremely talented. Sharaku member Odashima Masashi, who not only collects tapes and produces recitals but also performs, gave an accomplished recital at Sharaku's year-end party in 1991.

For some passionate fans, performing the repertoire of a favorite performer represents an act of reverence. San'yūtei Enshō VI, in particular, seems to evoke this kind of intense veneration among his fans. Some of them commemorated the 13th anniversary of Enshō's death by performing his material at a small hall in the Chiba shopping center where he suffered his fatal heart attack. A few of these performers had never even heard Enshō perform live. They learned the stories by watching the master's videos, and consequently picked up his mannerisms, rhythms, and pronunciation.

Conclusion

Over two hundred years ago, *ren* (networks of amateurs who wrote poetry and dabbled in literary wordplay) contributed to the invention of rakugo. When rakugo took root as a professional performance art, fans gathered at local yose. Present-day fans make use of electronic networks—telephones, broadcasting media, and computers—to experience rakugo and communicate their responses to it. New media facilitate the reproduction and dissemination of rakugo performance documentation. Cyberspace houses a new kind of yose for fans to gather and exchange information and opinions. Webpages offer fans and hanashika alike a chance to spout their opinions as well as inform their networks about performances and other significant rakugo-related events.

Amid all these new developments, certain older styles of fan behavior endure. Rakugo production is, by and large, less commercially driven than many other kinds of popular entertainment. It is small scale enough that fans can show their loyalty to performers by arranging recitals for them and buying up tickets. Fans have personal access to many storytellers. They often treat performers to drinks, and show their support financially when their favorite hanashika undergoes professional and personal rites of passage. In return for their donations and their loyalty, fans enjoy a great deal: the appreciation of performers, sometimes acknowledged publicly (gifts are displayed on stage on certain formal occasions, for example), the satisfaction of supporting an art form that they love, the creation of a social community, and the opportunity to imagine and even perform a fictional identity.

Performers generate an undercurrent of erotic desire in their fans and patrons, which manifests as a wish to possess the actor. In some fans, this desire further translates to a wish to possess the world that the actor represents. According to Imao Tetsuya (Raz 1983:205), fans yearn thereby to realize their own existence. Hanashika may not provoke as overt an erotic response as a female impersonator in kabuki. But as representatives of the world of play, hanashika awaken longings in their audiences and contribute meaning and focus to their existence. While many rakugo stories preach the value of hard work and ethics, a number also offer alternative, sometimes subversive role models. These stories celebrate the *san-dō-raku* (three amusements [debaucheries] of drinking, gambling, and buying women). Hanashika sometimes describe themselves as *asobi-nin* (playboys, goof-offs, gamblers). They joke that they visit prostitutes as part of their artistic training Rakugo's identification with tradition, with the past, may render these unacceptable behaviors less offensive. On the other hand, it is storytellers' and their stories' very affirmation of human nature in all its baseness that, to some extent, accounts for the genre's appeal. Hankering after the world of play, audiences attempt to possess hanashika and rakugo, not only by initiating personal contacts, but also by acquiring knowledge of the art and through documenting and archiving performances. Additionally, they seek to possess rakugo through reenactments, such as pilgrimages to geographical sites affiliated with stories or rakugo history, and through their own performances of rakugo, both as vocal impersonators, punsters, and amateur storytellers. Very few fans will give up their day jobs to live the allegedly carefree life of a storyteller. But they may fantasize a playful alternative to their daily grind by immersing themselves in rakugo culture, or by imitating hanashika speech. Rakugo may thus validate leisure among fans who tend to be wedded to their work.

In her discourse analysis of a rakugo tale, Mary Sanches notes how violation of speech events in rakugo comments on the absurdity of the play world and thereby implies the "realness" of the world of work (1975:304). By differentiating themselves from hanashika, fans indeed reaffirm their identity as upstanding citizens. But rakugo fans also seem to recognize the importance of laughter and *asobi* (play) in their lives. As a kind of play, fan activities are emergent, and thus productive. They harbor transformative potential. Hanashika model some of the possibilities for self-making inherent in play when they assume the identities of fictional characters. Both as fictional characters and in their personas as performers, they serve as paradigms to their fans for acting out other ways of being, and provide a stock of images for fans to draw on. Among these images, the idea of play itself may possess a special power to inspire rakugo fans' re-creation of themselves, even if these re-creations exist only in their imagination.

Notes

1. Although Sharaku membership includes women, I only encountered men at their meetings.

2. Rakugo is popular in the Osaka–Kyoto metropolitan area, and may be heard live throughout Japan, when performers tour. This study is limited to a consideration of Tokyo rakugo.

3. In the early 20th century, fans of the all-women's musical theater Takarazuka were also subjected to a similarly parodic classification (Robertson 1998:151).

4. He does not mention whether this method is still practiced. While sushi appeared in the green room from time to time on special occasions when I worked backstage in 1991, it seems to have been presented by established patrons, not would-be odan.

5. In terms of the "islands-in-space" model elaborated by Condry (chapter 1, this volume), otaku groups would be viewed as equivalent and autonomous. To some degree this may hold true for rakugo fandom. However, the variety format of the yose, which brings together performers of diverse styles, also attracts a diversity of fans. At live performances, fan groups cannot remain islands in space. As differing fan styles come into contact and clash, some fans may declare themselves superior.

6. The rakugo story, *Nedoko* (The Sleeping Place), is about a landlord, an incompetent amateur gidayū singer, who forces his tenants to listen to him croak through a recital.

References Cited

Fiske, John
    1992   The Cultural Economy of Fandom. *In* The Adoring Audience: Fan Culture and Popular Media. Lisa A. Lewis, ed. Pp. 30–49. London: Routledge.

Huizinga, J.
    1950   Homo Ludens: A Study of the Play Element in Culture. Boston: Beacon Press.

Jensen, Joli
    1992   Fandom as Pathology: The Consequences of Characterization. *In* The Adoring Audience: Fan Culture and Popular Media. Lisa A. Lewis, ed. Pp. 9–29. London: Routledge.

Katō Hidetoshi
    1971   Gendai no yose (Contemporary yose). *In* Yose: wagei no shūsei (Yose: A collection of verbal arts). Geinoshi kenkyūkai, eds. Pp. 265–278. Tokyo: Heibonsha.

Koyama Kan'ō
    1985   Rakugo zatsugaku (Rakugo miscellanea). Tokyo: Gurafusha.

Nakano Motomichi
    1991   Hataraku godaime 'Kokontei Shinsho' hakken (Discovery of the working 'Kokontei Shinsho'). Rakugo saakuru shi Sharaku, 33 (December): n.p.

Nedoko Gyaruzu (Nedoko Gals)
1984   Yose suzume (Yose sparrow), 9 (December).
1985   Yose suzume (Yose sparrow), 10 (January).

Nobuhiro Shinji
1986   Rakugo wa ikani shite keisei sareta ka (How rakugo was established). Tokyo: Heibonsha.

Raz, Jacob
1983   Audience and Actors: A Study of Their Interaction in the Japanese Traditional Theatre. Leiden: E. J. Brill.

Robertson, Jennifer
1998   Takarazuka: Sexual Politics and Popular Culture in Modern Japan. Berkeley: University of California Press.

Sanches, Mary
1975   Falling Words: An Analysis of a Japanese Rakugo Performance. In Sociocultural Dimensions of Language Use. Mary Sanches and Ben Blount, eds. New York: Academic Press.

Schodt, Frederick
1996   Dreamland Japan: Writings on Modern Manga. Berkeley: Stonebridge Press.

Shively, Donald.
1978   The Social Environment of Tokugawa Kabuki. In Studies in Kabuki: Its Acting, Music and Historical Context. James Brandon, William Malm, and Donald Shively, eds. Pp. 1–61. Honolulu: University of Hawaii Press.

7

Vinyl Record Collecting as Material Practice

The Japanese Case

SHUHEI HOSOKAWA AND HIDEAKI MATSUOKA

Acquiring and retaining arrays of objects is surely not a uniquely modern disposition, but collecting practices do reflect and constitute the social formation of taste and taste communities. Within modernity's material culture, the vinyl phonograph record, as a key symbol of modern sound reproduction, has been a frequent focus of systematic collection. This is certainly true for Japan, where vinyl records are the intensely sought objects of a small world of ardent collectors. In this chapter, we consider three sets of issues about this collecting form in Japan: (1) the appropriation of foreign music in 20th-century Japan as the historical context of record collecting; (2) the material and aesthetic specificity of vinyl discs within the culture of collecting industrial products, including its relationship with print media and the market; and (3) collectors' construction of personal and collective identities through their seeking, buying, and selling of such records.

Record Collecting and Modernity

Phonograph technology was invented by Thomas Edison in 1877, and only 11 months later in 1878, a British physicist experimented with the first wax cylinder phonograph in Japan (Kurata 1979:13). Wax cylinders did not become collectors' items at the time. They were scarce and deteriorated easily after about a dozen playbacks; they were seldom used to record music but rather were used in street spectacles and for the curiosity of recording human voices. Recording sound to vinyl discs was developed in the United States in 1888 by the German-born immigrant Emile Berliner, who patented his machine as the "gramophone." Rapidly expanding manufacture and sales of the gramophone from the beginning of the 20th century (Gronow 1983) not only increased consumers but also collectors of gramophone "records," which were used much more for recording music.

Disc-recording technology was first brought to Japan in 1903 by Fred Gaisberg, the most famous globe-trotting producer in the early record industry (Hosokawa 1998; Moore 1999:ch. 8). Whereas in the West famous opera songs and parlor melodies were the best-selling early recordings, in Japan, it was *rōkyoku* (a narrative genre accompanied by the *shamisen* [a three-stringed instrument]) that sparked the popularity of this new technology. Thus far we have found no contemporary references to "rōkyoku collectors," probably because the available repertoire was too small and all the recording artists were still alive. Another reason for their absence may have been the low status of the genre; the rōkyoku audience was predominantly working class and could not afford to collect phonograph records.

The industrialization meant the accumulation of stock and repertoire as well as the planned production targeted to the consumers diversified according to economic standing, taste and other factors. It is no accident that the record collection became visible in the 1910s and emerged from Western classical music listeners. For this timing coincided with the advent of Taishō internationalism and *kyōyōshugi* (culturalism), in which the rising middle class and the students were vehemently interested in things overseas and eager to possess new Western knowledge. It was also a period when *shumi* (taste) came to play a significant role in forming a mass consumer society (Jin'no 1994). Western music was a recognizable cultural icon of "refined taste." Such a status made it easy for Western music to penetrate in the upper middle class in the 1910s and 1920s. Phonograph recordings often provided the only audible access to Western music pieces that were rarely, if ever, performed, even in Tokyo.

Around 1910, a professor at the Tokyo Music School organized one of the first record concerts with discs of the Victor Red Seal label, a well-known series specializing in Western classical music. These imported, expensive items were popular with wealthy families whose children attended Gakushūin, an elite private school tied to the imperial family. They played Caruso, Melba, Joachim, and other famous artists. Another group of Western classical music fans established l' Union des Gramophonophilis (The Gramophone Union) around 1915 or 1916 (Iwasaki 1936). These clubs helped form a Western classical music audience who could not afford to buy the imported records and audio sets. Just as amateur associations in the West might inspire Japanese travelers and students overseas, the organizers had a clear intention of "enlightening" the people who had little accessibility to the splendid music. Some record stores started importing Western discs around 1910, and the wealthy students and Western-influenced writers rushed to patronize them. Stores such as Jūji-ya Music Shop and Yamano Music

Shop, both in Tokyo's Ginza, became cathedrals for Western music lovers. Vinyl collection in Japan thus began in conjunction with the accumulation of a new urban consumerism.

"Listeners' guides" for Western classical music first appeared in the 1920s. Unlike rōkyoku, this music was generally acknowledged as kyōyō (high culture), but the knowledge for its appreciation had not been circulated much in Japanese journalism. Since many authors—the first generation of "music critics"—read English, French, or German, or all three, they primarily drew their criteria of "masterpieces," "maestros," and "good records" from Western sources, although this was rarely mentioned in their works. But by adopting Western canonical standards in such music periodicals as Gekkan Gakufu (Monthly Music), Ongakukai (Music World), Ongaku Sekai (The World of Music), and Ongaku to Chikuonki (Music and Phonograph), they guided their readers toward the Western sensibility. The connoisseurship was thus "borrowed" and authenticated.

One of the first listeners' companions in Japanese, Hattori Ryūtarō's 1924 Rekōdo no eramikata to kikikata (How to Select and Listen to Records) parodied and criticized record collectors:

These days one finds some who display such a thorough knowledge of records as if they were phonograph shop sales clerks. They walk the streets clutching records under their arms, pretending to be those who live a "cultured life." We, the more serious and sincere music devotees, dislike these alleged music fans who show off records. We equally dislike the pretentious youth who have only a passing and superficial knowledge about music. [Hattori 1924:11–12]

Since the word bunka (culture) at the time signified high culture, vinyl, Hattori indicates, connoted high status and, as we will discuss later, discographic knowledge was something to be shown off. This quote also revealed a conflict between "sincere" music lovers like Hattori himself and "alleged" aficionados, who knew much about records but little of the music. The real music lovers, he believed, should know the details of the composition, the composer, the performance, and the performers rather than the sound reproduction technology. In the same year Ōtaguro Moto'o, one of the founders of music criticism in Japan, dismissed recordings as "canned music," which he might have picked up from reading a similar controversy in the imported music journals (Kurata 1979:264–265).

Ōtaguro's position was later opposed by Nomura Araebisu, another widely read music critic before the war, who questioned whether a concert could provide a genuine listening experience, given its distracting visual elements and disruptive audience noises (1931:8–10). He insisted on the aesthetic value of "sound itself," favoring armchair listening in domestic spaces. He further questioned if it was really better to listen to a live performance of a mediocre Japanese violinist or a superb recording of a virtuoso like Fritz Kreisler. Even in the 1930s, Western artists rarely toured Japan, and only a handful of Japanese professionals performed on stage. Recordings thus were not only indispensable but also canonical for music lovers and critics. The reviews by the known critics deeply affected the prestige and sales of records.

Publication of discographies in highbrow music magazines started in the 1930s, revealing a widening interest in systematic collecting among the record buyers. The subjects of these discographies—artists such as Benny Goodman, Duke Ellington, and Fritz Kreisler and titles such as "St. Louis Blues"—were indices of the early favorites of record collectors.

The Music Café as Public Record Collector

As phonographs and records diffused widely through urban life in the 1920s and 1930s, record collecting became a distinctive practice, and the collectors came to form a diffuse but recognizable community. This was associated with the establishment of *ongaku kissa* (music cafés), cozy spaces with vast record collections featuring particular genres (e.g., Western classical music, jazz, tango) and excellent audio equipment. The first of these appeared in Tokyo around 1929 (and closed by 1941). There were at least forty music cafés in the metropolitan area, which developed from the stylish "cafés" that had been in vogue since the mid-1920s. They targeted urbane youth who appreciated the new music but were unable to afford to buy it. Like ballroom and theater reviews, these music cafés were indeed considered "hip." They were overwhelmingly a male domain since men were far freer than women to consume time and money outside the home; music and dance periodicals in prewar Japan also had predominantly male readership.

Although attractive waitresses were sometimes topics of gossip among café goers, the main attraction was the opportunity to listen to good music with excellent sound equipment; indeed, the connoisseurs sometimes made fun of the waitresses' musical ignorance. Customers could request what they wanted to listen to, and many music cafés served as salons for small "taste communities" as well as record clubs. Café advertisements had such boasts as "Come and listen to the best Credenza phonograph!" and "We present you the latest Brunswick [jazz label] catalogue." Acquiring imported records was crucial for the reputation of music cafés. Significantly, none played Japanese music—either classical or popular—although Japanese music generally had larger audience shares and sold more records than foreign genres. This suggests that music cafés were designed to maintain the taste distinction of a "niche" public, nurturing dilettante, taste-based community.

Although they were forced to close during wartime, music cafés reappeared in the 1950s. Many of them enforced silence among their customers, sustaining a solemn atmosphere for revering immortal giants like Furtwengler and Coltrane.

Music cafés were vital to the local scenes of jazz, Western classical music, tango, and other foreign music until the 1970s. By then, lower prices for imported records and hi-fi stereo sets gave ordinary listeners increasing private access (Derschmidt 1998).

Reproducing the Aura

Now we turn to individual record collectors. Susan Pearce (1995) has distinguished three modes of collecting—the souvenir, fetishistic, and systematic—based on the relationship of the collecting subject to collected objects. In souvenir collecting, she notes that "the individual creates a romantic life-history by selecting and arranging personal memorial material to create what . . . might be called an object autobiography, where the objects are at the service of the autobiographer" (p. 32). In fetishistic collecting, by contrast, "the objects are dominant and . . . are allowed to create the self" of the collector, who just responds to his obsessive need by gathering as many items as possible (p. 32). The third type, systematic collecting, is based on an intellectual rationale that emphasizes the completeness of assembled items. As Pearce notes, these three modes are not exclusive, and individual collections can embody all of them (see also Eisenberg 1987: chs.1, 3, 9, 11).

Most collectors we have interviewed have confirmed the three features of Pearce's model, articulating a desire for systematicity, the lure of the market, and the fatal attachment to the objects as indispensable elements in their transition from ordinary record listeners to passionate collectors. Let us consider each of these.

First, owning large numbers of records is necessary but not sufficient for recognizing oneself as a "collector." For instance, a music writer employed by a small record company owns four or five thousand records of African music, but he does not identify himself as a record collector as he once did in the 1980s, when he collected records systematically according to genres, countries, and special artists. He abandoned the self-recognition of "African music collector" when he married and was getting interested more in the life behind the recorded sound than in completing his archive. We might say that in his case an anthropological interest has replaced a collector's enthusiasm. Another collector, who is proud of his near-complete collection of the original issues of ECM (a German jazz and contemporary music label), began collecting from dissatisfaction with the randomness of his record library, which resulted from his eclectic-taste-based buying. He wanted to own "something special which has not yet been found on others' shelves." He found the ECM music attractive, so he decided to dedicate himself to completing the whole catalogue independent of his aesthetic judgment. The systematicity gave him the intellectual pleasure of knowing the catalog and recording profiles, the standard price of each issued record, the purchase price he negotiated with dealers, the degree of difficulty in "digging" out each record, the locations of secondhand record stores, his participation in international auctions, and the competition against rival collectors. He likened his collecting to working on a jigsaw puzzle: He has a clear sense of the complete figure and is searching for the missing pieces. Discography is indispensable to setting a goal and to knowing the full pattern.

Second, one of our informants was a jazz collector who has nearly one thousand cassette tapes and mini discs privately recorded from the radio and from live club performances; however, he does not identify himself as a "collector" because such private recordings have no limits in quantity (and thus no completeness to be achieved) and the tapes, even if they capture rare performances, have no market value (though he sometimes exchanges his tapes for others). Private recordings have no "catalogue" as records have. He also has some one hundred CDs but feels no greater attachment to them than to records. He buys them just because he likes to listen to them. The "I-like-therefore-I-buy" behavior is, for him, still quite different from that of the collector, who is oriented toward market value.

Finally, for many collectors, the record is more than the means for music listening. It is a total object composed of visual, graphic, material, and audible elements. As demonstrated by the flood of picture books of old record jackets, such jackets are the most appraised visual feature, even by noncollectors. An interviewee told us that what really motivated his collection of the original ECM record label was the superb cover artwork. Some collectors have even focused on the outer sleeve (called the *obi*, a strip with a description of the record and blurbs wrapped around the jacket itself, which was developed in Japan in the early 1960s), the typography and the layout of the central label, and the type of center hole in the record itself. The jazz record producer and collector Ogawa Takao notes, "To me, a [secondhand] record without an outer sleeve is as worthless as a tea cup with a crack" (VV. AA. 1996–97, vol. 1:100). A fixation with such particular elements is often dismissed as fetishistic by noncollectors for whom vinyl records are merely a manufactured medium for listening to music. However, collectors develop their own criteria of authenticity and aesthetics for their favorite industrial products. As with stamp and coin collectors, they will pay for the smallest discernible details. W. J. T. Mitchell (1986:191) noted that Marx labeled commodities as fetishes to reveal how the most mundane products of daily use could have attached to them the most extraordinary (irrational) value. In this sense it is true that Japanese record collecting is fetishistic.

Japanese jazz enthusiasts have been attributed with discovering the "deep groove," a deeper microgroove than ordinary cutting, in the Blue Note jazz records manufactured in a New York factory for some years during the 1950s (personal communication with Fred Cohen, the owner of Jazz Record Center, New York City, 1995). This feature, enthusiasts claim, can carry much better sound quality—which is to say, a higher fidelity to the live performance—than an ordinary groove. Japanese collectors assembled a list of such deep-grooved records, which affects market pricing and taxonomic passion.

Another group of jazz collectors favors the "heavyweight disc," which is thicker and heavier than the normal disc and which, they believe, allows a more stable tracing by the needle and results in better sound. Such an attention to manufacturing details is common to many industrial product collectibles, including coins, stamps, cameras, electric guitars, model guns, miniature railroad cars, Barbie dolls, and Hawaiian shirts. What outsiders consider to be fetishism is to insiders a fine-grained attention to systematizing material differences.

Many vinyl collectors' ultimate dream is to possess brand-new factory-sealed records. As philatelists desire mint stamps, vinyl collectors highly value the material "virginity" of records. Such mint records command higher prices than used records not only because of the physical condition of the disc itself but also because of the jacket, the label in the middle of the disc, the outer sleeve, and other elements that noncollectors do not perceive. This search for the perfect-condition record often heightens the quest for completing a series. Wealthy collectors will exchange, at a premium, a record for a mint or better condition example of the same to move closer to the ultimate goal of a complete mint series. They may own a pair of the "same" records—one for their collection, the other for playing.

Record collectors often mention the aura of "original" releases. A jazz collector remarked with considerable feeling that

an original release immortalizes the sound of the performance by certain inspired musicians in a certain studio on a certain date—a one-and-only performance in the world. It's miraculous. It's a miracle because no other moment in human history had the airwaves I listen to now, thirty or forty years later. The reissues and the digital rerecordings have never given me such a thrill.

The digital transfer and stereo conversion of monaural analog recordings, two technical procedures common in today's record industry, are anathema to him. Like many vinyl collectors, he believes that these digitized products lack aura. They claim that technological interventions distance the rereleases and CDs from the sound source.

Such a cult of the original is akin to book collectors' search for first editions. Original record collectors, though, emphasize the indisputable sound quality of the original issue. To paraphrase Roland Barthes (1982), the originals have a "grain of sound," a materiality and physicality embodied in sound. The aura of industrial products is different from what Walter Benjamin (1969) once characterized as something related to the uniqueness of aesthetic experience and the one-ness of the object of art. But even industrial products can have aura if one is sensitive to the small but salient singularities in the series.

Generally, the worship of original issues is more common among jazz and Western classical music collectors than among, say, rock and pop collectors. While Miles Davis collectors rarely show interest in Italian or Swedish releases of *Kind of Blue*, many Beatles collectors are not satisfied with completing the original Parlophone issues and tend to further search out all local releases, the reissues with local art-works. Their different standard for authenticity may be due to the different record-ing techniques of jazz and rock. Because jazz recording usually valorizes unique unrepeatable improvisation, it seldom utilizes tape editing. As a result, fans believe the recordings are the legitimate trace of what the musicians really played. This is why jazz records and discography meticulously credit the recording session person-nel, place, and date. The session is the origin, the authentic site for jazz recording. Some jazz records are famous for including the studio sound check because the lis-teners can compare the performance with the real sound of cymbal, trumpet, piano, bass, and other instruments. For these reasons, Japanese jazz collections are heavily biased toward the acoustic combo recordings of the 1950s and the 1960s. The younger musicians since the 1970s are popular in the general record industry but they are marginal in the collector's market. (We leave aside here collectors of vocal jazz, whose taste practices differ from instrumental jazz collectors.) The ideology of "high fidelity" and the intimacy of the audio set are also true to Western classical music recordings. This is demonstrated by parallels in Japanese mainstream jazz and Western classical music magazines such as *Suingu Jānaru* (Swing Journal; since 1947) and *Rekōdo Geijutsu* (Record Art; since 1952), two magazines that always review audio equipment in the same way they treat the recordings.

Rock recordings, by contrast, often use tape editing, overdubbing, and other "postperformance" devices in the studio, which many jazz fans regard as "gim-micks." Even the stereophonic sound reproduced on the record does not always originate from the session. Such procedures dilute the value of the "original" version and stimulate interest in other elements as a result.

If jazz and Western classical music collectors represent the authenticity-ori-ented end of the record collection spectrum, we find at the other end collectors of obscure records such as elevator music and nonmusic (e.g., narration, language courses, documentaries). Their topics are often classified as "miscellaneous" or "to be classified." Unlike jazz and Western classical music, the most systematized collector regimes, they have no established catalogue or market control. There are no predictable ways to locate desired discs, and they must resort to scrap deal-ers and flea markets. Indeed, their pleasure often lies in finding value in the "trash" few collectors are interested in and in constructing counterhegemonic as-semblages out of the unfashionable. As with the recent popularity of "elevator music," their collections may occasionally gain some exchange value, but this is rarely the case. They are peripheral within the record collector community that is already on the fringe of mainstream society. These trash record collectors often collect other items such as pulp fiction, tabloid pornography, science-fiction novels, B-movies, and other mass-produced but poorly regarded "miscel-lanies." Mainstream society's disrespect for these collectors is indeed crucial to their identities as outsiders even in the record-collector world, which itself is already marginalized.

Printed Grooves: Authenticity and the Music Press

As we have argued, the print media have exerted a decisive influence on record collectors and vice versa. Reviews, information, and essays have heightened Japanese record collectors' desires and also have established aesthetic standards by canonizing specific records, artists, and labels. In particular, *Rekōdo Geijutsu* and *Suingu Jānaru*, the two thick (approximately four hundred pages) monthly magazines for classical music and jazz, respectively, are recognized as canonical. It is no coincidence that these are the two musical genres that have been available as recorded music since the 1930s and have motivated such institutions as music cafés, the circulation of used records, and the production of catalogues and discographies. The audiences for both are predominantly the upper-middle-class or white-collar workers and intellectuals with the time and money for consumption and collection.

As with many other Japanese music periodicals, a key feature of *Rekōdo Geijutsu* and *Suingu Jānaru* are the large number of record (and now CD) reviews. *Suingu Jānaru* anoints a monthly "Gold Disc" (selected by the editors and a panel of critics) and chooses an annual Gold Disc (through a poll of critics and readers), and these carry much weight with readers and the music industry. The majority of the Gold Discs have been recordings from the past or by well-established artists. *Rekōdo Geijutsu*'s annual Record Academy Award is given to what the periodical considers the best Western classical recordings. The small gold seal of a Record Academy Award, which looks like a small vintage champagne bottle, is affixed on record jackets, and is prominently visible in store displays and marketing campaigns. Although many magazines have such an award system, none has been able to equal the prestige of *Rekōdo Geijutsu* and *Suingu Jānaru*. These two magazines and the genres they represent retain top spots in the Japanese music status hierarchy.

Certainly providing the information and reviews of commercial recordings is essential to listeners' guides throughout the world (e.g., *Diapason* for Western classical music, *Downbeat* for jazz), but Japanese guides distinctively not only showcase new releases but also highlight reissues and prestige *meiban* (master recordings). Every time Carl Böhm's Mozart symphonies or Sonny Rollins's "Saxophone Colossus" (or *sakkoro* as it is affectionately nicknamed in Japanese jazz jargon) are reissued, the journals feature them as the newest "must" item for all listeners.

Japanese listener's guides are also unusual in indicating the appropriate "level" of the records and CDs, such as those "for the beginner," "for the advanced listener," and "for the dedicated collector." By establishing the "routes" and "stages" for gaining cultural distinction, the editors attempt to control the aesthetic and historic legitimacy of the music they cover. Like judo or ikebana masters, the conservative critics often insist on a "back-to-basics" philosophy, rebuking those beginner listeners who are inclined to buy records graded for "advanced" audiences in order to pretend to be experts. A fanatical collector who claims a complete set of Rolling Stones' releases advises that one has to collect the official items first, before moving to the unofficial "bootlegs." Such a sequence is the "fanatics' Way" (Otaka 1998:83). In other words, records are graded as an indication of the collector's knowledge, economic standing, and cultural distinction. Little has changed since Hattori's 1924 parody and criticism of record collectors.

Such an emphasis on basics reinforces the reverence for record (and now CD) collecting. Profiles in these magazines usually stress the commitment and passion of noted collectors and the serendipity, good luck, and mistakes in their experiences. It seems that the quirkier the collector, the more popular the article. Through these published profiles, which match the voyeuristic desires of readers and exhibitionistic pride of collectors, even beginners discover just how demanding the *dō* (the "way" of a discipline or practice) is of record collecting.

This broad respect for collectors and connoisseurship has prompted a number of discographic publications. As we have seen, *Rekōdo Geijutsu* and *Suingu Jānaru* have driven a rising popularity of Western classical music and jazz since the 1950s. In 1987, a small publisher issued a discography titled *Kanzen Burū Nōto gaido* (Complete Blue Note Guide; VV. AA. 1987). The whole catalogue of this prestigious jazz label is arranged in chronological order, with short reviews; details of recording date, place, and personnel; and a small photo of the jacket cover. Because of its surprising sales (it is used by foreign collectors and record stores even though they do not read Japanese), the publisher subsequently produced volumes for other historical labels such as Prestige and Riverside, two distinguished jazz labels in the 1950s and 1960s.

An important difference between Japanese and Western discography conventions is that Western record catalogues supply recording dates and matrix number (number of master source), while Japanese discographies always feature record jacket photos with the data. A Western discography resembles a telephone book in size and look—pages filled with columns of numbers and names (undecipherable to the outsiders), while the Japanese counterpart is more akin to a shopping catalogue, a handy volume immediately useful for purchase; the records here are less catalogued as historical documents and more showcased as commodities circulating in a market. This is one more indication of the direct link of the Japanese collector media with a consumer economy.

It is symptomatic of recording-oriented consumerism that many Japanese music books for general readership also contain discographic information of music quoted. This is also true for translations whose originals had no such data. For example, the Japanese translation of Peter Manuel's *Popular Musics of the Non-Western World* (1988), a standard reference book of "world music," adds disc information in the translator's notes (sometimes even with jacket photos). A scholarly work is thus made useful as a consumer guide.

Grooves in the Market

Most record collectors are aware that records are essentially commodities. This is a basic difference from the freely circulating, privately recorded concert tapes (only when a bootlegger makes illegal discs from these source tapes do they acquire a price and become collector objects).[1] There are several sources of record prices, including books, auctions, brochures, and price lists issued by secondhand record stores. Collectors are always browsing record stores and carefully monitoring price guidebook lists.

Interestingly, Japan has no domestic record price books despite the large number of collectors. Rather, Japanese collectors refer to foreign sources, such as *Goldmine's Price Guide to Collectibles Jazz Albums 1949–1969* (1992) and *The Mainstream: Jazz Reference and Price Guide 1949–1965* (*O'Sullivan Woodside Record Collectors Reference and Price Guide*, Vol. 1), both of which have international reputations as standards. The order price lists distributed by influential record stores in the United States and other countries are also consulted. This lack of domestic price lists may be due to the limited readership of Japanese publications in the international market (except for the jazz label lists mentioned previously) and by record stores' efforts to price their commodities by themselves. This may be the reason for the scarcity of record auctions in Japan (although many Japanese collectors participate in international auctions abroad). Instead of auctions, Japanese record stores quite often present "fairs" or bargain sales for very specific record types (e.g., a "Swedish progressive rock" fair or "Japanese early 1960s female pop singers" bargain sale). And in major cities throughout Japan, there are annual record fairs, where vintage analog record stores from several cities converge to display their treasures. Collectors' enthusiasm reaches its peak at these fairs.

The popular music critic Otaka Toshikazu reported on two record markets in Tokyo during the summer of 1992. One of them, the All-Japan Record Festival opened at 11 a.m., but people began arriving as early as 4:30 a.m. As soon as the doors opened, collectors rushed into the hall and started battling one another to find and purchase their favorites. What he found most dramatic were collectors who dashed to the records on the wall (the most rare and valuable) and tore them off. Otaka observed that the attendees seldom looked at each other but were intent on browsing; he depicted them as "hunting dogs attacking their game" (1998:145). Nonetheless, he discovered that the early birds did not always catch the best worms. Often those coming later and browsing in a less hectic atmosphere had good luck finding what the earlier buyers overlooked. Each collector, he concluded, has his own tactics at such fairs.

Otaka also reported on the Tokyo International Music Exposition, which attracted some three thousand visitors despite the 1,000 yen ($8) admission. Its name was not an exaggeration; some thirty Japanese record stores were joined by about forty foreign dealers from the United States, the United Kingdom, Australia, and Italy. The vintage vinyl market is global, and Japan's position within it is privileged. The Internet of course has further connected the international and the domestic record markets in terms of commodities and price.

Collectors' relationships with the market are ambiguous. For example, a fan of Group Sounds records (a Japanese electric guitar band of the late 1960s) publicized his collecting needs through fanzines and general magazines, and became widely recognized as the "Group Sounds collector." Such publicity, understandably, has the double-edged effect of bringing forth sought-after records but also inflating prices. In this case, his collecting created a market for Group Sounds, such that one of his final acquisitions, a single by the obscure group, cost more than 300,000 yen (about $2,500 at the time). Even mediocre music can be worth gold overnight, and such drastic changes in market profile often affects collectors' strategies.

For instance, when publicity inflates the popularity and the price of the Blue Note originals, a Blue Note collector of modest means must decide whether to stick with the label despite the near impossibility of reaching completeness, or perhaps to admit reissues as part of his Blue Note collection, or even to shift to a more affordable but lesser known label. In other words, he must choose between an incomplete or mediocre collection of a famous label and a top-notch collection of a more obscure one. Of course even obscure records and record labels can become expensive overnight. In this case their collectors are applauded and envied for their foresight (although we found that the collectors themselves are seldom prescient about market value, but rather just working within limited means). Unlike antiques and art objects, there are no professional speculators and institutional collectors of records. Nevertheless, price is often the measure by which collections are appraised.

To define the profile of one's desired repertoire is an important step from ordinary listener to committed collector. There are no "record collectors" or even "jazz record collectors," but rather there are collectors of certain categories. For instance, there are collectors of soprano saxophone jazz recordings, of "Take the A Train" versions, of recordings done in Paris, of air-check bootlegs, of Detroit jazzmen, of song titles that contain place names, of jazz in ex-communist countries, and so on. One collector specializes in all records that have a connection to Andre Previn as composer, conductor, and pianist (VV. AA. 1996–97, vol. 1:17–19). The choice of "theme" depends not only on one's finances but also on one's personal narratives. The more precisely one specifies the range of one's collection, the more "advanced" (or "fanatic") he feels himself as a collector. More than the size of the collection it is the specificity that matters to many collectors. It is this singularity that defines their collector identity.

Shopping with the Enemy

Although the accelerated circulation of written and oral information targeted at collectors is reducing price differentials among dealers, there are still "great finds" here and there. Browsing record stores is no less important than scouring the price books. In addition to discovering a good buy, collectors frequent record stores to pick up current news of general market situation, bargains and sales, and store openings and closings. For regular customers, conversation with store managers and salesclerks is a necessary back channel for information.

Many of our interviewees confirmed that knowing one or two reliable store-keepers is indispensable not only for completing one's collection but also for breaking the collector's solitude. Many secondhand record storekeepers are or were themselves collectors and have "professional" knowledge about the records. They are professional not only because of their encyclopedic and cross-referential knowledge but also because of their relationship with collectors. That is, theirs is not a peer-competitive tie of buyer to buyer, but a commercial connection of seller and buyer. Knowing a friendly store manager will help fill out a collection by finding items in auction or from other collectors; they know and try to meet the needs of their regular customers. Such a supportive relationship always has another dimension because collectors are also suspicious about the pricing, especially when they discover much lower pricing elsewhere.

This is often where luck enters. Many collectors' stories have at least one episode about luck, about how they unexpectedly encountered something they had long sought or about how cheaply they bought a vintage record in a tiny unknown shop in a small town. The more one knows the structure and flow of record market, the less one "wastes" money for "rubbish." In this sense some compare collecting with gambling.

How can one know the location of treasure islands in the back streets? *Rekōdo mappu* (Record Map; VV. AA. 1988) is a guide of more than five hundred record stores in Japan with maps, addresses, and short comments. Before it first appeared in 1988, many collectors had their own small "territories" or their regular routes and stores. Now, however, *Record Map* has revealed what had been the secret refuges of particular collectors to a wide readership. To a jazz collector and store owner who has seen several customers with the book tucked under their arms in his or her store, the book has destroyed "the pleasure of discovering a tiny but high quality shop unpublicized in magazines and located far from the metropolitan center" as well as reducing the "probability of making a good buy behind the back of peer collectors because everyone knows every store" (interview by the authors, April 2000). In other terms, though, *Record Map*, revised every year, has liberated the record-collector world from an esoteric circle of experts.

Conclusion: Collecting Selves, Completing Shelves

Our research has been concerned with the significance of recordings in the reception of foreign jazz and classical music in modern Japan, with systematicity as a key concept of collection, with the relationships of record collectors to the print media and market and to each other as a subworld, and with the construction of personal identity through attachment to a material product and the sound it produces.[2]

Collecting records (or other objects) is a solitary practice, based on an exclusive and exclusionary relationship between subject and object. Collectors are ambivalent about their peers; it is a small world that is simultaneously supportive and antagonistic. Fellow collectors are the only ones who can appreciate the value of collected records but at the same time are fierce rivals. These mixed feelings of rivalry and sympathy demand a subtle communicative strategy from collectors, who may show off some acquisitions to some peers but hide the same or other records from others. There is much guessing, while communicating, of the level (or "extraordinariness") of a collection in terms of quality and quantity. Envy, jealousy, boasting and contempt are among the emotional qualities of collectors. Like *otaku* (nerd fans) of *manga* (comic art books and magazines) and other popular culture productions, record collectors are connected only through the objects they possess and those they seek to possess. Because none of the objects belong to individuals jointly (even spouses do not share collections), the individual collectors are competitive with one another. Their passive solitude is caricatured by their jargon for the record rack in record stores. They call it the *esabako* (feed box); they just "peck" the feed provided by the dealers as if they were broilers in the cage.

As we have argued earlier, record collecting displays all three dimensions of Pearce's (1995) model: souvenir, fetish, and system. In fact, many collectors and collectors' narratives emphasize the latter two, while downplaying the first. That is, they insist on differentiating themselves from the general audience who listen to reproduced music only from fondness and memory. But recollection is often the core motivation of collectors. For example, a Rolling Stones collector once sold his entire collection (4,500 records) except the 200 records that had intimate memory associations for him (VV. AA. 1996–97, vol. 1:62). In part because of severe housing limitations in Japan, many collectors have a similar experience of selling their entire collections (or a major share) after they felt that they had achieved a goal of completeness. Such periodic selling certainly stimulates a market flow and a circulation of commodities. All the record collectors we interviewed agree that it is ultimately the sound cut in the black grooves that matters. It is the sound that evokes recollection even if they rarely play their precious acquisitions (on collection and recollection, see Stewart 1991). The advent of the phonograph meant that "music [became] a thing," as Evan Eisenberg put it succinctly (1987:ch. 2; on Theodor Adorno's similar conclusion, see Levin

1990; on the general aesthetic discussion of recorded sound, see Hosokawa 1991). That records are material objects that reproduce sound is an essential trait, compared with posters, T-shirts, character goods, autographs, and other collectibles and ephemera.

The fanaticism of collectors is colloquially rendered in Japanese as *byōki* (a sickness). Because the collectors are aware that they are labeled as perverse, obstinate, narcissistic, and esoteric, they rarely show off their collector's identity to outsiders. Such a stereotyping reinforces the affective bond with the collectors' world in spite of the constant rivalry among each of the members. Such a conflict between extremity and moderation is pertinent to the construction of collector's identity.

Acknowledgments

We are grateful to the following interviewees who generously collaborated with us: Ebihara Masahiko, Ishikawa Satoshi, Oyama Satoshi, Segawa Masahisa, Sugihara Yukihiro, and Takahashi Hiroshi. A preliminary version of this chapter was presented at the JAWS Conference at the National Museum of Ethnology, Osaka, Japan, in March 1999.

Notes

1. Of course, sometimes items distributed for free (for example, Christmas records by The Beatles) have become expensive market goods because of their rarity.

2. In this chapter we have left aside several important issues because they deserve more attention than we can give them here. First, we have not dealt with the relationship of record collectors and audiophiles. Though some can purchase as many records and audio sets as they want, many give priority to one over the other. A limited budget is the most common reason for this. But is this sufficient to explain the difference between an orientation toward the music and an orientation to the sounds? Second, we have also left aside the issue of gender. Why are almost all record collectors, audiences, and performers in this genre male? Will Straw (1997) explains the homosocial structure of the record-collecting community by the close ties between masculinity, power, and taxonomic knowledge. He may be correct here, but this still fails to account for the passion among females for collecting artists' goods such as posters and dolls (see Stevens, chapter 3, this volume). Third, we have not examined the recent influence of the Internet. The emergence of internet auctions such as eBay has certainly changed the profile of record collecting in Japan. A remarkable number of Japanese collectors are thought to use eBay, which allows direct access to American and European vinyl markets. The number of analog discs featured on eBay is enormous (for example, on April 5, 2002, 7,019 records were being offered). eBay is also significant for its search function. One can search by label, name of player or composer, title of record, and other fields. The sophisticated search function is tending to split

the sales market. Showing some of his prized eBay purchases to one of the authors, a vinyl collector added that collectors tend to focus on famous labels like Blue Note and Prestige in jazz and UK Decca in classical music; the concentration of bids for such labels is driving up eBay prices over vinyl stores. On the other hand, rare records of lesser known labels tend not to draw collectors' attention and can be found at prices below those of vinyl stores. This is where a new niche is emerging. As the collector noted, "You can get very rare records cheaply if you search eBay thoroughly." Finally, we have passed over the DJ and the club music scenes in which the vinyl records regain their musical and practical values because club DJs and collectors have quite different views of record value.

References Cited

Barthes, Roland
    1982   Le grain de la voix. *In* L'obvie et l'obtus. Pp. 236–245. Paris: Éditions Du Seuil.

Benjamin, Walter
    1969   The Work of Art in the Age of Mechanical Reproduction. *In* Illuminations. Hannah Arendt, ed. Harry Zohn, trans. Pp. 219–253. New York: Schocken Books.

Derschmidt, Eckhart
    1998   The Disappearance of the "Jazu-Kissa": Some Considerations about Japanese "Jazz-Cafés" and Jazz Listeners. *In* The Culture of Japan as Seen through Its Leisure. Sepp Linhart and Sabine Frühstück, eds. Pp. 303–315. Albany: State University of New York Press.

Eisenberg, Evan
    1987   The Recording Angel: Music, Records and Culture from Aristotle to Zappa. London: Picador.

Gronow, Pekka
    1983   The Record Industry: The Growth of Mass Medium. Popular Music 3:53–75.

Hattori Ryūtarō
    1924   Rekōdo no eramikata to kikikata (How to select and listen to records). Tokyo: Arususha.

Hosokawa Shuhei
    1991   Rekōdo no bigaku (The aesthetics of records). Tokyo: Keisō shobō.
    1998   The Edisonian Era in Japan: The Early Years (1877–1914). *In* Studies in Socio-Musical Sciences. Joachim Braun and Uri Sharvit, eds. Pp. 191–203. Ramat-Gan: Bar-Ilan University Press.

Iwasaki Masamichi
    1936   Omoide no chikuonki ongakukai (Memories of gramophone concerts). Rekōdo ongaku (Record music) (November): 46–52.

Jin'no Yuki
    1994   Shumi no tanjō: Hyakkaten ga tsukutta teisuto (The invention of taste: The taste that department stores made). Tokyo: Keisō Shobō.

Kurata Yoshihiro
 1979   Nihon record bunka-shi (Cultural history of recording in Japan). Tokyo:
         Tokyo shoseki.

Levin Thomas Y.
 1990   For the Record: Adorno on Music in the Age of Its Technological Reproduc-
         tivity. October: 23–47.

Manuel, Peter
 1988   Popular Musics of the Non-Western World: An Introductory Survey (Hiseiyō no
         popyurā ongaku). Nakamura Tōyō, trans. New York: Oxford University Press.

Moore, Jerrold Northrop
 1999   Sound Revolutions: A Biography of Fred Gaisberg, Founding Father of
         Commercial Sound Recording. London: Sanctuary Publishing.

Mitchell, W. J. T.
 1986   Iconology: Image, Text, Ideology. Chicago: University of Chicago Press.

Nomura Araebisu
 1931   Chikuonki to rekōdo tsū (Connoisseurs of phonographs and records). Tokyo:
         Shiroku shoin.

Otaka Toshikazu, ed.
 1998   Rekōdo korekutā shinshiroku (Who's who of the record collectors). Tokyo:
         Myūzikku Magazine-sha.

Pearce, Susan M.
 1995   On Collecting: An Investigation into Collecting in the European Tradition.
         New York: Routledge.

Stewart, Susan
 1991   On Longing. Durham: Duke University Press.

Straw, Will
 1997   Sizing Up Record Collections: Gender and Connoisseurship in Rock Music
         Culture. In Sexing the Groove: Popular Music and Gender. Sheila Whitely, ed.
         Pp. 3–16. New York: Routledge.

VV. AA.
 1987   Kanzen Burūnōto gaido (Complete Blue Note Guide). Tokyo: Jazu hyōron-sha.
 1988   Rekōdo mappu (Record map). Tokyo: Gakuyō shobō.
 1996–97 Oto no shosai (The drawing rooms of sound). 2 vols. Tokyo: Ongaku no
         tomosha.

8

Girls and Women Getting Out of Hand

The Pleasure and Politics of Japan's Amateur Comics Community

MATTHEW THORN

Of all the productions of Japanese popular culture in the second half of the 20th century, the most highly developed and commercially successful has been *manga* (comic art magazines and books), and the closely related *anime* (film, video, and digital animations). It is hard to exaggerate their commercial success and influence. Manga magazines and books represent more than one-third of unit sales (and nearly one-quarter of gross revenues) of all publications in Japan. In 2001, more than 1.9 billion manga magazines and books were sold, with gross revenues totaling 531 billion yen ($5 billion). Many of those sold were *shōjo manga* (girls' comics) or so-called ladies' comics (intended specifically for adult women).[1]

A recent survey reported that 42 percent of Japanese women between the ages of 20 and 49, and 81 percent of teen girls read manga with some regularity.[2] At any time, there are more than one hundred manga magazines in circulation that target female readers of many different age brackets and specific tastes. The best selling of these, *Ribbon* (published by Shueisha), has a monthly circulation of well over one million copies. Nearly all the artists who create shōjo manga are women, and the most successful of them, such as *Sailor Moon* creator Takeuchi Naoko, are multimillionaires.

The subject of Japanese comic art has drawn a number of studies, and I myself have extensively studied commercial shōjo and women's manga,[3] but my attention here is directed to another, equally remarkable development of the manga world in Japan, which is the proliferation of what are known as *dōjinshi*.

These are self-published manga by amateur fan–artists, working either alone or in groups, producing what are inspired by, in tribute to, or a takeoff of popular commercial manga series. This chapter focuses on this creative outpouring by female manga fans, and especially on the venues in which they are displayed and circulated.

In this world of self-publication, artists and writers find—or rather create—avenues of expression beyond those offered by mainstream, commercial publishing. This may sound like a modest undertaking, but in fact there are a great many people who do care to buy such wares, and they do so at events known formally as *dōjinshi sokubai kai*. The term literally means a market of self-published magazines, but participants tend to call them simply *ibento* (events). They are enormous public gatherings of amateur artists and writers selling the comic books, fiction, illustrations, and so forth that they have created to anyone who comes to buy them.

These gatherings can indeed be huge events. The largest by far is the Tokyo Komikku Māketto, or "Comic Market," a semiannual, multiday convention attended by an estimated 400 thousand people (see http://www.comiket.co.jp/). However, even the smaller, one-day events held in cities throughout Japan are attended by thousands and even tens of thousands. Those who flock to these events—to buy what the artists create or simply to revel in the happening—find alternatives to mainstream publications and also discover—or rather create—a powerful, if sometimes fragmented, experience of community.

Most strikingly—at least it was to me when I first encountered this community—the majority of participants are women and girls. These fanzine conventions, from the awesome Tokyo Comic Market to the smallest local events, are in many ways about gender and sexuality, both in what one finds in the pages of the books offered for sale and in what goes on between and within the convention participants themselves. This chapter explores some of the gender politics—personal and public, abstract and concrete, artistic and pragmatic—in this community that has grown so large that "counterculture" seems an inappropriate label.

The first dōjinshi market I ever attended was held in Osaka in August 1993. At the time, I was conducting research on readers of shōjo manga, and I had heard from several informants about amateur, self-published manga that focused on stories of same-sex love between boys or men. This theme, known as *shōnen ai* (boys' love), first appeared in commercial shōjo manga in the early 1970s. It enjoyed tremendous popularity for about a decade, but by the late 1980s, this was waning.[4] However, my informants reported that it remained the dominant theme in amateur manga for girls and women, and that these manga enjoyed an enthusiastic and devoted following.

Arriving at the convention center on the morning of the event, I found myself amid tens of thousands of people, overwhelmingly female, anxiously awaiting the event to begin. When the gates were opened, there was a rush as experienced fans, armed with the event's catalog and map, hurried to the booths of the "major" *sākuru* (circles) before the lines grew too long. "Circle" refers to an individual or group of people who publish something to be sold at an event. Although the majority of dōjinshi circles today are actually single individuals, the term remains as a carryover from the days of mimeographing, when self-publication was beyond individual means.[5] Examining the catalog, I found that the circles—more than five thousand in number—were grouped by genre. Most of the genre labels, such as Cyber Formula, Trooper, and Entertainment, were incomprehensible to me at the time, but to the side of one of the four halls was a modest-sized group of booths labeled "shōjo manga, et cetera." For someone studying shōjo manga, this seemed the obvious place to begin.

There I found, not original manga done in the shōjo manga style, as I had expected, but rather takeoffs of commercial shōjo manga, most of which featured some degree of romantic tension between two male characters. For example, about eighteen of the circles featured takeoffs on Yoshida Akimi's popular shōjo manga, *BANANA FISH* (Yoshida 1998). Yoshida's original story had a heavy homoerotic slant, but these fans had expanded that element, or extended it to secondary male characters from the same story. I was further puzzled that only this corner of this one hall was classified as "shōjo manga." If over 80 percent of the participants were women and girls, what was the rest of the material on display?

I soon realized that my confusion stemmed from misunderstanding the nomenclature. For example, the section of tables I first examined was labeled "shōjo manga" because they featured takeoffs of commercial shōjo manga. The kind of original amateur manga I had expected were in another section labeled "original"—although such original manga accounted for only about seven percent of all the circles. Almost all of the rest were takeoffs of various types of commercial manga and animation. These are generally called *parodi* (parody), although the term does not necessarily have the connotation of satire implicit in the original English term. Most of these parodies—that is, most of the material offered for sale—were classified loosely as *yaoi*.

Yaoi is an acronym for the phrase, "<u>Ya</u>ma nashi, <u>o</u>chi nashi, <u>i</u>mi nashi" (No Climax, No Resolution, No Meaning), which was coined in the late 1980s to describe this new genre of amateur manga. Until the mid-1980s, the amateur manga world was composed largely of would-be professional manga artists, amateur manga critics, and the fan clubs of professional artists. In 1985, however, a group of young women artists began producing a series of spin-offs of the popular boys' soccer manga *Captain Tsubasa*, in which the two young male heroes were portrayed as lovers. Of course, the original manga, created by a male artist with a young male audience in mind, had no such theme of homosexual love. Like many boys' manga, it is a story of male friendship, bonding, and rivalry. But these female fans read into the story—its setting and characters—the possibility of male bonding yielding to homoerotic desire.

This formula—which came to be synonymous with yaoi—proved to be a stunning hit, and similar *Captain Tsubasa* takeoffs began to appear in huge numbers, rapidly increasing the population of the amateur manga community. *Captain Tsubasa* was followed by takeoffs of such boys' manga and animation hits as *Saint Seiya, Tenkuu Senki Shurato, Yoroiden Samurai Trooper,* and *Ginga Eiyū Densetsu.* Such internationally renowned manga as *Dragonball* and *Slam Dunk* have also been subjects of intense yaoi-ization.

The term *yaoi* refers to the fact that some of these takeoffs did not purport to be fully developed stories, but were rather just scenes and snippets, *oishii tokoro dake* (only the yummy parts). What constituted a "yummy part" was usually a scene in which the two male protagonists are brought by circumstance into physical contact with each other. There is an awkward moment, and then one makes an aggressive move, perhaps initiating a kiss. The other resists, but it is clear that the feelings are mutual. Some artists will end the scene here, preserving the tension between the two. Others will treat readers to several pages of skin, tangled sheets, sweat, and other bodily fluids. Many so-called yaoi manga, however, are genuine stories, often with plots stretching over many volumes, leading some fans to suggest alternative meanings of the acronym, such as "Yamete, oshiri ga itai" (Stop, my ass hurts).

I should note here that an almost identical genre developed in the English-speaking world, quite independently of yaoi. Known as "slash," this fan-lit pairs male protagonists from such television programs as *Star Trek, Blake's 7, Babylon 5,* and *X Men* and casts them as lovers (Bacon-Smith 1992; Jenkins 1992; Penley 1992). Like yaoi, these takeoffs of commercial programs have been created largely by and for heterosexual women. Also like yaoi, they range from restrained portrayals of homoerotic tension to explicit depictions of sexual intercourse. Unlike yaoi, the form they take is usually text-based fiction or illustrations.

Yaoi fans are usually surprised to hear that there is an English-language equivalent to yaoi, but it seems that most slash fans have become aware of the Japanese counterpart to the genre they love, due primarily to the introduction in the mid-1980s of a fan-produced, unauthorized translation of several volumes of Aoike Yasuko's commercial shōjo manga *Eroika yori ai o komete* (From Eroica With Love). *Eroica* portrays the adventures of a flamboyant and unabashedly gay art thief, who goes by the nickname Eroica, and the rigidly masculine German intelligence officer who hunts him. Although the manga, which was produced in the 1970s and early 1980s, was never fodder for many yaoi artists in Japan (an openly homosexual element tends to take the mischievous fun out of yaoi-izing), it has enjoyed a passionate following among certain slash fans, who have produced a large body of fiction and illustrations based on *Eroica.* Knowledge of yaoi outside Japan has since grown exponentially, thanks to the Internet. There is a yaoi category on Yahoo!, and a search of the web for the term *yaoi* will turn up thousands of fan pages from around the globe.

The independent rise of identical genres in Japan and the English-speaking world is a striking coincidence. I have received e-mail from women around the world who stumbled onto my shōjo manga home page and were stunned to find that many Japanese women enjoy the same kind of male love stories they themselves do. Clearly, there is something about this formula that pushes the buttons, so to speak, of a certain demographic of women throughout much of the industrialized world. Later, I will suggest just what that something might be.

What distinguishes yaoi from slash and other similar genres is the scale. As I will describe, yaoi has become a mainstream form, enjoyed by hundreds of thousands of women and girls. In the English-speaking world, however, slash fiction engages only a very small community, which has endured the contempt of the wider science-fiction fandom for more than two decades. Perhaps because of Western homophobia, slash fans are both scorned by others and compelled, it would seem, to justify their hobby to themselves and to the world. Many slash fans are "closeted," and very secretive about their hobby, although the Internet is leading to a massive "coming out." Many fear outside persecution, including being sued for copyright infringement. In the current environment of open lobbying for homosexual rights, some fans seem to feel the need to justify slash to the gay community, or even to reform slash in such a way as to make it more palatable or "politically correct." Among yaoi producers and fans, I have seen no such tensions, and I want to discuss why this might be.

With the introduction of yaoi, attendance figures at the Tokyo Comic Market shot from five digits to six. Stories began to appear regularly in the mass media about the amateur manga world, and various groups saw potential profits to be made. Commercial publishers began publishing anthologies of amateur yaoi-style manga and scouted popular amateur artists, such as Ozaki Minami (who once specialized in *Captain Tsubasa* takeoffs) and Kōga Yun (who made her mark with *Saint Seiya* takeoffs). Other entrepreneurs, noting the relative isolation of fans and artists living outside the Tokyo area, formed companies to organize events such as Comic City and Comic Live throughout Japan. Today, there are roughly a dozen commercial magazines dedicated to the genre, and the ranks of artists working in such magazines are, of course, recruited directly from the amateur manga world. For reasons of copyright law, most such magazines do not print blatant takeoffs of other commercial manga or anime, but instead feature original stories incorporating similar themes. I know of one case, however, in which a pair of male pop singers, known as "access," authorized an "official" yaoi-style manga featuring themselves as lovers. This was tied in with various promotions, and I was left with the impression that this very popular duo was formed from the start with a yaoi marketing angle in mind. Needless to say, for the duration of their (rather brief) popularity, there were also plenty of unauthorized yaoi-izations of the duo to be found at the Comic Market and other events.

Meanwhile, back at that event in 1993, I was feeling overwhelmed. There was a powerful energy in the air; this space belonged to these girls and women, and they were reveling in it. I envied the electric sense of community they shared, but I did not have the courage to initiate many conversations.

I should note that there were some men there. By my rough estimate, they were perhaps 15–20 percent of the participants, and they were mostly clustered in one corner of one hall around a section of tables labeled *bishōjo* (beautiful girls.) "Beautiful Girls" refers to what are essentially pornographic manga created largely by and for heterosexual men, and featuring female characters below the age of 18. At the time, I knew little about this genre and the men who were creating and enjoying it. Certainly the aura I felt emanating from that corner was, well, creepy. The few women whom I asked about it characterized "that corner" and the men occupying it in similarly unflattering terms. In retrospect, it seems that the perceived "creepiness" may have been a factor of numbers; there simply were not enough men to create an atmosphere of relaxation and festivity comparable to that enjoyed by the women. Indeed, today the Tokyo Comic Market draws far more male participants than it did a decade ago, and though the materials they sell and buy are the same, the atmosphere is far more cheerful, and I do not hear the female participants complaining about the men as much.

At three o'clock, the close of the event was announced over the public address system, and there was a burst of applause from both buyers and sellers. Here and there bouquets of flowers changed hands, presumably as congratulations for a job well done. As I lingered, my eye was drawn to a cluster of six young women. They were taking group photographs, and at the center was a woman with short hair wearing black jeans, a white blouse, a black vest, and black leather gloves with the fingers cut off. I thought she looked really cool, and her more femininely dressed friends seemed to think so, too. They giggled and fawned, and she seemed to enjoy the attention. It was as if a scene from the all-female Takarazuka Review was being played out before my eyes. What I was seeing may have been an expression of homoeroticism, plain and simple, but I suspect it was something more complex. I left my first event feeling that I had only scratched the surface.

In the summer of 1995, feeling somewhat oriented to the world of dōjinshi and yaoi, I attended my first Tokyo Comic Market. The Comic Market was first held in 1975; it featured 33 circles and drew about six to seven hundred participants. According to Yonezawa Yoshihiro, the current head of the Komikku māketto junbi kai (Comic Market Preparation Association), the Comic Market was founded as a forum for free expression at a time when Japanese popular culture was characterized by homogeneity and a lack of outlets for alternative media. Today, the Comic Market is a dual organization. The real work is carried out by the Comic Market Preparation Association, a nonprofit organization of volunteers. A legal corporation, Comiket Incorporated, exists in conjunction to facilitate such business matters as the renting of space and the handling of taxes. The Preparation Association today consists of 1,800 volunteer staff, whose only compensation is travel expenses and, literally, a free lunch. Since the market is held only twice a year (a three-day summer gathering and a two-day winter event), the vast majority of staff have little organizational experience. They are overseen by a small core of veteran Comic Market staffers who bear the real burden of running this enormous event.

The Preparation Association proclaims in its literature that the Comic Market is open to anyone willing to follow its rules, but in fact the number of circles who would like to sell their wares at the Comic Market greatly exceeds the capacity of the facilities. The Comic Market is currently held at the imaginatively named Tokyo Big Site, a fairly new convention center that is the largest in Japan. The Summer 2001 Comic Market featured 35,000 circles over three days. Those 35,000 were selected by lottery from 52,000 applicants, which means that roughly one-third were rejected. The number of attendees was 480,000.[6]

The Comic Market was as enormous as I had been led to expect, yet I could not help feeling that this giant of all fan events lacked the intense energy, the palatable sense of community, that I had felt previously in the smaller events I had attended. Comic Market organizers I spoke with concurred. Yonezawa told me that the event had grown so large and so segmented that it lacked the overall sense of community it once had, and which can still be found in many smaller gatherings. Nonetheless, in spite of this sprawl, the Comic Market did retain a festival-like character—a liminal space and time, where participants could shed many of the restraints of mundane society.

Many of those coming to these conventions create and wear elaborate costumes, modeled on characters from their favorite manga, anime or video games. Known as *kosupure* (costume play or cos-play for short), this is so popular at the Comic Market and other events that dressing rooms are provided and rules have been created to avoid cos-play-related trouble. Each day of the event, an average of forty-five hundred people (80 percent female) register for dressing room access.

It is said that the first cos-play ever performed at a fan event in Japan was that of a young woman portraying Tezuka Osamu's character Umi no Toriton (Triton of the Sea) back in 1978. But contrary to popular belief this performance took place not at the Comic Market but at the "Ashicon" science-fiction convention, and was performed by none other than the then 20-year-old Kotani Mari, now renowned as a critic and author of science fiction.[7] According to Minoura (1998), cos-play in the context of the Comic Market was originally intended as a role-playing fantasy. The cos-player could "become" the character she or he admired, if only for a day. By the late 1980s, however, the point of cos-play became not to pretend to be a favorite character, but rather to be photographed. Photographers (mostly male, many working for shady pornographic magazines) began to come in hordes, and for the first time there began to appear cos-players who had no involvement or even interest in selling or buying books, but were strictly there to be seen. Such cos-players choose characters based less on their own taste than on what they think will attract the most photographic attention. Friction began to develop between the cos-players and the traditional participants, who saw the newcomers (and photographers) as a major nuisance. Comic Market organizers, rather than banning cos-play, segregated it, creating dressing rooms (the use of which requires registration) and setting aside a large space specifically for cos-players and their photographers. (Photography outside the cos-play area is strictly forbidden to anyone not registered as a member of the press.) Rules were also created to prevent accidents (e.g., no costumes with sharp protrusions). Of course, as long as one follows the safety rules, she or he can wear anything that does not require a change of clothes (which is to say, anything one would not mind being seen wearing on a train), so there is plenty of "cos-play lite" to be seen beyond the cos-play area.

Cos-play often entails cross-dressing, so that one sees women dressed as the dashing, úniformed heroes of *Gundam Wing* alongside men dressed as *Sailor Moon*. One occasionally witnesses eroticized teasing, particularly on the part of cross-dressed cos-players, who will make suggestive comments to or fondle fellow participants of either sex, who are usually happy to play along. When cross-dressing is involved, there are always multilayered heterosexual and homosexual tensions. When a woman dressed as a man makes a pass at another woman, she is "playing at" heterosexuality, but the fact that she is biologically a woman creates an obvious homosexual element. If the other woman is herself dressed as a man, then the two are "playing at" male homosexuality, yet there is also a suggestion of female homosexuality, since both are biologically women, and, because each woman is ostensibly reacting to the performed "masculinity" of the other, there is a heterosexual nuance as well. Similarly, when a woman dressed as a man is flirting with a man dressed as a woman, there is a double-reverse heterosexual element, yet, again, since each is reacting to the performed gender of the other, there is also an element of homosexuality.

Similar erotic play has been noted in carnivals and other liminal settings, but it is the term *queer* as used by Alexander Doty that I believe best captures both the cos-play itself and the fans and creators of amateur manga's most popular genre, yaoi. In *Making Things Perfectly Queer*, Doty uses the term *queer*

> to question the cultural demarcations between the queer and the straight . . . by pointing out the queerness of and in straights and straight cultures, as well as that of individuals and groups who have been told they inhabit the boundaries between the binaries of gender and sexuality. . . . Queer would . . . describe the image of Katherine Hepburn dressed as a young man in Sylvia Scarlett, as it evokes a complex, often uncategorizable, erotic responses from spectators who claim all sorts of real-life sexual identities. [Doty 1993:xv–xvi]

Even when one is cos-playing a character of the same sex, I believe one is very much "playing gender." Women who in daily life might be seen as plain are transformed into pheromone-exuding ultrafemales, and similar sorts of men can suddenly become icons of idealized masculinity.

One might argue that the entire amateur manga world, and not just the cos-play aspect, is finally about gender and sexuality. It is not just the cross-dressing cos-players who are queer. When I ask creators and fans of yaoi why they like the genre, they often equivocate. One standard response is that stories of heterosexual romance, such as those common in shōjo manga, are boring because they are predictable. When one yaoi artist, who makes a living as a professional manga artist's assistant, offered this reason, I pointed out that yaoi tended to be as formulaic as heterosexual romance stories. She laughed and replied, "Yes, but this is the formula I like." Another fan expanded on this, saying that a heterosexual romance is always limited by the fact that the heroine and the hero, no matter what the circumstances, are ultimately following society's mainstream norm of mating. In a yaoi story, the two male characters are inexorably drawn to each other, in spite of social proscriptions and their own desire to avoid such a taboo relationship (see Figure 8.1). The inadequacy of this reasoning is that it does not explain why the taboo relationship has to be one between two men, rather than two women or some other pairing or grouping.

Most of the women and girls I have asked have simply said they like such stories: "They're exciting." "They're moving." "They're beautiful." These stories give them pleasure, and that is good enough for most readers. The stories tend to be almost stubbornly apolitical. Most of the characters insist, "I'm not gay, I'm just passionately in love with this one person, who happens to be a man." That such a relationship is taboo is the sine qua non of the genre, but that fact is never addressed politically. In fact, some gay male activists in Japan have blasted yaoi as offensive to homosexuals.

Some readers have told me they enjoy the stories because they present an idealized masculine world. Some speak of despising femininity, and even of wishing they had been born male, rather than female. For most such women, yaoi and boys' love allow them to indulge in the fantasy of loving a man *as a man*, or, to rephrase it, as an equal, free of predefined gender expectations. In her book *Yaoi genron* (1998), Sakakibara Shihomi, herself a popular yaoi-style novelist, describes herself as a gay man in a woman's body (a "female-to-male gay" transsexual). S/he suggests that this condition may be quite common among fans of this genre and may, in fact, be the reason for its existence.[8] Nonetheless, I think there is an undeniable voyeuristic element, because most readers and artists are, in fact, females.

Many fans also clearly take pleasure in seeing their male characters suffer. It is common for male characters to be raped, even (or perhaps most notably) by the men who love them. This, too, suggests that, while readers may imagine themselves in the place of one of the male characters, they may be objectifying them at the same time. It may be that some artists (not to mention their readers), by projecting experiences of abuse onto male characters, are able to come to terms in some way with their own experiences of abuse.

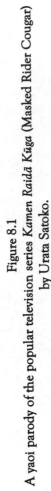

Figure 8.1
A yaoi parody of the popular television series *Kamen Raidā Kūga* (Masked Rider Cougar)
by Urata Satoko.

This aspect of projection has been noted by others. The feminist sociologist Ueno Chizuko has asserted that "male homosexuality [in shōjo manga] was a safety device that allowed [girls] to operate this dangerous thing called 'sex' at a distance from [their] own bodies; *it was the wings that enabled girls to fly*" (1998:131). Shōjo manga essayist Fujimoto Yukari has argued that, through the abuse to which women artists and writers subject male characters, and which is particularly prominent in yaoi, "women are freed from the position of being unilaterally violated, and gain the perspective of the violator, of the one who watches" (p. 140). Fujimoto has even asserted that this genre is rooted in women's self-loathing. For girls, she says, sexuality is a thing to be feared and ashamed of, not something that can be explored frankly and aggressively. Artists use the voices of male characters to express contempt for women's sexual passivity and timidity, and yet, ironically, in doing so they force readers to face the unjust standards that Japanese society imposes on women. Fujimoto writes, "In other words, these [expressions of] misogyny reverse themselves, exposing the mechanism that makes women's self-loathing inevitable, and begin to reverberate as words of understanding for [the position of] women" (p. 141). Finally, noted shōjo manga artist Takemiya Keiko, best known for her boys' love classic, *Kaze to ki no uta* (The Song of the Wind and the Trees) has also argued that the boys' love genre is a "first step towards true feminism" (1993:82).

There can be little doubt that both the artists and the readers who are drawn to boys' love and yaoi are unhappy with mainstream norms of gender and sexuality. And while they speak fondly of *otoko no sekai* (world of men), and seem to prefer masculinity over femininity, yaoi artists and writers show contempt for "straight" masculinity, just as they scorn standardized femininity. In every yaoi story, there is a *seme* (an aggressor), and an *uke* (a recipient or "target"). The seme comes to accept his feelings early on, and pursues the uke until he relents. It can be said that the story climaxes when the uke abandons conventional masculinity and, in a sense, accepts that he is *hen*, a word that can be translated as "strange," "odd," or "queer."[9]

Perhaps the reader can thus understand why I characterize this genre and its fans as "queer." The women and girls in this community may never display their dissatisfaction with mainstream norms of gender and sexuality in front of their more conventional peers, but they give expression to it in the liminal space of the "event," and every time they read or draw or write a story in this genre.

Fans acknowledge the subversive potential of their passion when they jokingly describe it, as they so often do, as *yabai*, *abunai*, or *ayashii*, words meaning "dangerous" or "suspect."[10] But beyond the treatment of gender and sexuality in these stories, there is another subversive potential in this community. Feminists, both in Japan and elsewhere, have noted that mass media tend to be male dominated because access to its expensive technology and labor is limited to the corporate capital that has so marginalized women. Manga is an exception, however; like literature, it is a medium that requires very little capital, and this may be an important reason why it has become a lucrative form of income for so many women artists. Amateur manga, in turn, while generating income only for the most popular artists, provide women and girls with an inexpensive means of self-expression, utterly free of editorial restrictions. In commercial manga magazines, by contrast, the top editors are almost all male, and will not publish pieces that violate "editorial policy." Yet even commercial publishers have created "alternative" manga magazines as well as lines of novels dedicated to this genre. They can be bought in any Japanese bookstore and even many convenience stores. And those looking for the "hard stuff" can join the hundreds of thousands of women and girls who make the trek to the Comic Market and similar events.

Considering these characteristics of yaoi fandom, I think we can appreciate why yaoi and slash-style fan productions find favor among a certain demographic cohort of women in many industrialized nations. I would argue that what these fans share in common is discontent with the standards of femininity to which they are expected to adhere and a social environment and historical moment that does not validate or sympathize with that discontent. In the case of America, I find that it is primarily women from rather conservative backgrounds who are presently drawn to this genre. They are more often from small towns or rural areas than from metropolitan centers, and it may well be that their home communities are at such a point of development as to expose profound contradictions between their current socioeconomic structure and ingrained gender values. Such situations give rise to what Betty Friedan forty years ago labeled the "feminine mystique." For most middle-class urban and suburban women, those felt contradictions manifested themselves in the 1970s and fueled the women's lib movement. It may be, though, that the initial wave of proto-feminist consciousnes is still moving slowly through the pink- and blue-collar classes in more provincial regions, inspiring new fans of the slash genre along the way. Indeed, my impression is that the heyday of slash was in the late 1970s and early 1980s, when feminist consciousness was finally permeating the mainstream to an unprecedented degree.

One precondition for slash and yaoi fandom is an awareness of homosexuality, which nonetheless remains largely abstract. Direct familiarity with homosexuality as practice may inevitably dilute the thrill of slash, which draws on a sense of taboo violation. Further, the introduction of overt politics into a romance narrative is a turnoff to many readers. Thus it may be that slash (and yaoi) simply do not appeal to women who feel less constrained by gender constructs (which is to say, those raised in a more progressive social environment with more developed feminist consciousness) and for whom homosexuality has little sense of taboo.

Statements of fans of slash and yaoi from other countries (including Italy, Brazil, Mexico, and the Philippines) with whom I have corresponded support this view. These fans complain that they are considered by family and peers to be perverts indulging in unhealthy fantasies, or are so worried about eliciting such reactions that they keep their interest to themselves, "coming out" only to a small number of fellow fans.

In the case of Japan, the enormous popularity of yaoi in both urban and rural areas indicates to me that the society as a whole may be lodged in Freidan's "feminine mystique" phase. Although there has been an indigenous feminist movement in Japan for more than a century, progress made during the 1970s (when the boys' love genre first appeared and gained popularity) and the early 1980s (when yaoi took off in the amateur manga world) halted abruptly with the burst of the economic bubble in the late 1980s. Similarly, awareness of homosexuality is widespread yet severely distorted, and gay political activists have been largely frustrated in their attempts to influence public discourse. In short, conditions are ripe for this genre to flourish. If we accept Takemiya's argument that boys' love is a first step toward feminism, then it may be that mainstream Japanese women have yet to take the second or third step. They stand on the threshold, in a liminal space, fraught with contradictions and ambiguities, where yaoi remains a salient attraction.

Nonetheless, we must acknowledge that even in Japan the majority of women do not find yaoi or boys' love particularly appealing. One person I have interviewed about yaoi and slash is an American woman with a singular biography. Once a great fan of slash, she discovered yaoi and was so drawn into that genre that she went on to learn to speak and read Japanese fluently, and now works in Tokyo as a professional editor of commercial yaoi anthologies. She feels strongly that an attraction to both slash and yaoi is "hardwired"; if you've got it, you can't avoid it, and if you don't, it's meaningless to you. This is essentially what Sakakibara (1998) argues, though in different terms, when she claims that yaoi fans are "gay men born in women's bodies." Although traditional, essentialist notions of gender were debunked by feminism, feminist formulations of radical constructionism have themselves come under serious scrutiny. Nature and nurture may condition one another in complex ways, and it may be that notions like a "gay man in a woman's body" (or a "lesbian in a man's body"), and indeed the concept of "transsexuality" are awkward attempts to describe manifestations for which we still lack an adequate analysis. My own conviction from a decade of researching shōjo manga and yaoi is that such is the case with these fans, although it will require much more to substantiate this claim.

But what of the men and the boys who participate in this community? In the first event I attended, males and females seemed to go their very separate ways. Notable exceptions were those men who could be found, not in the Beautiful Girls section ogling pornographic manga for men, but at the yaoi tables chatting excitedly with women and girls. In contrast to the drab men in the Beautiful Girls corner, these men and boys were very fashion conscious, sometimes even partially or wholly cross-dressed. Some of these males may have been gay, but not all. Here were men who understood, or at least were trying to understand, what these women were doing in their manga- and text-based fiction, and were communicating with them. But they were a very small minority.

In the summer of 1998, I attended the Comic Market for the first time in three years, and was struck by certain changes, most particularly by the gender dynamics of the participants. The Tokyo Comic Market has always been attended by more men and boys than are most other such events. As I noted earlier, men accounted for only fifteen or twenty percent of participants at the 1993 event I attended. At the 1995 Comic Market, I estimated that maybe forty percent of participants were male. At the Summer '98 Comic Market, males seemed to account for nearly fifty percent of participants, although the gender distribution varied over the three days according to the genres featured on a given day. Still, female participants could no longer simply ignore male participants. Males, on the other hand, seemed much livelier and sociable than in earlier events where they were an unwelcome minority. Sitting on a spread of lawn outside the convention center as the final day of Comic Market 54 drew to a close, I watched the other participants and analyzed the gender dynamics.

Pornographic manga featuring female characters below the age of 18 are still the mainstay of amateur manga for men. But this time my impression was that these manga may be more complex and less disturbing than I (and others) had first assumed. For example, most of the manga ostensibly featured young girls, yet those girls were usually portrayed with enormous breasts and very womanly hips. Only a small minority portrayed characters that appear to be prepubescent. The lust expressed was clearly lust for sexually mature women, so the young age given the characters must be signifying something else (perhaps a fear of socializing with adult women). Furthermore, the content was often comical, and not always easily dismissed as misogynistic. Interestingly, most of these manga, like yaoi, featured homosexual relationships, but portrayed female couples, not male couples.

Anne Allison finds in *ero manga* an obvious and dominant "male gaze," and she insists "that *ero manga* are misogynistic is undeniable" (1996:78). Shigematsu has argued, to the contrary, that "the *manga* text functions as a mechanism that is capable of placing the reader's gaze in multiple positions" (1999:137). She writes that

> identifications are more oscillating and fluid, shifting and incomplete, moving among multiple contradictory (psychic) sites that are constituted differently depending on the specific history and experiences of the subject. Some of these possible sites might be expressed as: I desire to be the object of desire/I hate the object of desire/I conquer the object of desire/the object of desire wants me/the object of desire hates me. [p. 136]

Nothing illustrates this fluidity of identification more vividly than the image of a man cross-dressed as a favorite heroine standing in line to buy a pornographic amateur manga featuring that same heroine. If, as Sakakibara argues, yaoi fans are gay men in women's bodies, then it would be fair to suggest that many fans of amateur Beautiful Girls manga are, as it were, lesbians in men's bodies, and not simply misogynists.

I would further stress that that these amateur manga are, first and foremost, a medium of social interaction and not strictly, as I had first assumed, a solitary fantasy. To be sure, there on the lawn of Big Site I saw the occasional single male fan poring over his day's purchases. But most of the men were in all-male groups, sometimes as many as twenty or thirty in number, chatting and laughing and clearly enjoying the company of peers. Some carried a duffel bag containing the costume—perhaps Sailor Moon?—they had worn that day. However attractive or unattractive they might have seemed to passing women as potential social partners, their behavior was quite convivial.

Moreover, they were mirrored by very similar all-female groups. There on the same lawn sat women who, like the men, would probably not be the target of much romantic attention from the other sex. Like the men, they sat together, laughing and enjoying each other's company. In the men's shopping bags (bearing the design of Comic Market 54) were amateur manga, probably produced by men very much like themselves, labeled "Beautiful Girls." In the women's shopping bags were amateur manga, also probably produced by women very much like themselves, labeled "yaoi." To accept, uncritically, the latter as good, and reject, uncritically, the former as bad, would be a mistake. In a sense, the two genres mirror each other, and speak to the desires of those who, by choice or circumstance, do not fit neatly into society's prescribed norms of gender and sexuality. They do not see themselves as the conventionally beautiful characters who inevitably get the perfect guy or girl in mainstream media for women or men.

But there on the lawn I also observed mixed gender groups—men and women, sitting together, chatting and laughing and enjoying each other's company. Where had I seen this pattern before? I had seen it, it occurred to me, in the high schools where I had done my fieldwork: the girls who socialized only with girls, the boys who socialized only with boys, and the girls and boys who socialized together. Of course, similar patterns can be found in the United States, but in a "couple-oriented culture" such as the United States, where one is expected not only to have a mate but to display that mate frequently and publicly, the pressure to interact with the opposite sex may be greater.

What struck me particularly, though, sitting there on that lawn, was that these three configurations were not entirely distinct from one another. Women would join groups of men, men would come over to groups of women, and the gender proportions of the mixed groups would change. There was fluidity. There were signs of crossing boundaries, which were not abstract, as in the costume play, but mundane and real. There were also couples here and there, holding hands and smiling—couples who had probably met through their participation in this culture, and who may not have seemed likely, at first glance, to find romance anywhere.

In drawings and in words, revolution is easy. In fiction, one can rewrite the world, remodel human relationships, with the stroke of a pen. Here, at the Comic Market and in countless smaller venues throughout the country, throughout the year, women and men paint worlds so outrageous that the mainstream media will not touch them. But out there, on the lawn, on the street, in the home, in the workplace, the stakes are much higher. Even those who dream the wildest dreams become timid when confronted with the weight and complexity of social reality.

But let us look again. These women and men, dismissed by so many as otaku, as reclusive geeks, were taking small risks. They were crossing lines that many others could not cross. They were finding their own place, making their own way, while most of the societal mainstream was taking the easier, socially sanctioned course. They were holding hands, talking to one another, enjoying each other's company.

The barriers between the women and the men, and between the masculinity and the femininity within us all, can be thick and high. There is mutual suspicion, mutual misunderstanding. But, as their manga testify, these fanzine aficionados had always been suspicious of the barriers.

Notes

1. It is impossible to be precise about the numbers because while figures for sales of manga magazines are available by genre, there are no similar figures for sales of manga books by genre. Manga magazines for girls and women account for nine percent and seven percent, respectively, of all manga magazine sales. My research shows that women prefer buying books over magazines more than men, and I believe it reasonable to assume that those percentages would be somewhat higher for sales of manga books. These and other statistics in this paragraph are drawn from the 2002 edition of *Shuppan shihō nenpyo* (Annual Report of Publishing Indices).

2. Mainichi shimbun 2001. The survey was conducted September 1–3, 2000. There were 3,232 respondents, all 16 years of age or older. Of the respondents, 1,681 (52 percent) were female.

3. For further English-language information on shōjo manga and the manga industry in general, see Kinsella 2000; Schodt 1986, 1996; Thorn 2001). Additional articles and resources can be found at my website: http://matt-thorn.com.

4. The starting point of this genre is a matter of debate. The first shōjo manga story to suggest romantic love between boys was probably Hagio Moto's 1971 short piece, "Jūichi-gatsu no gimunajiumu" (November Gymnasium). Set in a German boarding school, it features two identical boys who eventually learn that they are twins who were separated at birth. This story was, in fact, a spin-off of a longer story idea she would not publish until 1974, Tōma no shinzō (The Heart of Thomas). Whereas "November Gymnasium" merely

carries homoerotic connotations, *The Heart of Thomas* is explicitly about romantic (though never physical) love between boys, and there is even a strong, however implicit, suggestion of a homosexual gang rape. Both stories were inspired by Jean Delannoy's 1964 film, *Les Amities Particulieres* (This Special Friendship), which features a romance between two boys in a boarding school. In 1976, shōjo manga artist Takemiya Keiko published *Kaze to ki no uta* (The Song of the Wind and the Trees), the first shōjo manga to portray romantic and sexual relationships between boys. Takemiya says there were nine years between original conception and approval for publication, because she refused to remove or fudge the sexual aspect. All three stories were published in *Bessatsu Shōjo Komikku* (Special Edition Girls' Comic), a then-new magazine read by primary-, middle-, and high-school girls. The editor in chief at the time, a man named Yamamoto Jun'ya, gave artists an unusually free rein and was often willing to take risks in order to publish manga he judged to have artistic or literary merit. *Special Edition Girls' Comic* became a forum for a new generation of female manga artists, and boys' love.

5. There remain, however, many genuine circles, with multiple members. Most high schools and universities in Japan have *manga kenkyū kai* (manga study groups), which are essentially clubs for amateur manga artists or would-be manga critics. In my fieldwork on the community of girls' comics, I participated in the manga study groups of two high schools. Many such clubs participate collectively in events, although neither of the two groups I was affiliated with did so; several members, however, did attend events regularly and a few paired or teamed up with other amateur artists to participate as circles independent of the school clubs. The presence of pornographic material at comic mart events and the well-publicized efforts of certain groups of citizens and educators to suppress such material and even ban events have made it difficult for minors to participate openly and in an organized fashion. Teenagers have created alternatives in the form of small, local events comprised almost entirely of high-school and middle-school manga clubs. I attended one such event, and it seemed to me that the students—and perhaps the girls particularly—felt more at ease there than do high-school teens who attend "grown-up" events. They may also feel less self-conscious about the level of their cartooning skills.

6. It would seem the process of selection may not be entirely egalitarian. Yonezawa noted in a 1998 interview that there are about three hundred circles, classified as "Emergency Exit Circles," who receive what he calls "special treatment." These circles are so designated because they draw long lines—as many as two or three thousand customers at a time—and therefore must be located by the emergency exits (actually large, shuttered doors used to move things into and out of the halls) so that the lines can be routed outdoors where they will not block traffic in the halls. Yonezawa did not indicate if the special treatment referred only to where successful applicants are placed or whether such circles were guaranteed a table.

7. This is according to Kotani's own rather comical résumé on the Science Fiction and Fantasy Writers of Japan website: http://www.sfwj.or.jp/member/KOTANI-MARI.html.

8. The title of Sakakibara's book is, in fact, very difficult to translate. *Genron* is a neologism coined by Sakakibara consisting of the character 幻 (gen) meaning "fantastic," "elusive," or "illusory," and the character 論 (ron) meaning "argument," "discussion," or "theory." It may be seen as a pun on the homonymous 原論 (genron), which means

"principles" or "basic theory." Sakakibara's book is a comprehensive and subtly argued analysis of the genre of gay male fiction for women, though many critics argue that her assertions are too extreme.

9. There is, in fact, a popular manga series that takes transsexuality and homosexuality as its primary theme. It is simply titled *Hen* (Queer). Surprisingly (to me, at least), this manga was created by a man and published in a manga magazine geared toward young men. It is important to note, however, that the word *hen* is not used in the sense that *queer* is in the English-speaking world today. The English word *queer* (pronounced *kuiaa* in Japanese) is a recent import, though it seems to be known to few outside gay and lesbian circles.

10. They also betray a sense of shame about their interest in the genre. Although, as I mentioned earlier, my own impression is that Japanese fans of yaoi are less self-conscious than are English-speaking fans of slash, Sakakibara (1998) argues strongly that yaoi fans are wracked by shame. But while slash fans seem compelled to justify their interest, yaoi fans, according to Sakakibara, seem to try to avoid self-analysis by avoiding stories with weighty themes and pursuing ever more pornographic or fantastic stories.

References Cited

Allison, Anne
    1996   Permitted and Prohibited Desires: Mothers, Comics, and Censorship in Japan. Boulder, CO: Westview Press.

Bacon-Smith, Camille
    1992   Enterprising Women: Television Fandom and the Creation of Popular Myth. Philadelphia: University of Pennsylvania Press.

Doty, Alexander
    1993   Making Things Perfectly Queer: Interpreting Mass Culture. Minneapolis: University of Minnesota Press.

Fujimoto Yukari
    1998   Watashi no ibasho wa doko ni aru no? Shōjo manga ga utsusu kokoro no katachi (Where do I belong? The shape of the heart as reflected in girls' comics). Tokyo: Gakuyō Shobō.

Jenkins, Henry
    1992   Textual Poachers: Television Fans and Participatory Culture. London: Routledge.

Kinsella, Sharon
    2000   Adult Manga: Culture and Power in Contemporary Japanese Society. Richmond, Surrey: Curzon Press.

Mainichi shimbun
    2001   Mainichi shimbun dokusho yoron chōsa (Mainichi Newspaper survey of reading habits). Tokyo: Mainichi shimbun.

Minoura
    1998   Kosupure shi: furusato o motomete hanaichimonme (History of cos-play: Hanaichimonme in pursuit of home). *In* Kokusai otaku daigaku 1998 nen:

saizensen kara no kenkyū hōkoku (International Otaku University 1998: Research reports from the front lines). Pp. 1–14. Tokyo: Kōbunsha.

Penley, Constance
1992   Feminism, Psychoanalysis, and the Study of Popular Culture. In Cultural Studies. Lawrence Grossberg, Carrie Nelson, and Paula Treichler, eds. Pp. 479–500. New York: Routledge.

Sakakibara Shihomi
1998   Yaoi genron yaoi kara mieta mono (An elusive theory of Yaoi). Tokyo: Natsume Shobō.

Schodt, Frederik L.
1986   Manga! Manga! The World of Japanese Comics. Tokyo: Kodansha International.
1996   Dreamland Japan: Writings on Modern Manga. Berkeley: Stone Bridge Press.

Shigematsu, Setsu
1999   Dimensions of Desire: Sex, Fantasy, and Fetish in Japanese Comics. In Themes and Issues in Asian Cartooning: Cute, Cheap, Mad, and Sexy. J. A. Lent, ed. Bowling Green, OH: Popular Press.

Takemiya Keiko
1993   Josei wa gei ga suki? (Do women like gays?). Bungei shunjū (June): 82–83.

Thorn, Matt
2001   Shōjo Manga—Something for Girls. Japan Quarterly 48(3):43–50.

Ueno Chizuko
1998   Jendāresu wārudo no <ai> no jikken (Experimenting with <love> in a genderless world). In Hatsujō sōchi: erosu no shinario (Apparatus of arousal: Scenarios of eros). Pp. 63–82. Tokyo: Chikuma shobō.

Yoshida Akimi
1998   Banana Fish. Matt Thorn, trans. San Francisco: Viz Comics.

Zenkoku shuppan kyōkai/Shuppan kagaku kenkyūjo (The All Japan Magazine and Book Publisher's and Editor's Association/The Research Institute for Publications)
2002   2002 Shuppan shihyo nenpyō (2002 annual report of publishing indices). Tokyo: Zenkoku shuppan kyōkai/Shuppan kagaku kenkyūjo.

Glossary of Japanese Terms

abunai: Dangerous

aidoru: (lit., "idol") Referring to young pop singers

akeni: Traditional luggage

angura: underground

angura fōku: Underground folk

anime: Film, video, and digital animations

asobi: Play (as in leisure)

asobi-nin: Playboys, goof-offs, gamblers

au: (lit., "to meet") Used to describe attending a concert

ayashii: Suspect

banzuke: Tournament ranking sheets released two weeks before each tournament

bishōjo: Beautiful girls; essentially pornographic manga created largely by and for heterosexual men, and featuring female characters below the age of 18

bunka: Culture

bushidō: The way of the warrior

byōki: A sickness

chaya: (lit., "teahouses") Companies that guide the audience during a sumo tournament

dafu-ya: Ticket scalpers

dai-nekkyō: Wild enthusiasm

dasai: Outdated, uncool

dekata: Guides employed by the teahouses, who lead sumo spectators to their seats

deshi: An apprentice

dō: The "way" of a discipline or practice

dōjinshi: A self-published book or magazine; associated most commonly with amateur manga

dōjinshi sokubai kai: (lit., a market of self-published magazines)

Edomae no asobi: True Edo-style play or fun

enka: An old-fashioned, sentimental genre of Japanese popular music, commonly dubbed expressive of "the heart–soul of Japanese" *(Nihonjin no kokoro)*

esabako: A feed box

famirii: (lit., "families") Loose networks of rappers who perform together and collaborate on each other's albums

fuan: (lit., "fan")

fushōji: Scandal

gei o sodateru: To cultivate a performer's artistry

geinōkai: The (Japanese) world of entertainment

genba: The "actual site" of a scene or experience

gidayū: The declaimed narrative accompaniment to the Bunraku puppet theater

goshūgi: Tips to performers

gottsan: A formal expression of gratitude in the world of sumo

gyōji: Referees

hanashi: A broader term for rakugo

hanashi no kai: Comic storytelling assemblies (contests)

hanashika: Rakugo storytellers

happi coats: Light blouse jackets, often decorated to be worn by participants in a matsuri, baseball fan clubs, business groups on excursions, and so forth

hen: Strange, odd, or queer

heya: Sumo stables; the place where wrestlers live and practice

hiiki: Fan, patron, favor

hiiki jōren: A steady fan

hyōbanki: Booklets that are guides to actors

ibento: An organized event or function

iemoto: Stem family system

iemoto-style: A business model based on the traditional stem family structure

ikebana: The Japanese art of flower arranging that emphasizes form and balance

ikigai: What one lives for; a reason for living

inakamono: Country bumpkins

inaka-teki: Rural

irotsuki mawashi: Tournament silk loincloth

jisaku jien: Self-made, self-performed (music)

jimusho: (lit., "office") An artist management agency

jōren: Regular audience; "professional" spectators and leaders of an audience community

judo: A sport developed from jujitsu that emphasizes the use of quick movement and leverage to throw an opponent

kabuki: Traditional Japanese popular drama performed with highly stylized singing and dancing

kachi: Triumphs

kaigyaku: Parody

kaihō: (Fan) newsletter

kakae rikishi: When sumo wrestlers compete against each other to enhance the glory of their feudal domain

kakegoe: Audience interjections during kabuki performances applauding a well-executed pose or delivery of a line

kakko ii: Cool style

kakko warui: Uncool

kanjin-zumō: Charity sumo

kanjōsei: Emotion

kankeisha: Associate

karaoke: Singing to prerecorded accompaniment

karaoke box: A room rented to a small group of friends for singing along to favorite pop songs

kata: Long-standing explicit "forms"

kataribe: Storytellers of ancient times

Kattobase: "Let it rip!"

kayōkyoku: Japanese pop music

keshō-mawashi: The decorative apron that top wrestlers wear during their ring-entering ceremony

ki-jyaaji kumi: (lit., "yellow jackets") Officers of the Private Alliance of Tiger fan clubs who lead the cheers at Kōshien Stadium

kōenkai: Support group or fan club

kōenkaichō: The president of the supporter group

kōensha: Supporter

kokoro no sasae: To nurture fans' hearts and souls

kokugi: The Japanese national sport

kokugi sumo: Sumo as the national sport

kokumin: National subjects

kokutai: National polity

Komiketto: An abbreviation of Komikku Maaketto or the "Comic Market"

kosupure: Costume play

koten: Classical

kyaku: (lit., "customer" or "guest") Term for audience

kyōyō: High culture

manga: Comic art magazines and books

maniakku: (lit., "maniac") An obsessive fan

masu-seki: Box seats in sumo stands

meiban: Master recordings

monomane: Imitation

mon-tsuki hakama: Formal clothing with family crests

moriagaru: Audience excitement

mukashi-biiki: The "good-old-days" fan who waxes nostalgic for the theater of the past and has no interest in young stars

mukanshin: Unmoved

mukoyōshi: A husband adopted into his wife's family to continue that house line

nagaya: Edo-period tenement row houses

neta: Musical samples

netsuretsu na fuan: Intense fans

Nihon hōsō kyōkai (NHK): Japan's public broadcasting corporation

Nihonjin no kokoro: The heart–soul of Japanese

nobori: A large banner that announces either the name of the heya or the wrestler

Noh/No: Classic Japanese dance-drama having a heroic theme, a chorus, and highly stylized action, costuming, and scenery

nyū myūjikku: "New music" produced out of the folk song tradition

obi: The outer sleeve of a record

ochi: A punch line

ochiken: Amateur school rakugo clubs

ōendan: Fan clubs; fan supporter groups

oiribukuro: Special envelopes made by the Japanese Sumo Association used to give gifts to people associated with sumo

oishii tokoro dake: Only the yummy parts

okamisan: A stable master's wife

okkake: (verb) A variation of "to chase"; a fan who follows a particular performer and makes an effort to catch all of his appearances

okkake: (noun) Steady fans; "chasers"

okome: (lit., "rice") Term for money in the special language of sumo

okyakusan: (lit., "customer" or "guest") Polite term for audience

omiyage: Souvenirs

omoiyari: Empathy

ongaku kissa: Music cafés, cozy spaces with vast record collections featuring particular genres (e.g., Western classical music, jazz, tango) and excellent audio equipment

onna no kimochi: The feelings of women

orijinaru: Original

oshare: Classy

otaku: (lit., honorific word for "house" or "you") Began to supplement "mania" to mean "hard-core aficionados" in the early 1980s; the term evokes an image of nerdy youths comparing comic book collections or reeling off trivia about a favorite singing star

otoko no sekai: A world of and for men

otsukare sama: Comment to someone for a job well done

oyakata: A stable master, who runs the heya

ōzumō: Professional sumo

parodi: Parody (without the English term's connotation of satire)

rakken: Abbreviation for rakugo kenkyūkai, or rakugo research association

rakudoru: Rakugo idol; a combination of *rakugo* and the Japanese–English word *aidoru* (idol)

rakugo: Traditional comic storytelling.

ren: Networks of amateurs who wrote poetry and dabbled in literary wordplay

Rokkō oroshi: The Hanshin Tiger anthem

rōkyoku: A narrative genre accompanied by a shamisen (three-stringed Japanese instrument)

sābisu seishin: A performer's "spirit of service"

saigo no zeitaku: The last luxury

sākuru: (lit., "circle") An individual or group of fans who create and publish something to be sold at comic conventions

san-dōraku: The three amusements (debaucheries) of drinking, gambling, and buying women

seitai: Ecology

seme: An aggressor

sharaku: Unconventional, free, unconstrained

shibai tsū: A theater expert who possesses a detailed knowledge of everything connected with the theater, theater history, and actors

shibai-zuki: A theater fan who is addicted to the theater itself

shikiri-sen: Starting lines

shinjinrui: (lit., "the new human breed") A popular media term for youth culture during the economic bubble of the 1980s; somewhat analogous to American yuppies

shisetsu: Private

shōjo manga: Girls' comics

shōnen ai: The manga theme of boys' love

shufu bunka: Housewife culture

shumi: Taste

slash: English-language comics that pair male protagonists as lovers

sōgo shintō: Mutual interpenetration

soto: Outsiders

sumō-dō: The way of the wrestler

taiken: Bodily experience

taiko: Large Japanese drums

taikomochi: Male geisha who entertained at parties in the old licensed quarters

taishū: The masses

tanimachi: Sumo patrons

tanran-zumo: Sumo performed in front of the emperor

tegata: The autograph of the wrestler signed over a print of the wrestler's hand on the standard autograph board (the wrestler typically dips his hand in either black or vermilion ink)

tekiya: Itinerant stall operators and hucksters at markets and carnivals

tengu: A long-nosed, birdlike mythical creature known as a boaster; a derogatory term for people who think highly of their own abilities (in the arts or other fields)

tengu-ren: Serious amateur performers who consider themselves on a par with professionals

teuchi renjū: Hand-clapping clubs

tezukuri: "Handmade" (folk music)

tokai-teki: Metropolitan

tokoyama: Hairdressers for sumo wrestlers

tora-kichi: (Hanshin) Tiger-crazy

toshiyori-kabu: Elders' stocks

uchi: Insiders

uchiage: Postperformance parties

uke: A recipient or target

yabai: Dangerous or suspect

yaji: Jeers

yakuza: Japanese organized crime groups or individuals

yaoi: An acronym for the phrase "Yama nashi, ochi nashi, imi nashi" [No Climax, No Resolution, No Meaning]

yasuragi: To soothe people (fans)

yobidashi: Name announcers

yose: Theaters in Osaka and Tokyo where rakugo is performed

yūjo kabuki: Prostitute kabuki theater

yukata: A light cotton kimono

Contributors

Lorie Brau is assistant professor of Japanese in the Department of Foreign Languages and Literatures at the University of New Mexico. She received her Ph.D. in performance studies at New York University. She is currently finishing a book on her research on contemporary rakugo.

Ian Condry is assistant professor of Japanese Cultural Studies in the Foreign Languages and Literatures Department of the Massachusetts Institute of Technology. He is writing a book about Japanese hip-hop and maintains a website: http://iancondry.com.

Shuhei Hosokawa is an associate professor at the International Center for Japanese Culture in Kyoto, Japan, specializing in musicology and popular culture. Among his books are *Rekōdo no bigaku* (The aesthetics of records) (Keisō shobō, 1991) and *Karaoke Around the World* (coedited with Tōru Mitsui) (Routledge, 1998).

William W. Kelly is professor of anthropology and Sumitomo Professor of Japanese Studies at Yale University. He is currently completing a book on Japanese professional baseball. His website is http://research.yale.edu/wwkelly.

Hideaki Matsuoka is professor of international communication at Shukutoku University in Japan. He received his Ph.D. from the Department of Anthropology at the University of California–Berkeley in 2000. His dissertation dealt with how and why Japanese-Brazilians and other Brazilians followed a Japanese New Religion in Brazil.

Carolyn S. Stevens is senior lecturer in Japanese Studies at the Melbourne Institute of Asian Languages and Societies, University of Melbourne. She is the author of *On the Margins of Japanese Society: Volunteers and the Welfare of the Urban Underclass* (Routledge, 1996).

Matthew Thorn is associate professor in the Department of Cartoon and Comic Art at Kyoto Seika University. He is also a Ph.D. candidate in the Department of Anthropology at Columbia University. His website is http://matt-thorn.com.

R. Kenji Tierney completed his Ph.D. in the Department of Anthropology at the University of California–Berkeley and is a postdoctoral fellow at the East Asian Institute at Columbia University. He is presently completing a book on sumo provisionally titled *Wrestling with Tradition*.

Christine R. Yano is associate professor in the Department of Anthropology at the University of Hawai'i–Manoa. She is the author of *Tears of Longing: Nostalgia and the Nation in Japanese Popular Song* (Harvard University Asia Center, 2002).

Index